An Introduction to Medieval English Literature

An Introduction to Medieval English Literature
1300–1485

ANNA BALDWIN

 palgrave

© Anna Baldwin 2016

All rights reserved. No reproduction, copy or transmission of this publication may be made without written permission.

No portion of this publication may be reproduced, copied or transmitted save with written permission or in accordance with the provisions of the Copyright, Designs and Patents Act 1988, or under the terms of any licence permitting limited copying issued by the Copyright Licensing Agency, Saffron House, 6–10 Kirby Street, London EC1N 8TS.

Any person who does any unauthorized act in relation to this publication may be liable to criminal prosecution and civil claims for damages.

The author has asserted her right to be identified as the author of this work in accordance with the Copyright, Designs and Patents Act 1988.

First published 2016 by
PALGRAVE

Palgrave in the UK is an imprint of Macmillan Publishers Limited, registered in England, company number 785998, of 4 Crinan Street, London, N1 9XW.

Palgrave Macmillan in the US is a division of St Martin's Press LLC, 175 Fifth Avenue, New York, NY 10010.

Palgrave is a global imprint of the above companies and is represented throughout the world.

Palgrave® and Macmillan® are registered trademarks in the United States, the United Kingdom, Europe and other countries.

ISBN 978–0–230–25036–9 hardback
ISBN 978–0–230–25037–6 paperback

This book is printed on paper suitable for recycling and made from fully managed and sustained forest sources. Logging, pulping and manufacturing processes are expected to conform to the environmental regulations of the country of origin.

A catalogue record for this book is available from the British Library.

Library of Congress Cataloging-in-Publication Data

Names: Baldwin, Anna P.
Title: An introduction to Medieval English literature : 1300–1485 / Anna Baldwin.
Description: New York : Palgrave Macmillan, 2015. | Includes index.
Identifiers: LCCN 2015038897| ISBN 9780230250369 (hardback) | ISBN 9780230250376 (paperback)
Subjects: LCSH: English literature—Middle English, 1100–1500—History and criticism. | Civilization, Medieval, in literature. | BISAC: LITERARY CRITICISM / Medieval.
Classification: LCC PR255 .B29 2015 | DDC 820.9/001—dc23
LC record available at http://lccn.loc.gov/2015038897

Contents

List of Text-boxes	ix
Acknowledgements	x
Note on Quotation from Middle English Texts	xi

Introduction	1
(a) A Guide to Literature in a Period of Change	1
(b) Manuscripts and Readers	4
(i) The development of manuscripts in the period	4
(ii) Medieval habits of writing and reading	6
(iii) Modern readers	8
Sources and Further Reading	9

1 The Poor Commons: Literature and Social Change	13
(a) The Black Death, Decline of Serfdom and the Great Rising of 1381	15
Example Text: Ploughing Scenes in *Piers Plowman*	18
(b) The Drama	26
(i) Religious Drama: Mystery Play Cycles	27
Example Text: The Wakefield (Towneley) *Cain and Abel*	29
(ii) Religious Drama: Saints' Plays and Morality Plays	32
Example Text: *Mankind*	34
(iii) Secular Drama and the folk tradition	35
Texts, Sources and Further Reading	38

2 The Poor Commons: Education and Dissent	44
(a) Homiletic and Confessional Literature	45
(b) Sermons	47
Example Text: The Sermon *Of Servants and Lords*	49
(c) The Lollards and their Literature	51
Example Texts: *Piers the Plowman's Crede* and *The Ploughman's Tale*	55
Texts, Sources and Further Reading	58

3	**The Urban Middle Class: Satire, Debate and Political Advice**	**61**
	(a) Urban Communities and Political Crisis in the Reign of Richard II	62
	(b) Estates Satire	65
	Example Text: (i) Langland's *Prologue* to *Piers Plowman*	66
	Example Text: (ii) Chaucer's *General Prologue to the Canterbury Tales*	68
	(c) Venality Satire on the Misuse of Money	73
	Example Text: (i) *Wynnere and Wastoure*	76
	Example Text: (ii) The Vision of Lady Meed in *Piers Plowman* 2–4	79
	(d) Complaint and Political Prophecy	83
	(e) Political Advice	84
	(i) Idealised and general advice	84
	Example Text: Hoccleve's *Regement of Princes*	87
	(ii) Personal Political Advice	88
	Example Texts: *Richard Redeless* and *Mum and the Sothsegger*	90
	Texts, Sources and Further Reading	94
4	**The Urban Middle Class: Tales of Women and Marriage**	**100**
	(a) Story Collections	101
	(i) Gower's *Confessio Amantis*	102
	(ii) Chaucer's *Canterbury Tales*	104
	(b) Statements about Women and Marriage in the Frame Narrative of the *Canterbury Tales*	107
	Example Text: (i) The *Wife of Bath's Prologue*	108
	Example Text: (ii) The *Merchant's Prologue* and opening of his *Tale*	111
	Example Text: (iii) The *Franklyn's Tale* Fr.5, 761–86	114
	(c) Chaucer's *Fabliaux*	115
	Example Texts: The *Miller's Tale* and *Reeve's Tale*	117
	Texts, Sources and Further Reading	119

5 The Community of the Church: Religious Lyrics and the
   English Mystics   124
   (a) Affective Devotion to God   126
       (i) The devotional lyric   127
       (ii) Richard Rolle's mystical prose   130
   (b) The Negative Way   132
       (i) Walter Hilton, *The Scale of Perfection*   133
       (ii) The *Cloud* Author   134
   Example Text: *The Cloud of Unknowing*: the explanation
       of the *Cloud*   135
   (c) The Women Mystics   137
       (i) Julian of Norwich   137
   Example Text: Julian's Metaphor of Jesus the Mother   141
       (ii) Margery Kempe   144
   Example Text: The *Book of Margery Kempe* seen
       from three viewpoints   145
   Texts, Sources and Further Reading   149

6 Religious and Moral Stories   154
   (a) Saints' Lives   155
       (i) The Legends   155
       (ii) Modern and medieval readers   157
       (iii) Literary hagiographers   159
   Example Texts: Chaucer's *Second Nun's Tale* and
       Bokenham's *Life of St Cecelia*   162
   (b) Popular Romances   165
       (i) Romances of adventure   166
       (ii) Sentimental Romances and 'Breton Lays'   167
       (iii) Homiletic Romances   169
   Example Texts: *Émaré* and Chaucer's *Man of Law's Tale*   170
   (c) Moral Examples   173
   Example Text: (i) *Patience*   176
   Example Text: (ii) Chaucer's *Clerk's Tale*   180
   (d) Religious Dream Visions   184
   Example Text: *Pearl*   188
   Texts, Sources and Further Reading   191

7 Aristocratic Love — 198
(a) The European Tradition of Writing about Love — 199
  (i) Classical and post-Classical texts — 200
  (ii) 12th- and 13th-century Love Allegories and Handbooks — 202
  (iii) Some 14th-century European Love Visions and Romances — 205
(b) English Love Lyrics of the 14th and 15th centuries — 208
(c) English and Scottish Love Visions — 211
  (i) Chaucer's Love Visions — 211
Example Text: The *Parliament of Fowls* — 212
  (ii) Love Visions of English and Scottish Chaucerians — 215
(d) English and Scottish Love Romances — 220
Example Text: (i) Chaucer's *Troilus and Criseyde* — 222
Example Text: (ii) Henryson's *Testament of Cressid* — 228
Texts, Sources and Further Reading — 232

8 Chivalric Romances — 239
(a) England at War — 241
(b) The Principal Sources for English Arthurian Romance — 243
  (i) Geoffrey of Monmouth — 243
  (ii) Chrétien de Troyes and his immediate imitators — 244
  (iii) The French Vulgate Cycle and beyond — 245
(c) Fourteenth-century English Arthurian Romance — 247
  (i) *Yvain* — 248
  (ii) The *Stanzaic Morte Arthur* — 249
  (iii) The *Alliterative Morte Arthure* — 250
Example Text: *Sir Gawain and the Green Knight* — 251
(d) The Fifteenth Century: Lydgate and Malory — 259
Example Text: The closing Books of the *Morte Darthur* — 265
Texts, Sources and Further Reading — 269

Index — 277

List of Text-boxes

William Langland	19
Alliterative Poetry	25
Lollard Principles	52
Geoffrey Chaucer	69
Debate Poetry	75
Thomas Hoccleve	86
John Gower	102
Richard Rolle	130
Julian of Norwich	138
Margery Kempe	145
The *Pearl*-poet	175
Religious Dream Visions	185
English Rhymed Forms	206
John Lydgate	216
Thomas Malory	261

Acknowledgements and Dedication

When I was half-way through writing this book I lost my ability to read print, and although modern technology enables me to continue reading and writing through my computer, this excellent machine has a tendency to mangle Middle English. So for the last two years Felicia McCormick has been reading me the texts which I wanted to discuss, with ever-increasing enthusiasm and skill, and so she is the book's metaphorical midwife (her previous profession). Two graduate students at the Centre for Medieval Studies, where I used to teach here in York, Jenn Bartlett and Anna Clarke, trawled through bibliographies for further up-to-date material. Numerous friends were inveigled into accompanying me to libraries, Margaret Clark and Sue Sessions being the most persistent seekers, and the staff at the Cambridge English Faculty Library have been particularly helpful. Both Barry Windeatt and Derek Pearsall have given me academic help, through their excellent books and articles, and more personally; Derek in particular has taken considerable trouble to sort out some problematic parts of my text. My editor at Palgrave, Rachel Bridgewater, and her incisive peer-review team have considerably strengthened the book as a whole and Jocelyn Stockley and Felicia have combed out my haphazard typography. My daughter Ruth has assisted with editing, and my husband Tom has both encouraged me and provided every kind of practical support.

I dedicate this book to the York Quakers, and hope that all such true students of Friendship, together with students of literature, will find this book a helpful introduction to the extraordinary poetry and prose of the Middle Ages.

Note on Quotation from Middle English Texts

In accordance with Palgrave policy, all archaic letter-forms have been replaced by their modern equivalents, þ (thorn) being represented as *th*, and ȝ (yogh) as either *gh* or *y*. The Middle-Scots use of *qu* where we would use *w* has been left unchanged. Wherever possible, an accessible on-line version has been used for quotation.

Introduction

(a) A Guide to Literature in a Period of Change

This Guide will describe literature written during a period of change which transformed England for ever, and which inspired dynamic, varied and excellent writing. One key change was a decisive shift towards the greater use of written English, the language spoken by most people. In 1300 English had already changed from Old English to the various dialects of Middle English (this Guide will not cover Early Middle English literature written before 1300). However, very few texts written before this were in Middle English. Clerics usually read and wrote Latin, and the aristocracy and many townsmen often spoke and usually wrote in French. But by 1400, the central date for this Guide, the picture was very different. From 1362 English was spoken in the law courts and Parliament, and it was much more commonly used in business, administration and education, though records were usually kept in French until well into the fifteenth century (see Salter 1983, p. 36). Though clerks still usually wrote for each other in Latin, they were increasingly writing in Middle English for a widening audience of lay readers; many of these were themselves writing in a growing variety of genres. By 1500 there was a considerable corpus of texts we can think of as 'literature' in Middle English, particularly from the rich period of the later fourteenth century, but also from the fifteenth. When Chaucer, Gower and their followers made the decision to write substantial works in English, including within them much culture and learning from Europe, and adopting the London / East Midlands dialect which is the ancestor of Standard English today, the English language and literature had won a place in the world alongside French and Latin.

This linguistic change reflects and hastens profound changes in medieval society. By the later fourteenth century, when Middle English literature found its voice, the old hierarchies were being challenged: serfdom was melting away, and the towns were expanding and filling with new migrants and enterprising foreign traders. Furthermore, the authority of Church, Pope and King were being questioned by ordinary men and women as well as by revolutionaries and heretics. More and more people could read and readers were no longer exclusively members of a clerical and aristocratic elite, or exclusively male. They included an expanding middle class who enjoyed books in English, in a variety of old and new genres. Churchmen worked hard to supply the increasing demands of pious lay people for religious books in English – Saints' Lives, Romances, Allegories, Lyrics, Debates and Homilies of every kind. But they could not hold back the tide of Middle English texts produced by the proto-protestant Lollards, even by burning their books and even the writers themselves. These reformers encouraged and fed lay literacy in working-class men and women with an organised programme of writing and translation, and there are more copies of their Bible translation than of any other work in Middle English. Thus Lollardy was supporting a revolution in literacy which could only be satisfied by the development of printing from the 1470s. My cover illustrates the development of lay and indeed female literacy, as the virgin reads while Joseph minds the baby.

As early as the Great Rising in 1381, working-class access to dangerous religious ideas was believed to have led to political revolution, but in fact the political establishment of the later Middle Ages was destroying itself from within. Richard II alienated the most powerful noblemen in his government and they deposed him in 1399, a pattern which was repeated again and again in the Wars of the Roses. Those wars ended in 1485 with the accession of Henry VII, and as that is also the date on which Caxton brought out Malory's *Morte Darthur* in print, it seems a good date on which to conclude this book.

These social forces and political events are so significant a context to the literature of the period that I have used the changing structure of medieval society to structure this Guide. I will move through the different 'estates' or classes of society, including the political events and social developments most relevant to each as I go. Without suggesting a hard and fast 'readership' for the texts I cover (for there is not enough evidence to make such claims), I will place them into groups of genres, and relate each group, in a pair of chapters, to the estate which they seem to address, or whose representatives they often describe. I start my survey with the group of genres addressed to the poor commoners at the bottom of the social scale, those who in the traditional medieval theory of the estates 'work for all'. This estate was addressed almost entirely in 'religious' literature, such as Drama and Sermons, but I include other genres which describe their way of life, and also survey the Lollard texts which addressed the literate commoners. I will look in Chapter 1 at the peasantry, who though largely illiterate were pressing hard for social change, and in Chapter 2 at the urban poor and their desire for religious freedom. In the next pair of chapters I will turn to secular (non-religious) literature and look at the genres which seem to address the more sophisticated urban dwellers, the middle class of craftsmen, professionals and merchants, together with aristocrats and clergy who shared their interests. I will look in Chapter 3 at the genres which directly analyse society, and which respond to current social and political change, including Richard II's deposition. In Chapter 4, I will look at more recreational reading, stories about women and marriage, setting these too in their social context. I will then turn back to religious literature and look at the genres which were written and read by the clergy, who 'pray for all'. As I said above, many religious texts were now read by lay people, and at least two I discuss were written by women. I will look in Chapter 5 at the devotional and expressive writing of poets and mystics (or would-be mystics), and in Chapter 6 at the more popular genre of religious and moral stories. Finally I shall turn to the group who had most wealth and power, the nobility who 'fight for all', now being diluted – or regenerated – by an aspiring group of middle-class gentry. The literature the nobility had traditionally read was in French, and so I will begin Chapters 7 and 8 with a fairly detailed explanation of the continental traditions, ideas and legends about love and chivalry. I will then describe the sophisticated Lyrics, Dream Visions and Romances which gave the readers of this new literary English language a truly European culture.

My aim is to provide the reader with a variety of information and tools with which to approach a comprehensive range of medieval texts. Therefore as well as contextualising the literature as I have described, I also introduce the pre-eminent authors, both by describing their careers (in a series of text-boxes), and by including significant sections of their work in Example Texts, which are embedded within each chapter. Thus Chapter 1 includes analyses of Langland and of Dramas; Chapters 2 and 3 include passages from Langland and Chaucer, whose works are also discussed in greater detail in Chapters 4 and 7; Chapter 5 includes analyses of passages from the two women authors, Julian of Norwich and Margery Kempe; Chapters 6 and 8 include discussion of different poems from the *Gawain* manuscript; Chapter 7 will use a text by Henryson; and Chapter 8 will introduce Malory. I will also use passages from lesser-known authors, significant at the time, as Example Texts. I will try to cover all the literary genres and traditions in which writers of English were working. At the end of each Example Text you will find questions, which might ask you to relate the whole text to the information that has been provided, or to discuss the originality of the author's own voice, or how he comments on the social or ideological context in which he writes. In this way I hope to avoid handing out ready-made interpretations, and I return these wonderful texts to you, the reader. Each chapter will end with its own *Sources and Further Reading* bibliography.

(b) Manuscripts and Readers

Before I begin, however, I would like to suggest some of the differences between medieval and modern readers. I will start by describing the effect on writers and readers of a manuscript culture and look at how this was already changing before the revolution caused by the introduction of printing in 1476. To understand why writers made certain choices that you find strange, it may help you to use the super-sharp tools of modern literary criticism to dissect rather than to destroy these archaic texts.

(i) The development of manuscripts in the period

Until the late fourteenth century, manuscript production in England and Wales took place chiefly in religious houses (including friaries and the homes of the secular clergy as well as monasteries), the two universities, and a few London workshops. Almost all these manuscripts are in Latin, or occasionally in French. The manuscripts in Old and Middle English which survive, particularly if they are not religious, are generally provincial, and are usually associated with monasteries or noble households (see Boffey and Edwards 2011, p. 87). Many of these English texts are quite modest, perhaps produced at the request of a local lord who wanted a translation of a French romance, or a Life of his patron saint. But some much more ambitious provincial manuscripts do survive, such as the collections of poems known as the *Harley Lyrics* in British Library MS, Harley 2253 (Ludlow, 1340s) and the Vernon Manuscript (West Midlands, 1390s). The earlier texts of the 'Alliterative Revival' (*Wynnere and Wastoure*, the *Alliterative Morte Arthure*, and *Sir Gawain and the Green Knight*: mid- to late fourteenth century) are also provincial, using a North or West Midlands dialect, though, like Langland, their authors may well have lived also in London. The lives of many prominent families 'spanned London and the provinces... it was a restless not a static society... which discouraged the isolation of particular areas and classes of people' (Salter 1983, pp. 63–4).

Toward the end of the fourteenth century, London began to dominate manuscript production. The richly-decorated Auchinleck Manuscript (London, 1340s) demonstrates that groups of scribes there could produce an ambitious book by the middle of the fourteenth century, but the growing body of London book artisans did not form a Guild until 1403, and were not known generally as 'stationers' until the 1440s (see Christianson 1989, p. 88). Langland, Chaucer, Gower, and Hoccleve all lived in London, and by the end of the century their very popular texts were being copied professionally under private commission in small workshops. Such manuscripts, for example the Ellesmere Manuscript of the *Canterbury Tales*, could be as ornate as the products of the monasteries, so one of them could be given to a noble patron who had commissioned it from the writer. Gower claims that the first version of the *Confessio Amantis* was commissioned by King Richard II, and Chaucer says that Queen Anne asked him to write the *Legend of Good Women* (see Prol. F. 496–7). English manuscripts of this quality begin to be mentioned in wills, a tribute to their importance. Evidence that the middle classes were becoming book owners can be gleaned from the inventories of two bankrupt grocers, and from the wills of minor gentry like Sir John Paston, who owned several English literary manuscripts in the fifteenth century (Salter 1983, pp. 35, 39).

Secure in a market for the works of Langland, Chaucer or Gower, the London stationers began to copy their books 'on spec' and to sell them directly to the public, as they had been doing with Bibles and Books of Hours. This development gave the 'publisher' power to find and favour a market, and paved the way for Caxton to influence English gentlemen through his very successful publishing projects. Caxton used paper in his printing press. Paper had been used increasingly for books written in English in the fifteenth century, though not for high-status productions like liturgical books or court records, which continued to be written on parchment. Paper could be as much as eight times cheaper than parchment, so this technological development contributed to the greater availability of books (see Lyle 1989, p. 28). By the beginning of the Tudor period there was fast developing a large secular readership of people who would buy books, and who wanted new genres to fit a new world.

(ii) Medieval habits of writing and reading

This history of manuscript production and transmission of medieval texts must have affected the way writers thought about their work. I will suggest here four areas where medieval attitudes to texts may be different from our own. In the first place, the monastic context of manuscript production may well have brought with it a valuing of tradition over originality. It is not surprising that vernacular writers claim to be following in the footsteps of a greater author when this had so long been a mark of quality in a religious text. Secondly, because texts had been associated with the church, it was natural to assume they should be edifying. Lyrics were generally seen as aids to devotion rather than personally expressive, and even romances were more often Christian in tone than mere adventure stories. Writers on political and social subjects, when they were not using satire, tended to adopt a didactic tone; Anne Middleton (1978) hears in some works a new voice of secular public concern about social good. Lighter reading was also seen to be good for one, a form of recreation which stilled the passions and had a generally hygienic and recuperative effect upon the soul. It took some time for the author to free his reader from a position of subservience, listening to and learning from a teacher. The more sophisticated authors play with this assumed relationship, or subvert it completely (see Olson 1982, chs 1–3, for discussion of this development).

Thirdly, the rarity and expense of manuscripts had led to an almost universal practice of reading communally. There is fourteenth- and fifteenth-century evidence that recreational reading, particularly of romances and histories, was a usual occurrence after dinner in large households, such as those of James I of Scotland while a 'prisoner' in England, or of the sons of Henry IV, who enjoyed reading Chaucer together according to their tutor Scogan (see Coleman 1996, ch. 5). Communal reading also occurred in lowlier circles, such as among the scholars and commoners of New College Oxford, who, it was said in 1379, were allowed to 'linger in the hall' after supper if a fire was lit, and 'study poems, chronicles of kings, and wonders of this world' (Coleman 1996, p. 136). Devotional reading, particularly by women, was a little more likely to be private, but here too the practice of communal reading prevailed, whether in the monastery (for example, to accompany meals) or in the pious household. Lady Cecily Neville, in the fifteenth century, used to have a holy man read Walter Hilton to her at dinner, and she discussed devotional works with a cleric and probably other members of her household. In *Reading Families*, Krug argues that 'medieval women took part in literate culture through the authority of membership in family-based social groups', so that reading empowered them within their community rather than being 'an expression of gendered rebellion' or dissent (Krug 2002, pp. 4–5).

The practice of communal or public reading may have affected assumptions about the authorial voice. There is evidence that poets read their own work aloud, and clearly, its impact would be enhanced by a dramatic reading style. I will be addressing the question of authorial voice in Chapter 4 in the context of the tellers of the *Canterbury Tales*.

This oral dimension to texts for which there would be few written copies also encouraged the author to write in poetry rather than prose. This is my fourth area of difference between medieval and modern assumptions about texts. Poetry has the advantage of locking the author's ideas more securely into particular phrases, allowing them to be remembered or copied with fewer mistakes. Accordingly, almost all the genres of Middle English are poetic, and it is more interesting to ask why a text is in prose than why it is not. For example, the mystics (apart from Rolle) wrote in prose, perhaps because they were more focused on expressing their complex experiences rather than teaching others (and possibly exposing themselves to accusations of heresy). Religious texts had long tried to overcome the problems of oral transmission by giving pictorial forms as aids to the memory, and Middle English writers also used allegory and verbal pictures to convey meanings and fix them into their listeners' memories. Even an apparently plain text like *Piers Plowman* is richly decorated with allegory; these techniques will be looked at in Chapter 1. A comparison between the verse religious stories discussed in Chapter 6 and the prose *Morte Darthur* discussed in Chapter 8, shows what is lost and gained by the shift to prose for narrative fiction, which printing made almost universal.

(iii) Modern readers

Although it is good to have these sorts of consideration in mind when exploring Middle English literature, there is no need to be constrained by them. The most sophisticated of the Middle English texts display a complexity of reader/author relationship, a use of ambiguity, and an inventiveness and unexpectedness equal to those of any modern text. We can also find in them a questioning of traditional assumptions about authority, gender and class, and a sensitivity to the changes which were overtaking the author's society. A discerning critic can also find, in less sophisticated texts, revealing material about a writer's often ambiguous attitudes, for example on the position of women. Our approach to texts has become much more self-conscious and modern critical theory can help us interpret our reception of these texts.

This Guide, for example, suggests that the reader should be aware of contemporary social and political pressures, which identifies it among the many kinds of 'critical historicism' discussed in Patterson's collection of essays on *Literary Practice and Social Change* (1990), and in Barr's *Socioliterary Practice* (2001). These studies variously articulate the cultural and social forces which bear upon both the writer and his or her modern reader. Patterson also uses anthropological 'practice theory' to refine the more traditional contexts of social critics, such as patriarchy or gender studies. Other books experiment with applying modern critical theory to medieval texts. A variety of such approaches can be found in *Medieval Texts and Contemporary Readers*, edited by Finke and Shichtman (1987; for example, Trevis exploring reader/response theory, or Renoir the effects of aurality on texts). Strohm in *Theory and the Post-modern Text* (2000) develops what he calls 'practical theory' by using such techniques as 'symbolisation' or psychoanalysis to focus on particular texts. Salter's *Popular Reading in English* (2012) interestingly compares modern theories of reading with medieval reading practice. I have brought criticism which uses such theoretical approaches into my accounts of Example Texts and into the Further Reading sections. But whether you approach a text in the *persona* of a medieval or of a modern reader, or of both together, does not matter, so long as the result is your greater enjoyment of this wonderful body of literature.

Sources and Further Reading

Medieval social and linguistic change (see also Chapter 1)

Miller, E. and Hatcher, J. (1995) *Medieval England: Towns, Commerce and Crafts* (Longmans).

Patterson, L. (ed.) (1990) *Literary Practice and Social Change in Britain 1380–1430* (University of California Press).

Salter, Elizabeth (1983) *Fourteenth Century English Poetry: Contexts and Readings* (Oxford University Press).

Strohm, P. (1989) *Social Chaucer* (Harvard University Press), pp. 1–10.

Wright, L. (1996) *Sources of London English: Medieval Thames Vocabulary* (Clarendon Press).

Medieval manuscripts and readers

Amtower, L. (2000) *Engaging Words: The Culture of Reading in the Later Middle Ages* (Palgrave Macmillan).

Baugh, A. and Cable, T. (1993) *A History of the English Language*, 4th edn (Routledge).

Boffey, J. (2012) *Manuscript and Print in London, c. 1475–1530* (British Library).

Boffey, J. and Edwards, A. (2011) 'English literary writings 1150–1400', in Gillespie, A. and Wakelin, D. (eds), *The Production of Books in England 1350–1500* (Cambridge University Press).

Christianson, C. P. (1989) 'Evidence for the study of London's late medieval manuscript-book trade', in Griffiths, J. and Pearsall, D. (eds), *Book Production and Publishing in Britain 1375–1475* (Cambridge University Press).

Coleman, J. (1996) *Public Reading and the Reading Public in Late Medieval England and France* (Cambridge University Press).

Green, D. H. (2009) *Women Readers in the Middle Ages* (Cambridge University Press).

Griffiths, J. and Pearsall, D. (eds) *Book Production and Publishing in Britain 1375–1475* (Cambridge University Press).

Hudson, A. (1989) 'Lollard book production', in Griffiths, J. and Pearsall, D. (eds), *Book Production and Publishing in Britain 1375–1475* (Cambridge University Press).

Krug, R. (2002) *Reading Families: Women's Literate Practice in Later Medieval England* (Cornell University Press).

Lyle, R. J. (1989) 'Materials: the Paper revolution', in Griffiths, J. and Pearsall, D. (eds), *Book Production and Publishing in Britain 1375–1475* (Cambridge University Press).

Meale, C. (ed.) (1993) *Women and Literature in Britain 1150–1500* (Cambridge University Press).

Middleton, A. (1978) 'The idea of public poetry in the reign of Richard II', *Speculum*, 53, pp. 94–114.

Morgan, N. and Thompson, R. (eds) (2008) *The Cambridge History of the Book in Britain, Volume II, 1100–1400* (Cambridge University Press).

Norton-Smith, J. (1974) *Geoffrey Chaucer* (Routledge).
Olson, G. (1982) *Literature as Recreation in the Later Middle Ages* (Cornell University Press).
Pearsall, D. (1989) 'Introduction', in Griffiths, J. and Pearsall, D. (eds), *Book Production and Publishing in Britain 1375–1475* (Cambridge University Press).
Reynolds, S. (1996) *Medieval Reading: Grammar Rhetoric and the Classical Text* (Cambridge University Press).
Salter, Elizabeth (1983) *Fourteenth Century English Poetry: Contexts and Readings* (Oxford University Press).
Strohm, P. (1989) *Social Chaucer* (Harvard University Press).

Modern critical theory applied to medieval texts

Amtover, L. (2002) *Engaging Words: The Culture of Reading in the Later Middle Ages* (Palgrave Macmillan).
Barr, H. (2001) *Socioliterary Practice in Late Medieval England* (Oxford University Press).
Classen, A. (2004) *Discourses on Love, Marriage, and Transgression in Medieval and Early Modern Literature* (Arizona Centre for Medieval and Renaissance Texts).
Cohen, J. (2001) *The Postcolonial Middle Ages* (Palgrave Macmillan).
Corbellini, S. (ed.) (2013) *Cultures of Religious Reading in the Late Middle Ages* (Brepols).
Finke, L. and Shichtman, M. (eds) (1987) *Medieval Texts and Contemporary Readers* (Cornell University Press).
Hansen, E. (1992) *Chaucer and the Fictions of Gender* (University of California Press).
Patterson, L. (ed.) (1990) *Literary Practice and Social Change in Britain 1380–1530* (University of California Press).
Salter, Elizabeth (2012) *Popular Reading in English c. 1400–1600* (Manchester University Press).
Strohm, P. (2000) *Theory and the Pre-modern Text* (University of Minnesota Press).
Strohm, P. (ed.) (2007) *Oxford Twenty-first Century Approaches to Literature: Middle English* (Oxford University Press).
Travis, P. W. (1987) 'Affective criticism: oral-formulaic rhetoric', in Finke, L. and Shichtman, M. (eds), *Medieval Texts and Contemporary Readers* (Cornell University Press).

General guides to Middle English literature (a selection)

Bennett, J. (1986) *Middle English Literature* (Clarendon).
Boffey, J. and Edwards, A. (eds) (2013) *A Companion to Fifteenth-century Englsh Poetry* (D. S. Brewer).
Brewer, D. (1983) *English Gothic Literature* (Macmillan).
Burrow, J. (1971) *Ricardian Poetry: Chaucer, Gower, Langland and the Gawain-poet* (Routledge).
Burrow, J. (2012) *English Poets in the Late Middle Ages: Chaucer, Langland and Others* (Ashgate).
Cannon, C. (2008) *Middle English Literature: A Cultural History* (Polity).
Corrie, M. (2008) *A Concise Companion to Middle English Literature* (Wiley-Blackwell).
Pearsall, D. (1977) *Old English and Middle English Poetry* (Routledge).
Turville-Petre, T. (2007) *Reading Middle English Literature* (Blackwell Introductions to Literature, Blackwell).

Chapter 1

The Poor Commons: Literature and Social Change

Medieval society was hierarchical; we will start at the bottom, with the poor and underprivileged who made up the majority of it. In this and the next chapter I will be discussing the 'illiterate readers' in the countryside and towns, the literature written with this audience in mind, and the literature which (though not necessarily addressed to them) described their changing experience and problems. This first chapter will look at the developments in the lives of the illiterate commoners, at the Black Death and the Great Rising of 1381, and indicate how some of these developments are reflected in the literature, particularly *Piers Plowman* and Religious Drama. The next chapter will look more closely at other kinds of literature designed for the illiterate poor, and at their educational development and ventures towards dissent in religion. Both chapters will therefore show the commoners experiencing and initiating change, and discuss writing which is in different ways seditious and far-thinking. However, in neither chapter can it be claimed that the rural or urban poor were the sole readers of the literature discussed, for it was written and read by educated people, both clerical and lay, and in the case of the Drama was supported by the very wealthiest and highest groups in society, as well as by the illiterate poor.

These commoners had traditionally been the rural peasantry, who probably made up ninety per cent of the population in the early Middle Ages. But during the thirteenth to fifteenth centuries more and more of them became urbanised. There had always been migrants from the villages looking for work in the towns, and as serfdom – which bound the peasants to their lord's estate or 'manor' – declined in the later fourteenth century, the trickle became a flood. As villages became market towns, and established towns expanded, and even became cities, there was an increasing need for them to maintain communication with the countryside, which provided them with food. The peasants themselves – still the majority of commoners – needed to sell their produce outside the villages because by the end of the fourteenth century many peasants were renting their land for cash, rather than being in feudal service. This overlap between the commons of town and country meant that they became a single audience in terms of their tastes and responses, though most of them could not read. Townsmen were still interested in the problems of peasants, and country people came from the country into the town to see the drama performances. In East Anglia, one of the most sophisticated parts of England, groups of actors even began to leave town to play in the larger villages. As we shall see in the next chapter, 'homiletic' or educational religious texts were preached to the poor in both the town and the country, sometimes with inflammatory results. Indeed, the most shocking event of the period, the Great Rising (or Peasants' Revolt) of 1381, can be seen as a coming together of the commoners of both country and town in an attempt to end the grievances which oppressed them all.

I will begin the chapter with a brief account of some of the social history of the time, the Black Death, the decline of serfdom, and the Great Rising. These events are reflected in the popular fourteenth-century poem by William Langland, *Piers Plowman*, my first Example Text, for although this poem as addressed to a reading community, it includes two ploughing scenes which illustrate social change. I will then give an account of the different kinds of plays that were written in Middle English. Although Secular Drama expected a particular audience, Religious Drama, as I have said, was enjoyed by all classes of society, literate as well as illiterate, being arguably the most 'literary' of the genres accessible to the poor commoners. It was generally performed by the urban commoners themselves, and many plays used contemporary social conditions to bring the Bible stories to life. I will give as my Example Texts two such plays, the Mystery (or Miracle) Play known as the Wakefield *Cain and Abel*, and the Morality Play *Mankind*, both from the fifteenth century. The central character of both these plays is a farmer, and can be compared with Langland's Piers, a figure who lies behind the 'Lollard' texts examined in the next chapter. Finally I will say something about the little which has survived of the oral tradition of literature, the secular ballads and plays handed down informally from one generation to another.

(a) The Black Death, Decline of Serfdom and the Great Rising of 1381

It is indeed its hunger for change which makes the estate of 'poor commons' the most interesting audience to write for and to try to influence. It was the class most affected by the economic and social changes that followed the Black Death, which probably halved the population between 1348 and 1361. This plague greatly diminished the labour pool, and increased the availability of land and employment opportunities, allowing the rapid development of a landowning 'middle' class of peasants in the countryside, and of shopkeepers and craftsmen in the towns. If the century after the Black Death was a 'golden age for the middle . . . peasantry' (Hilton 1985, p. 149), this availability of opportunity was even more evident in the towns (see Waugh 1991, chs 3 and 4).

As the villagers and artisans became more emancipated financially, they were increasingly finding their way to education. Priests often taught village boys practical reading skills, and there were opportunities for children to attend monastic and convent schools, on payment of a fee to their overlord. Such opportunities were multiplied in the towns, where the audience for literature became increasingly sophisticated. These educational developments will be discussed more in the next chapter. As commoners developed in wealth and education they aspired to take a larger part in social affairs, and resented restrictions on their freedom, particularly those imposed by the outdated institution of serfdom. This severely restricted their ownership of property, their wages, and their ability to move freely. Unjust customs had been exacerbated by recent unjust laws, not only the Statutes of Labourers, which aimed to keep wages and prices depressed after the Black Death (when labour was scarce and labourers powerful), but also the hated Poll Taxes. The Chancellor invented these as a means to pay for the renewal of the war in France by demanding 12 pence (in the Third Poll Tax – two weeks' wages for a ploughman) from every man and woman in the kingdom over the age of 15. Working men who had developed organisational skills, either in local village government or in the defence of the port towns from invasion, were – if we are to believe the Chronicles – 'corrupted' by disaffected preachers to offer an alternative to suffering these restrictions any more. The commoners could refuse to be bound by laws that they saw as unjust. They could combine in large groups and force their lords to change these laws and customs; they could threaten to kill lawyers who upheld them; and they could even march on London and punish the Chancellor and Chief Justice for their 'crimes against the people'.

In June 1381, a considerable body of commoners, largely peasants from Kent and Essex, marched to London, where they were joined by a great number of local craftsmen, artisans, apprentices, and other townsfolk. One of the rebels' stated aims was to 'slay all tyrants' – and in particular the Chancellor (Archbishop Sudbury) and the Treasurer (Robert Hales) who had instigated the Poll Tax. They succeeded in doing this on 14 June, executing them in the Tower itself. A more far-reaching aim of the rebels was to abolish serfdom altogether, and so they and other rebels in the country at large killed a number of lawyers, including the Chief Justice, and destroyed many legal records, hoping to institute a system in which master and servant, or lord and tenant, could make contracts freely. On 14 June, King Richard II himself rode to meet them at Mile End, east of the City, and offered them liberty from serfdom, amnesty for their revolt, and the punishment of (unspecified) traitors. 'Charters of manumission' from serfdom were quickly drawn up for the counties from which they had come, and to which some immediately began to return. However, according to some chroniclers, notably Walsingham and Knighton, many rebels wanted to go further in their demands, and 'end all lordship', in accordance with the supposedly egalitarian notions of their spiritual leader, John Ball. The *Anonimalle Chronicle* recounts that on the following day at Smithfield their leader, the Kentish Wat Tyler, made such outrageous further demands and with a dagger in his hand, that he was killed by the men surrounding the king. At this dangerous moment the fourteen-year-old king then courageously rode towards the infuriated rebels and offered to be their leader himself, but led them not to freedom but only to Clerkenwell, where they found they had lost the initiative. The sense of disappointment and failure must have been immense as they returned home in the following weeks to find the Charters of Manumission had been revoked the day after they had been granted. (See Dunn 2002, chs 4–6, for a detailed account of these events.)

The reaction to this abortive revolution was one of middle- and upper-class horror and outrage, as shown in all remaining records, including the Rolls of Parliament and the Chronicles. However, two of these also preserved some records of what the rebels themselves wrote, including 'coded' letters which use phrases from *Piers Plowman*. (These are discussed in detail in Justice 1994, ch. 3; the letters themselves are printed in Krochalis and Peters 1975, pp. 83–5, or Robertson and Shepherd, eds, *Piers Plowman*, 2005, p. 484.) The Chroniclers, as we will see in the next chapter (p. 50), blamed the revolt on itinerant preachers, and the fear of rebellion continued to fan the flames in which religious dissenters were burned in the following century. Literary conservatives like John Gower saw the rebels as animals in his *Vox Clamantis* (see p. 102 below). It is true that the rebels sullied their cause by the use of violence, murder and vandalism. During the week of riots in London and some other cities, the rebels attacked or sacked the buildings and foundations of hated lords and institutions, such as the Temple (the lawyers' church) and the Savoy (palace of the most powerful and corrupt of the king's uncles, the Duke of Lancaster), and they destroyed the Fleet prison and released its inmates. However, the real aims of the rebels were more or less achieved by the end of the century, as serfdom had been abandoned on most country estates and the peasants were either renting land under contract or 'copyhold', or purchasing it outright, employing one another and enjoying the common law rights of free citizens. The Revolt of 1381 may indeed have hastened this result, and it certainly prevented any further king from imposing a Poll Tax until Margaret Thatcher tried it in the 1980s.

Example Text: Ploughing Scenes in *Piers Plowman*

To illustrate the social changes that I have been describing, I would like to look at part of *Piers Plowman*, a poem too sophisticated to have been intended for an illiterate audience, but which is engrossed by its concern for the poor commons in the countryside and in London. Its enormous popularity suggests it was read to and by a broad audience; it was even used to provide a code for the rebels in the Great Rising (see Justice 1994, ch. 3).

The poem is a long 'Dream Vision' in an alliterative metre so plain and loose as to feel frequently like prose, but able to achieve dramatic effects and intricate word play when required (see the text-boxes on pp. 185 and 25). What is most immediately striking about it is its variety and inclusiveness, its vivid depiction of so much of the society with which this survey is concerned. There are scenes in the London markets, in the King's Council, in the households of lords and beggars, in the church, in the field, on the hills. Everywhere we see human drama, as men and women struggle to gain status and wealth or merely their daily bread; oppress others or try to control oppression; indulge in pleasure or try to love one another. The poem shows the world as a whole; its shifting cast of characters is confronted by political, economic, social and religious forces at once, as we are in real life. This universal confusion is epitomised by the bewilderment of the narrator, Will, who travels through the world and through his own mind, reporting the struggles of others while also struggling with himself. His very name, Will, is ambiguous, suggesting at once an individual called William, usually assumed to be the author William Langland, and the general human Will. This ambiguity makes his personal questions into ones which touch everyone. Indeed, although the poet offers us consistent values for judging the world – the values of Truth, of Justice, of Love, of Faith – he seems to expect his readers to work things out for themselves, and to find their own routes through the scenes and characters which confront them at every turn. Being so open-ended gives the reader dynamic choices; in a different way and for different reasons this is also the effect of the poet Chaucer, writing for a much higher class of people. *Piers Plowman* is relevant to the next three chapters of this Guide, but here I will focus on Langland's description of the changes in their way of life overtaking the poor commons.

William Langland

We know nothing definite about this author. Several manuscripts of his only known work, *Piers Plowman*, assert that it was written by a Robert or William Langland, and one (Trinity College Dublin MS 212) says that 'Willielmi de Langlond', was the son of 'Stacy de Rokayle, who died in Shipton-under-Wychwood in Oxfordshire'. This would suggest that he was from the minor aristocracy, which might explain his extensive knowledge of law and parliament. However, he himself implies that he is a poor man and that he comes from the Malvern Hills, which fits the dialect of some of the manuscripts. The poem exists in three main versions, which can be roughly dated by the contemporary events to which this most topical of poems alludes. It would appear that it was begun during the last years of Edward III's reign (A-text), rewritten shortly after Richard II's coronation in 1377 and the Papal Schism of 1378 but before the Great Rising of 1381 (B-text), and then rewritten again, possibly after the 'tyranny' of Richard II, 1382–6, one of the Statutes of Labourers (1388) and the rise of the Lollard movement in the late 1380s (C-text; see the next two chapters for descriptions of these events). This would mean that the author was alive between approximately 1330 and 1390. Unless the 'Will' of the poem is not the poet himself but an appropriate *persona*, we can also learn some details of his life from the poem, especially from C.5.1–108, B.12.1–28 and B.20.1–58. He lived in London on Corn Hill with his wife and daughter, and the poem is full of the sights and sounds of London, to where almost all its vibrant cast of characters come unless they were there already; even Christ seems to be crucified among the riff-raff of a London street. Langland has a deep and detailed knowledge of Christian learning, but (like Gower and Hoccleve) as a married man he could not have been a priest, but must have been only in 'minor orders', earning his living by no secular 'craft' but by such clerk's tasks as saying prayers for the dead (C.5.45–50). It is likely, however, that he was partly supported by patrons and readers, for his poem is included in some 56 manuscripts, a remarkably large number for a text written in English.

Sources: Hanna (1993); Bowers (1995).

The text of *Piers Plowman* is divided into a succession of 'Passus' or steps, beginning with a Prologue, and at several points Langland describes the peasantry, seeing them both literally and symbolically. The Prologue is a depiction of the different classes or 'estates' (discussed in Chapter 3 below), in which the author introduces himself as Will, a 'hermit' on the scrounge, a social parasite who has never done a decent day's work in his life. After a long episode of venality satire (also discussed in Chapter 3), we meet Will's opposite, Piers the Plowman, a true labourer whose Truth is the honest farming of food. Piers offers to lead the commoners, whom we have just seen confessing their sins, towards his kind of Truth by setting them to work like Adam: ploughing will be their penance for sin.

This scene, which occupies Passus 6 in the B-text, is a fascinating reflection of the social changes in the countryside, which I have just been describing. As we have seen, it was increasingly common for the tenants to rent the land, including the lord's demesne, and farm it themselves. Some of these peasants were rich enough to own their own ploughs, but it was rare for them to own an entire plough team as well, and others did not even own a plough. So they continued the tradition established under the years of serfdom and shared their beasts to make up a team, so that 'Ploughing not only provided the staff of life, but it depended on collective effort, so that ploughmen stood for co-operation and shared responsibility' (Dyer 1995, pp. 57–8). Piers indeed involves the whole village, women as well as men, the knight (and landlord?) as well as the ditchers, in the effort to grow food. Literally, Piers epitomises the new kind of peasant-employer who replaced the lord and who paid a wage but also relied on the co-operation of his peers. Symbolically he also epitomises service to Truth in its medieval sense of faith-keeping as well as honesty:

> 'I haue ben his folwere al this fourty wynter – ...
> I haue myn hire of hym wel and otherwhiles moore'. (5.542, 50)
>
> *folwere*: follower; *hire*: pay; *otherwhiles moore*: sometimes more (pay)

Returning to the literal sense of this community working in the half-acre, we can see at once that it has the typical disadvantage of a group of social equals: the leader has few sanctions to make the Waster work.

For although some of the labourers seem to be following the principles of Truth, working honestly and keeping faith with their employer, others

> seten ... and songen atte nale,
> And holpen to erye his half acre wilth 'How trolly lolly!' (B.6.115–16)
>
> *atte nale*: over a drink of ale; *holpen to erye*: helped to plough [ironic]

For a while Piers can withdraw wages and wheaten bread (214) to force Waster into working, but when the harvest comes in and labour is in short supply, Waster demands higher wages and wanders off the farm in search of them.

> And tho wolde Wastour noght werche, but wandren aboute,
> Ne no beggere ete breed that benes inne were (B.6.301–2)
>
> (Bread made with beans was used for cattle food.)

This situation closely reflects the labour problems in the decades suffering the visitations of the Black Death (1348–61), which Edward III's parliaments tried to solve by legislation. Between 1349 and the end of the century, Parliament passed a series of Statutes and Ordinances requiring all the able-bodied to work, to accept regulated levels of pay, and to remain with an employer for the full period of their contracts. The Wasters, 'Britoners' (discharged soldiers) and other landless labourers in Langland's story seem to be flouting all three principles of the legislation:

> Laborers that haue no land to lyue on but hire handes
> Deyned noght to dyne aday nyght-olde wortes; ...
> He greueth hym ageyn God and gruccheth ageyn Reson,
> And thanne corseth he the Kyng and al his Counseil after
> Swiche lawes to loke, laborers to greue. (B.6.306–16)
>
> *handes*: their hands are their only source of income; *Deyned not*: thought it beneath them; *night-old wortes*: yesterday's vegetables; *gruccheth*: grumbled

It does seem as though Langland approves the legislation as being in accordance with the teachings of God and Reason, in spite of the fact that its avowed aim was to keep the poor from bettering themselves (because of the fear of an economic collapse). The legislation was of course hated by the rural poor, providing an additional excuse for rebellion, and although it was enforced for a while, could not ultimately stop wages from rising during the later fourteenth century. Piers does not bring in the knight as JP, or the other justices appointed to enforce the legislation, and Langland ends the Passus with a warning that such irresponsible behaviour may well result in famine. In any case, Piers' ploughing enterprise seems to be only a partial success and we are not entirely surprised when Will abandons Piers and goes off on his own to find Truth in other ways.

However, when Piers returns in Passus 19, not to serve, but to plant Truth, Langland seems to have gone back in time to a traditional feudal manor. In a kind of recapitulation of the Prologue, Grace gives gifts to the various estates, culminating in the ploughman, who is once again made the leader. Here Piers clearly plays the part of St Peter, the first Pope, to whom Jesus specifically gave the power *To bynde and vnbynde* sinners (19.190; see Luke 22:60–2). But Grace, acting as a kind of feudal overlord, then gives him a series of jobs characteristic of a feudal model of service to a lord:

> For I make Piers the Plowman my procuratour and my reue,
> And registrer to receyue *Redde quod debes*.
> My prowour and my plowman Piers shal ben on erthe,
> And for to tilie truthe a teeme shal he haue. (19.260–3)
>
> *procuratour*: agent; *registrer*: registrar; *Redde quod debes*: render what is owed; *prowour*: purveyor; *tilie truthe*: plough truth; *teeme*: plough-team

A *procuratour* was an agent, a reeve (*reue*) was a servile villager responsible for organising a lord's tenant services and keeping his accounts; a *register* was a keeper of records including accounts; and a *prowour* was a purveyor who requisitioned supplies for a lord. Such titles would give Piers an isolating and necessarily unpopular authority over the other villagers, responsible for exacting payments and debts. Why has Langland returned to this older model of serfdom in his allegory of the early Church?

Before deciding that Langland is an arch conservative in disguise, we should note that this authoritative model for cultivating Truth in the world is less successful than the co-operative cultivation of actual corn had been in Passus 6. Piers himself only fulfils his manorial duties for a limited time: using a team of oxen – the four evangelists and the four famous 'Doctors' of the Church – he sows the *greyness* of the Cardinal Virtues (264–77), and prepares a barn called *Unitas* or *holy Chirche on Englissh* (331) to store the expected crops of Truth. Grace and Piers then leave the responsibility of growing Truth, and so being able to pay the debts they owe to Grace, to Conscience as King. Does this mean that the individual Christian cannot devolve his moral responsibility and Christian duties to the Church authorities but must follow an inner sense of right and wrong? This would suggest that the authoritative model of the Church has already changed into the more co-operative model we met in Passus 6. And indeed it seems as though Conscience is as weak a leader as Piers had been earlier. Soon we see that neither he nor his fellows can stand up for long against the attacks of Antichrist:

> Antichrist cam thanne, and al the crop of truthe
> Torned it [tid] vp-so-doun, and ouertilte the roote,
> And made fals sprynge and sprede and spede mennes nedes.
> In ech a contree ther he cam he kutte awey truthe,
> And gerte gile growe there, as he a god weere. (B.20.54–8)
>
> *ouertilte*: turned over; *tid*: quickly; *spede*: proper; *gerte*: made

Antichrist is a kind of anti-ploughman: his plough turns over the crop, not the soil, and cuts away the good plants (Truth) to let the weeds grow (Guile). Only a few Christians, the Fools, resist the hypocrisy and deceit with which Antichrist and Pride infuse the entire Church, and the Sins (such as Lechery and Covetousness) who follow in their wake. These few Fools retreat into *Unitas* but are corrupted from within by the Friars, and the poem ends in the fall of the Church. But is this the true Church which has failed, or a degenerate hierarchical structure 'ruled' by the Pope and his cardinals, who are concerned only to get the people to pay their debts in money?

> The contree is the corseder that cardinals come inne …
> Inparfit is that Pope that al peple sholde helpe,
> And s[ou]deth hem thaat sleeth swiche as he sholde saue. (B.19.431–3)
>
> *s[ou]deth hem thaat sleeth*: pays them who slay

These bitter words are spoken by a *lewed vicory* (413), who offers the alternative of a Church led by Piers Plowman, working (as we saw in Passus 6) for the whole community, and whose weak authority encourages Truth to grow within the individuals who try to follow him:

> Right so Piers the Plowman peyneth hym to tilye
> As wel for a wastour and wenches of the stewes
> As for hymself and hise seruaunts, saue he is first yserued. (19.438–40)
>
> *peyneth hym to tilye*: takes pains to plough; *wenches of the stewes*: prostitutes; *saue he is first yserued*: except that he is served first

It may be that Langland's understanding of the emancipation of the peasantry in secular society (and his contact with the Wycliffite ideas we will discuss in the next chapter) softens the apparently pessimistic ending of the poem. If Christians no longer obeyed the Church, and the Church had failed to obey Grace, then – in a world turned both upside down and inside out – morality and Grace might still be found in the individual heart. Conscience ends the poem with a prayer:

> Now ... sende me hap and heele, til I haue Piers the Plowman!
> And siththe he gradde after Grace, til I gan awake (B.20.385–7)
>
> *sende me hap and heele*: send me good fortune and good health; *gradde*: cried aloud

Questions on ploughing scenes in *Piers Plowman*

- Do the two ploughing scenes in the poem suggest to you a traditionalist or a reformist attitude to social developments? How do you interpret the use made by the rebels of quotations from the poem? (See Krochalis and Peters 1975, or Shepherd and Robertson (eds), *Piers Plowman*, 2005, for the texts.)
- Looking also at his imitation in *Piers the Plowman's Crede* (see Chapter 2, pp. 55–7), discuss the character and reception of Piers himself (if you can, include his appearances in B. Passus 16 and 18).
- Analyse Langland's cast of characters in Passus 6 and 19, looking particularly at the roles played by beggars, misfits and women.

Alliterative Poetry

A great deal of Middle English literature (including many of the texts discussed in these first two chapters) used alliteration, as a structural principle to enhance the poetry and to make it memorable. Poems of this type revive the Old English poetic tradition, so that their appearance between about 1350 and 1450 has been known as the 'Alliterative Revival'. Alliteration could be used with rhyme, as in the Wakefield *Cain and Abel* where there is a definite rhymed and scanned stanza but where each line usually includes alliterating letters. The virtuosic lyric poem *Pearl* and the lyrics of Dunbar show its effectiveness in rhymed stanzas. But traditionally it was used on its own, in the 'alliterative long line', characterised as follows:

- Each line divided into two half-lines separated by a pause, generally in a four-beat pattern though with a varying number of syllables.
- Half-lines are linked by a single alliterative letter or a consonant-group (sp, sk etc.), generally at the beginning of a word, or by the use of any vowel as an initial letter.
- The alliteration generally occurs on the two stressed syllables in the first half of the line and on the first stressed syllable in the second half (a a / a x).

Piers Plowman and poems following its lead (such as the Lollard poems discussed in Chapter 2 and the Advice for Princes discussed in Chapter 3) are written in a plain 'low style', with a rather loose approach to rhythm, stress and alliteration, allowing for realistic conversation, complex argument, or narrative. But occasionally it is lifted into set pieces of onomatopoeic action more characteristic of the older 'high style', which is further characterised by:

- the employment of unusual (often 'poetic') words to provide alliterating synonyms, including French technical terms, Scandinavian words from northern dialects, and Old English words from poetic or geographical contexts (see p. 175 below); for example, the use of *jesseraunt* (French: coat of mail), *carpe* (Northern: to speak), or *clogh* (Old English: cliff), which are words we would only expect to meet in alliterative poetry;
- repetitions of an idea in different variations in order to meet the demands of the alliterative metre and to create sound-effects.

> Alliterative poems written in this style cover a variety of subjects. They include virtuosi lyrics like *Swarte-smeked smethes* (Davies, ed. 1963, no. 115), Dream Vision debates like the *Parliament of Three Ages*, *Wynnere and Wastoure* and *Death and Life*, and in particular, verse Chronicles and Romances like the *Alliterative Morte Arthure*, the *Wars of Alexander*, and *Sir Gawain and the Green Knight*.
>
> Source: Turville-Petre (1977, ch. 4).

(b) The Drama

I will now turn to a genre of literature which healed the social divisions between rich and poor, free and unfree, learned and illiterate. From the first performances of the Mystery Plays in the later fourteenth century until their suppression with the Saints' and Doctrine Plays by the Protestants of the sixteenth, Religious Drama had been a force for unity. It enacted the experience of the lowest and the highest classes, it brought men together to put on these spectacles, and it was watched by the whole community, from the illiterate commoner who learned his Bible from the plays, to the lord or king who learned about his low-born neighbours from seeing their sufferings enacted by their representatives on stage. Indeed, the Mystery Play continues to be inclusive, for it is one of the two kinds of medieval literature still experienced fairly widely by non-specialists (the other being the Mystics). Morality Plays have a long history from before the first surviving Mystery Plays until well into the Renaissance. Secular Drama includes Pageants, staged for important civic occasions, and Interludes, performed at the Universities and Inns of Court. But Morality Plays can also use broad humour which would appeal to the commons of the villages and towns, and these audiences also enjoyed Mummers' Plays and Robin Hood Plays on summer festival days.

I will look first at the Mystery Play Cycles, using the Wakefield *Cain and Abel* as my Example Text, because it explores some of the problems confronting the peasantry in the period. I will then turn to the Saints' Plays and Moralities and look in more detail at *Mankind*, who is another peasant or at least a representative of Adam. Finally

I will briefly look at the Secular Drama, for which there are few texts, but from which we can trace influences on not only the Mystery Plays but also Renaissance Drama. I will also include the ballads, which although not plays are similarly relics of a vigorous oral tradition to which the illiterate could themselves contribute.

(i) Religious Drama: Mystery Play Cycles

Most of the surviving dramas of the later Middle Ages are retellings of the Biblical history of the world from the Creation to the life of Christ, and then on to the Last Judgement. These 'Mystery Cycles' (sometimes called Miracle Plays) were generally written by the clergy for performance by members of the town Guilds or 'Mysteries'. Records of plays of this kind survive from the fourteenth to the sixteenth centuries, and regular performances continued in some places until some years after the Reformation. Complete Cycles survive from York (probably the earliest, as it was in existence before 1376), Chester, Wakefield (or 'Towneley'), and the area around Bury St Edmunds (the so-called N-town Cycle); there is also a Cycle in Old Cornish. Records and occasional plays survive from the Cycles at Beverley, Newcastle, Coventry and Norwich among others. The audience were both townsfolk and country visitors of all classes, and performances of individual plays were given in wealthy households. The rich and powerful were eager to join the general audience; Richard II watched plays in London in 1397, and Queen Margaret watched the Coventry Cycle in 1457. Two of the Cycles may have been intended for a more rustic audience: Wakefield was only a small town at the centre of a large agricultural estate (the Manor of Wakefield in West Yorkshire), and the so-called 'N-town Cycle' seems to have been performed by a group of actors in Bury and then taken around the nearby small towns and villages as well, changing the name of the Cycle to suit the location ('N-town' mans 'any name' town).

The performance of Cycle plays was an expensive civic affair, paid for directly by the members of the Guilds, who not only staged individual plays but also put on a Guild procession on the following day. They vied with each other in the staging of their play and in the splendour of the (contemporary) costumes, but sometimes preferred to pay a fine to the city authorities to avoid the considerable expense that the production cost. These city authorities kept a tight control on the whole occasion, watching the performance to check that the actors were speaking the approved scripts. It is for this reason that the scripts have survived, mostly in city archives. The whole Cycle was generally performed on Corpus Christi Day (the first Thursday after Trinity Sunday, which can fall between 23 May and 24 June) or at Whitsun. The days are long then, but not all of the forty-nine extant York plays can have been performed every year, and the Chester Cycle may have extended its twenty-five plays over three days. The actors were generally members of the Guild, and were paid for their performances; they were all male (though see Normington 2004, pp. 91ff.). Professional musicians and singers were hired to enhance the performance. Each play was performed on a wheeled wagon, richly decorated, and sometimes with an upper structure to represent Heaven, or an enclosed space below the wagon to represent Hell. These wagons were pulled to the different 'stations' in the city (10–12 in the case of York, 5 in Chester, etc.), where scaffolds had been erected to seat the wealthier citizens and visitors (who paid for their seats) and where most of the audience watched for nothing. The actors frequently entered the same space, as Mrs Noah and her cronies, shepherds looking for the stable, or soldiers of Herod, making it impossible for them not to feel the relevance of the Biblical story to their own situation.

The playwrights were almost certainly local clerks, working in a definite and sophisticated tradition, and at first new writers made changes to the text (though this practice was later stopped by the civic authorities). The choice of episodes to write about quickly became traditional, focused on the Passion of Christ and the events from the Old Testament (like the Flood or the Sacrifice of Isaac) which made it necessary or which 'prefigured' it (Isaac is a 'type' of the sacrificed Christ). The Crucifixion would be followed by its consequences, the 'Harrowing of Hell' taken from the Apocryphal *Gospel of Thomas*, and the events of Easter, the Life and Death of the Virgin Mary (also Apocryphal), and the Last Judgment. Two writers have been 'identified' though nothing is known about them, in the two earliest Cycles, York and Wakefield/Towneley, which share a number of plays. The Towneley Cycle is named after the family who once owned the manuscript, but the plays were probably performed in Wakefield, a rising market town about twenty-five miles from York. The York Plays are recorded as being performed as early as 1378, and at least two of them, the *Dream of Pilate's Wife* and the *Crucifixion*, are said to be by the 'York Realist' whose grim comic writing contrasts painfully with his tragic portrayal of Jesus' sufferings. He possibly revised both these and eleven other plays, giving them a vigorous alliterative metre (see Turville-Petre 1977, pp. 122–3). It seems likely that the 'Wakefield Master' revised a copy of the York Plays for performance there some time in the mid-fifteenth century, filling them with references to places around Wakefield to reinforce their local identity, and adding other lively touches, like the devil Titivillus, to the *Last Judgment*. He also wrote fresh versions of six highly original plays which both reveal the reality of working people's lives and question God's relationship with them. He demonstrates a dangerous use of comedy that almost undermines the Bible story being told, and a particular interest in dramatic tyrants and villains. Both these characteristics are prominent in my Example Text, *Cain and Abel*, which focuses on a wicked ploughman and so provides an interesting contrast with the work of Langland. This would have been a topic very relevant to the Wakefield audience of farmers and those who had escaped from that life to become craftsmen and traders; all could understand, laugh and shudder at Cain's predicament.

Example Text: The Wakefield (Towneley) *Cain and Abel*

Instead of making Cain an unsympathetic type of the 'worldly man' (see the Chester *Cain and Abel*), the Wakefield master shows us a Cain who expresses the sufferings of a contemporary peasant, though we may feel he exaggerates his proximity to beggary:

> I am ich yere wars than othere –
> Here my trouth, it is non othere.
> My wynnyngys ar bot meyn ... (109–11)
> When all mens corn was fayre in felde
> Then was myne not worth a neld.

> When I shuld saw, and wantyd seyde, …
> Then gaf he me none of his,
> No more will I gif hym of this (122–7)
> And it is better hold that I haue
> Then go from doore to doore and craue (142–3)
>
> *wynnyngys ar bot meyn*: my profit is only small; *not worth a neld*: not worth a needle; *craue*: beg

If the audience sympathised with these complaints, would they have also sympathised with the way Cain then chooses the sheaves for his sacrifice? He treats this as a medieval tithe, a customary 'rate' which by the fifteenth century was far lower than the Biblical tenth of one's goods, and paid to the Church to maintain both the priest and some of his charitable responsibilities. Should we see Cain as a newly emancipated peasant unwilling to give up the corn he now produces for himself, or as a selfish individualist unwilling to fulfil his responsibilities to the community? As Helterman points out in an excellent essay on the play (1981), Cain uses the first person singular almost entirely, only addressing Abel as his brother in a moment of bitter irony (line 108), and by the end he has almost replaced him by his servant, Garcio. From the first moment he has wanted to dominate by violence (his beasts, his servant, even the audience), and it is plausible that he would be infuriated by his younger brother's citation of the *custom of our lawe* (69) or of what *our father us bad* (72). Can we see the murder as – if not justified – at least explicable in an older brother who feels his supreme father, God, has always preferred the other sibling (*Me thynk that God is not my freynd*, 302)? He rejects all manifestations of authority, by the Church and the community, by his brother, by his father and by God. Did this strike a chord with an audience who had recently thrown off the bonds of serfdom and who valued freedom and independence even when it must be achieved by violence?

The one constraint that Cain seems to accept is the payment of debt, a principle which was also important (though in a different way – see pp. 22–3 above) in the second ploughing scene in *Piers Plowman*. Garcio's mirroring ripostes to Cain insist on a tit for tat morality: *with the same mesure and weght / That I boro will I qwite* (50–1), and argues that since God *gaf me none of his / No more wil I gif hym of this* (126–7).

Abel criticises Cain's tithing seven times, and so Cain might well see God's rejection of his sacrifice as a confirmation of Abel's rejection of it, and so *aght* (owes) Abel for God's *foul despite* (insult: 314). Shouting *now is tyme that I hit qwite* (315) he kills Abel, immediately expecting the same punishment himself (356–64). This is the Old Testament principle of 'an eye for an eye', and it is typical of this playwright's quality to suggest that Cain's expectation that debt must be repaid, and crime punished, seems to be integral to his characterisation as a poor peasant, determined not to give anything away, not to be taken advantage of, not to lose his independence.

Many Old Testament plays (*The Fall of the Angels*, *Adam and Eve*, *Noah*) demonstrate how those who disobey the law receive what God here calls his 'malision' (355). In the long sweep of a complete Cycle, such plays contrast with those performing the New Covenant of mercy, most notably the *Harrowing of Hell*, in which Christ's death is shown to release humankind from punishment in Hell. It can be argued that this replacement of justice by mercy takes place within this single play. If Cain expresses the Old Testament insistence on a strict repayment of debt, Abel expresses the New Testament God who offers gifts to his people and expects a return only as a proof of gratitude. As Abel puts it:

> Yis, all the good thou has in wone
> Of Godys grace is bot a lone ... (116–17)
> Gif we hym parte of oure fee. (76)
>
> *wone*: dwelling; *fee*: profit

God also seems to be ready to pardon both Cain's bad sacrifice and his murder of Abel (370–3), thus giving him 'a releasse' (407). But locked in their Old Testament attitudes, neither Cain nor Garcio take God's 'release' seriously. Garcio uses it as an opportunity to mock Cain, and Cain himself ignores it as he goes to hide from other men (470) and predicts his ordained '*stall with Sathanas the feynd*' in Hell (465). Is it then God or Cain himself who is responsible for his own isolation and despair? Is the playwright warning his audience against the perils of being too independent, too focused on one's rights to trust the friendship of a brother, of the village, or even of God?

Questions on *Cain and Abel*

- Abel himself demands vengeance (328), and God threatens to punish evil-doers (295–6). To what extent does the playwright leave the play unresolved, with Cain triumphantly escaping justice and continuing on his violent way?
- How does the playwright deal with violent and immoral characters in this play (and the other plays attributed to him, particularly the more famous *Second Shepherd's Play*)? Does he simply achieve a comic or a realistic, rather than a moral effect?

(ii) Religious Drama: Saints' Plays and Morality Plays

Mystery Plays were only part of English medieval drama; there was also a flourishing tradition of individual non-Cycle Plays. The majority of these were Saints' Plays commissioned by churches for performance on their Saint's Day. Records of plays performed in over a hundred different churches survive from the twelfth to the sixteenth century, particularly in East Anglia. Saints' Plays rivalled the Cycle Plays in popularity, and indeed several Cycles once included a play on the Virgin Mary. However, very few of these survived the Protestant reformers; indeed, only three Saints' Plays in English remain, though there are many European examples to compare them with. These are on St Mary Magdalene, St Meriaseck and St Paul, and are all preserved in Digby MS 133. Saints' Plays were also presented by individual Guilds, partly to venerate the saint, partly to promote parish or guild, and partly to raise money. Thus the Guild of St George in Norwich in the late fifteenth century (Normington 2009, p. 42) sponsored a procession of an actor dressed as the saint and escorted as he marched round the town and into the countryside, where a play was probably performed. There were also plays which taught Christian belief, the Doctrine Plays, which continued the homiletic and celebratory programme of the Mystery Plays but in a more specifically Catholic way. Again the Reformation targeted the surviving texts, for there is also only one extant example of a Doctrine Play (the *Play of the Sacrament*, found in the same Digby manuscript). These had existed at least since the fourteenth century (the lost York Plays on the Creed and the Lord's

Prayer), and Chester, Bury and Croxton also had Sacrament Plays, suitable for the Feast of Corpus Christi. In 1467 in Beverley the clergy themselves presented a pageant explaining the Lord's Prayer. This type of homiletic drama had been further developed in the later period as part of the drive against Lollard heresies (see Chapter 2), but of course this made them particularly vulnerable to attack when the Protestants won the day in the sixteenth century.

The less obviously Catholic Morality Plays, which may have existed from the mid-fourteenth century (the Anglo-Irish *Pride of Life* manuscript dates from 1337), were a little more fortunate (see Davenport 1984). There are 'Vices', characters suggesting evil choices, in several of the Mystery Plays, for example, Herod as a type of Pride. But, in the Morality Plays, allegorical characters, with names like 'Vice' and 'Nowadays', are usually seen tempting an Everyman or Mankind figure. Several examples of texts survive, two of them (together with the Interlude *Wisdom*) edited by Eccles as *The Macro Plays*, after the seventeenth-century owner of the manuscript: *The Castle of Perseverance* (c. 1405), and *Mankind* (c. 1460), which I shall look at in more detail below. Later examples of such plays try to reinforce Catholic doctrine, particularly on the sacrament of penance, which, like the drama itself, had been much attacked by the Lollards. An example is the haunting Morality Play *Everyman*, which appears to be a translation into Middle English from the Dutch play *Elckerlijc* written in the later fifteenth century (see Walsh and Broos 2007, p. 1). Everyman is visited by Death at the opening of the play, manages to put him off for a short while, and goes round to his friends, Fellowship, Kinsmen and Good Deeds, asking them to come with him *A longe waye, herde and daungerous* (243) to make his *rekenynge* (99) before God. The only one to agree is Knowledge, with the wonderful lines (used for the *Everyman Library* motto):

> Everyman, I wyll go with thee and be thy guyde
> In thy moste nede to go by thy syde. (323–4)

She then introduces him to Confession and the sacrament of penance, which enables him to revive his own Good Deeds, a reassuring promise of salvation that the Lollards could hardly equal. The play is also evidence of a link with the strong Dutch dramatic tradition, which might explain why so many Mystery and Morality Plays seem to have been written in East Anglia. Morality Plays were probably taken from town to village by small troupes of professional actors, and they could be spectacular in their effects and staging, using gunpowder as part of the devil's costume, and five scaffolds, as in *The Castle of Perseverance*. However, Morality Plays could also be performed indoors.

I will now discuss a lively example of non-Cycle Drama, *Mankind*, which both reaches back to the medieval sermon tradition and looks forward to the sixteenth-century comedies.

Example Text: *Mankind*

The Morality Play *Mankind* was written about 1465, and as is usual in the genre, its characters are allegorical rather than Biblical so that its homiletic purpose is much clearer than in *Cain and Abel*, and yet its use of comedy is, if anything, even more startling. The playwright seems to have designed his play for a small troupe of travelling players who can double up on parts, and who seem to have performed in the villages around Cambridge, to some of which they refer by name, probably in the inn. The play can be enjoyed by the simplest of country audiences, for its use of farce and toilet humour and for a strong plot clearly relevant to their own situation.

Mankind is a simple countryman seduced by the devil Titivillus, and the Vices New Guise, Nowadays and Nough. He is seduced or driven away from healthy work into association with blasphemous criminals and malingerers, from whose company he is only rescued by the clerical Mercy, who persuades him to repent and try again. As is usual in such plays, the language 'reflects the opposition between sin and Truth' (see King 1994, p. 240): the vivacious slang of the Vice characters who tempt the body to have fun and do what it likes, and the 'English Latin' used by Mercy (and Mankind when he is with him) which epitomises the Christian education that should direct the soul:

> The temptacyon of the flesch ye must resyst lyke a man,
> For ther ys ever a batell betwyx the soull and the body. (226–7)

However, the verve and inventiveness of the language used by the bad characters tempts the audience as much as it tempts Mankind. For example, throughout the play the Vices take Mercy's spiritual metaphors literally, seeing the 'chaff of vice' as literal chaff, and replacing the 'food of words' with bread and ale. The playwright himself describes his own easy use of slang, blasphemy and comic song as a new form of writing, one which is replacing the Latin and Latinate English of the past:

> Many wordys and shortely sett,
> Thys ys the new gyse, every-dele. (104–5)
>
> *gyse*: fashion; *every-dele*: every bit

In this way the text celebrates the Vices it attacks, and anticipates the realistic comedies of the sixteenth century, such as *Patient Grissel* (a retelling of the story that Chaucer used in the *Clerk's Tale*), in which the Vice character, Sir Politic Persuasion, steals our interest by his clever wickedness. It should not be forgotten that Shakespeare knew the tradition and was influenced by it, as can be seen in characters like Richard III and Iago, who follow Titivillus or Sir Politic in delighting in their vice.

Questions on *Mankind*

- To what extent is the moral effect of the play undermined by the comedy? How does the playwright compensate for this?
- Compare the protagonists of *Mankind* with those of *Everyman*. In each case they are supposed to represent you, the individual member of the audience. How do the authors make them both individual and universal?

(iii) Secular Drama and the folk tradition

There was also an incipient Secular Drama. Civic spectacles, especially in London, could rival the great Church processions that they imitated; Richard II's dramatic Coronation Pageant (described in *Piers Plowman*, Prol. 112ff.), Queen Anne's entry in 1382, and Richard's

'Reconciliation' Pageant of 1392, set the standard for the many pageants of the fifteenth century. The streets were decorated to represent the New Jerusalem with castles and tableaux, the conduits ran with wine, and there were mechanical and human (singing) angels and scripted speeches for both the actors and the King (see Kipling 1997). Other late medieval towns held similar pageants, for example Henry VII was welcomed into York with spectacular pageantry in 1485, to signal the end of the Wars of the Roses.

More intimate, and less inclusive, were the 'Hall-dramas' presented indoors at feasts: entertainments which included music and recitation, and dramas described as Mummings or Interludes. John Lydgate (see the text-box on p. 216) wrote seven 'Mummings' for performance at festivals at the court and at the London companies and guilds, in the early fifteenth century. These are indoor versions of the kind of elaborate pageant staged outside for royal occasions by the city corporation, but they take the form forward towards the Masques of the Elizabethan period. Most of them have verses spoken by a single speaker, so that the actors are *mum* (mute). The Classical Gods and a fleet of ships are the centrepiece of a Mumming written for the Mercers, and the twelve tribes of Israel and the Ark of the Covenant delighted the Goldsmiths. The *Mumming of Hertford* (1430), however, has speaking parts for rustic men requiring their wives to cook for them, and for their shrewish wives complaining like any Wife of Bath (see Pearsall 1970, pp. 183–91; Benson 2006). Lydgate was one of the most sophisticated writers of the period, with commissions from royalty and the highest aristocracy, and celebrated for Classical Romances about Troy and Thebes. He was in fact a monk at the Abbey of Bury St Edmunds, and another Bury monk may have been responsible for the Interlude (or Morality) *Wisdom*, probably meant for performance in an aristocratic house, and dating from about the same time as *Mankind*. This is more of a satire than a Morality, showing young clerks and others retained by noble lords to the detriment of justice, and we hear about monks who leave their Order, and are finally given a moral path to follow (see Happé 1999, p. 44). Lawyers also put on plays for each other and in the early Tudor period small theatres were built in both Oxford and Cambridge to encourage this. Such dramatic experiments were at the opposite extreme from the folk drama I will now turn to.

Drama, stories, ballads and songs, were part of a thriving 'folk tradition' for which there are few surviving texts. Evidence of its existence is gleaned from such sources as Court Rolls, where glimpses not only of story topics but also of methods of narration can be discerned (see Olson 2008, pp. 87, 198). The late thirteenth-century comedy *Dame Sirith* is the sole survivor of a genre of *fabliau*-like plays reminiscent of Chaucer's comic tales (discussed in Chapter 4). The audience is entertained by a deceitful crone outwitting a sexy but naive girl. It is probable there were many more comedies equivalent to the surviving European examples of street theatre (such as the French *Pie and the Tart* and the Dutch *Blessed Apple Tree*). Although written Interludes were referred to as 'Mummings', the term is now usually reserved for the *Mummers' Plays*, which were performed for the commoners assembled to enjoy the festivities of Christmas or St George's Day (23 April). These were possibly very early (though no examples survive from before the eighteenth century) and are thought to have included a sword dance, a fight between St George and a Saracen Knight, the death of St George and his resurrection by a doctor (see Brody 1970). A medieval manuscript has also been discovered, in the 1473–5 part of the Paston family papers, of some lines from a Robin Hood Play. These too were traditional plays (associated with the ballads mentioned in the fourteenth century by Langland), performed at the May 1st Games. Contemporary Paston papers suggest that the actors in both the Robin Hood and St George Plays included yeomen of the local lord's household, again indicating the way that drama breaks down class divisions. In this fragment Robin has various sporting and archery contests with Guy of Gisbourne, whom he kills. We then see a dialogue between Little John and Will Scarlet about Friar Tuck and the Sheriff of Nottingham, all characters mentioned in the ballads (see Doel and Doel 2000, ch. 4). Phillips' recent collection of Robin Hood studies shows the growing interest in the plays and ballads associated with Robin: 'Robin Hood studies are interdisciplinary; they are concerned with popular culture ... national identity ... attitudes towards wilderness ... gender and masculine identities' (Phillips 2005, p. 9). Indeed, Pearsall relates the ideal of fellowship celebrated in what is possibly the earliest surviving Robin Hood Ballad, *Robin Hood and the Monk* (1450?), to the 'Great Society' of rebels against authority and injustice in 1381 (Pearsall 2006, p. 48). With Secular Drama including both Lydgate's Mummings and Robin Hood Plays it is clear that it does a good deal more than entertain the illiterate, but this was still one of its functions, and it is to other attempts to educate the commoners in matters of Faith that I would now like to turn, looking both at homiletic literature, and at the Lollard writing which, we have already seen, was expressing the discontents and the spiritual aspirations of this the lowest class of English people.

Texts, Sources and Further Reading

Texts: *Piers Plowman*

Duggan, H. N. (1994) The *Piers Plowman* electronic archive (Mosaic, jttp//Jefferson.village.virginia.edu/piers/report94.html).

Knight, T. and Ohlgren, H. (1997) *Robin Hood and the Monk*, in *Robin Hood and Other Outlaw Tales* (TEAMS Middle English Texts, http://d.lib.rochester.edu/teams/text/robin-hood-and-the-monk).

Robertson, E. and Shepherd, S. (eds) (2006) *William Langland: Piers Plowman* (Norton Critical Editions, Norton).

Schmidt, A. V. C. (ed.) (1995) *Piers Plowman: A Parallel Text Edition* (Longman).

Drama

Ashley, K. M. and NeCastro, G. (eds) (2010) *Mankind* (TEAMS Middle English Texts, http://d.lib.rochester.edu/teams/text/ashley-and-necastro-mankind). This is the text used for quotation.

Beadle, R. (ed.) (1982) *The York Plays* (Arnold).

Cawley, A. C. (ed.) (1956) *Everyman and Medieval Miracle Plays* (Everyman).

Cawley, A. C. (ed.) (1958) *The Wakefield Pageants in the Towneley Cycle* (Manchester University Press). This is the text used for quotation.

Davies, R. (ed.) (1963) *Medieval English Lyrics: A Critical Anthology* (Faber and Faber).
Eccles, M. (ed.) (1969) *The Macro Plays* (Early English Text Society, EETS o.s. 262).
Happé, P. (ed.) (1975) *English Mystery Plays: A Selection* (Penguin).
Happé, P. (ed.) (1979) *Four Morality Plays* (Penguin).
Pearsall, D. (1970) *John Lydgate* (Routledge).
Walsh, M. and Broos, T. (eds) (2007) *Everyman and its Dutch Original, Elckerlijc* (TEAMS, http://www.lib.rochester.edu/camelot/teams//daevbib.htm). This is the text used for quotation.

History and criticism on the commons during social change

Aers, D. (1994) 'Justice and wage-labour after the Black Death', in Frantzen, A. J. and Moffat, D. (eds), *The Work of Work: Servitude, Slavery and Labour in Medieval England* (Cruithne Press), pp. 169–90.
Aston, T. and Hilton, R. (eds) *The English Rising of 1381* (Cambridge University Press).
Barr, H. (2001) *Socioliterary Practice in Late Medieval England* (Oxford University Press).
Bothwell, J. et al. (2000) *The Problem of Labour in Fourteenth-Century England* (York Medieval Press).
Dunn, A. (2002) *The Great Rising of 1381: The Peasants' Revolt and England's Failed Revolution* (Tempus).
Frantzen, A. and Moffat, D. (1994) *The Work of Work: Servitude, Slavery and Labour in Medieval England* (Cruithne Press).
Goldberg, J. (2004) *Medieval England: A Social History 1250–1550* (Arnold).
Hanawalt, B. (1992) *Chaucer's England* (Medieval Studies, Minnesota University Press).
Hatcher, J. and Miller, E. (1995) *Medieval England: Towns, Commerce and Crafts* (Longman).
Heffernan, T. J. (ed.) (1985) *The Popular Literature of Medieval England* (Tennessee Studies in Literature, University of Tennessee Press).

Hilton, R. (1975) *The English Peasantry in the Middle Ages* (Oxford University Press).
Hilton, R. (1985) *Class Conflict and the Crisis of Feudalism* (Hambledon Press).
Justice, S. (1994) *Writing and Rebellion: England in 1381* (University of California Press).
Kean, M. (1990) *English Society in the Later Middle Ages 1348–1500* (Penguin).
Knight, S. (2000) 'The voice of labour in fourteenth-century English literature', in Bothwell, J. et al. (eds), *The Problem of Labour in Fourteenth-Century England* (York Medieval Press).
Mohl, R. (1962) *The Three Estates in Medieval and Renaissance Literature* (Frederick Ungar).
Newman, F. (1986) *Social Unrest in the Late Middle Ages* (Arizona State University).
Olson, S. (2009) *A Mute Gospel: The People and Culture of Medieval Common Fields* (Brepols).
Platt, C. (1997) *King Death: The Black Death and its Aftermath in Late Medieval England* (Routledge).
Rigby, H. (1995) *English Society in the Later Middle Ages: Class, Status and Gender* (Macmillan).
Rosener, W. (1985; transl. Sutzer, A., 1992) *Peasants in the Middle Ages* (Polity Press).
Salter, E. (2012) *Popular Reading in England c. 1400–1600* (Manchester University Press).
Strohm, P. (1989) *Social Chaucer* (Harvard University Press).
Waugh, S. L. (1991) *England in the Reign of Edward III* (Cambridge University Press).
Ziegler, P. (1969) *The Black Death* (Penguin).

Criticism on Piers Plowman and the peasantry

Aers, D. (1988) *Community, Gender and Individual Identity* (Routledge).
Alford, J. (ed.) (1988) *A Companion to Piers Plowman* (University of California Press).
Baldwin, A. (2007) *A Guidebook to Piers Plowman* (Palgrave Macmillan).

Barr, H. (2001) 'Blessed are the horny hands of toil': Wycliffite representations of the peasant', in *Socioliterary Practice in Late Medieval England* (Oxford University Press).
Bennett, J. W. (2006) 'The curse of the Plowman', *Yearbook of Langland Studies*, 20, pp. 214–26.
Bowers, J. (1995) 'Writing the author's life', *Yearbook of Langland Studies*, 9, pp. 65–90.
Cole, A. (2003) 'William Langland's Lollardy', *Yearbook of Langland Studies*, 17, pp. 25–54.
Dyer, C. (1995) '*Piers Plowman* and ploughmen: a historical perspective', *Yearbook of Langland Studies*, 8, pp. 155–176.
Hanna, R. III (2009) 'William Langland', in Scanlon, L. (ed.), *Cambridge Companion to Medieval English Literature 1100–1500* (Cambridge University Press; also available as Cambridge Companions Online).
Kirk, E. (1998) 'Langland's plowman and the recreation of fourteenth-century religious metaphor', *Yearbook of Langland Studies*, 1, pp. 1–21.
Krochalis, J. and Peters, E. (ed. and transl.) (1975) *The World of Piers Plowman* (University of Pennsylvania Press).
Marshall, C. (2001) *William Langland: Piers Plowman* (British Council, Northcote House).
Pearsall, D. A. (1977) 'The Troilus Frontispiece and Chaucer's audience', *Yearbook of English Studies*, 7, pp. 68–77.
Pearsall, D. (1988) 'Poverty and poor people in *Piers Plowman*', in Kennedy, E. D. et al. (eds), *Medieval English Studies presented to George Kane* (Cambridge University Press); reprinted in the Norton edition of *The Canterbury Tales*.
Putnam, B. (1908) *The Enforcement of the Statutes of Labourers in the Decade after the Black Death: 1349–1359* (University of Columbia).
Rentz, R. K. (2011) 'Half-acre bylaws: harvest-sharing in *Piers Plowman*', *Yearbook of Langland Studies*, 25, pp. 95–116.
Rosener, W. (1985; transl. Sutzer, A., 1992) *Peasants in the Middle Ages* (Polity Press).
Simpson, J. (1990) *Piers Plowman: An Introduction to the B-text* (Longman).
Turville-Petre, T. (1977) *The Alliterative Revival* (D. S. Brewer).

The Drama

Beadle, R. (ed.) (1994) *The Cambridge Companion to Medieval English Theatre* (Cambridge University Press).

Beckwith, S. (2012) 'Language goes on holiday: English allegorical drama and the Virtue tradition', *Journal of Medieval and Early Modern Studies*, 42(1), pp. 107–30.

Benson, C. D. (2006) 'Civic Lydgate: the Poet and London', in Scanlon, L. and Simpson, J. (eds), *John Lydgate: Poetry, Culture and Lancastrian England* (University of Notre Dame Press).

Briscoe, M. G. and Harvey, N. L. (eds) (1989) *Contexts for Early English Drama* (Indiana University Press).

Brody, A. (1970) *The English Mummers and their Plays* (University of Pennsylvania Press).

Cox, J. and Kaslan, D. (eds) (1997) *A New History of Early English Drama* (Columbia University Press).

Chewning, S. M. (2005) *Intersections of Sexuality and the Divine in Medieval Culture: The Word made Flesh* (Ashgate).

Clopper, L. (2001) *Drama, Play and Game: English Festive culture in the Medieval and Early Modern Periods* (Chicago University Press).

Davenport, W. A. (1984) *Fifteenth-century English Drama: The Early Moral Plays and their Literary Relations* (D. S. Brewer).

Davidson, C. (2001) 'Violence and the saint's play', *Studies in Philology*, 98(3), 292–314.

Doel, F. and Doel, G. (2000) *Robin Hood: Outlaw or Greenwood Myth* (Tempus).

Edminster, W. (2012) 'Acting out: popular subversive themes in the English biblical drama', *Medieval Perspectives*, 27, pp. 7–25.

Grantley, D. (1994) 'Saints' plays' in Beadle R. (ed.) *The Cambridge Companion to Medieval English Theatre* (Cambridge University Press).

Grantley, D. (2007) *English Dramatic Interludes 1300–1580: A Reference Guide* (Cambridge Books Online).

Happé, P. (ed.) (1984) *Medieval English Drama: A Casebook* (Macmillan).

Happé, P. (1999) *English Drama before Shakespeare* (Longman).

Harper-Bill, C. (ed.) (2005) *Medieval East Anglia* (Boydell and Brewer).

Helterman, J. (1981) *Symbolic Action in the Plays of the Wakefield Master* (University of Georgia Press).
Hordis, S. and Hardwick, P. (2007) *Medieval English Comedy* (Brepols).
Kahrl, S. (1985) 'Secular life and popular piety in medieval English drama', in Heffernan, T. (ed.), *The Popular Literature of Medieval England* (University of Tennessee Press).
King, P. M. (1994) 'Morality Plays', in Beadle, R. (ed.), *The Cambridge Companion to Medieval English Theatre* (Cambridge University Press).
Kipling, G. (1997) 'Wonderful spectacle: heater and Civic Culture', in Cox, J. and Kaslan, D. (eds), *A New History of Early English Drama* (Columbia University Press).
Kolve, V. A. (1966) *The Play called Corpus Christi* (Stanford University Press).
Nolan, M. (2006) 'The performance of the literary Lydgate's Mummings', in Scanlon, L. and Simpson, J. (eds), *John Lydgate: Poetry, Culture and Lancastrian England* (University of Notre Dame Press).
Normington, K. (2004) *Gender and Medieval Drama* (D. S. Brewer).
Normington, K. (2009) *Medieval English Drama* (Polity Press).
Olson, S. (2008) *A Mute Gospel: People and Culture of the Medieval English Common Fields* (Institute of Medieval Studies).
Pearsall, D. (1970) *John Lydgate* (University of Virginia Press).
Pearsall, D. (2006) 'Little John and *Robin Hood and the Monk*', in Phillips, H. (ed.), *Robin Hood: Medieval and Post-Medieval* (Four Courts Press).
Phillips, H. (2005) *Robin Hood: Medieval and Post-Medieval* (Four Courts Press).
Richardson, C. and Johnston, J. (1991) *Medieval Drama* (Macmillan).
Ryan, D. (2003) 'Playing the Midwife's part in the English Nativity Plays', *Review of English Studies*, 54(216), pp. 435–48.
Scanlon, L. and Simpson, J. (eds) (2006) *John Lydgate: Poetry, Culture and Lancastrian England* (University of Notre Dame Press).
Scherb, V. I. (1999) 'Blasphemy and the grotesque in the Digby Mary Magdalene', *Studies in Philology*, 96(3), pp. 225–40.

Chapter 2

The Poor Commons: Education and Dissent

In the early Middle Ages the illiterate laity relied on church experience to acquire and deepen their Christian understanding and much of their knowledge of the world. In church they could see and be taught about the wall paintings, statues and stained glass, hear sermons from the pulpit and be led out on processions, which might include religious songs and even some drama. Pilgrimages could extend their experience but these too were to church buildings, dedicated to local or Biblical saints (see Finucaine 1977, ch. 2; Riches 2006). But in the thirteenth century, under the educational drive promoted by the Fourth Lateran Council of 1215, bishops instituted a kind of 'national curriculum' for the laity, to enable them to deepen their Christian life outside the churches (see Boyle 1985). One very significant way in which this was done was through the Drama, which taught the principal Bible stories in some detail to those who could and who could not read. But Bible knowledge was only part of the educational programme required of the clergy. They were themselves to learn, and then to instruct their flock, in the key principles of Christian belief and practice: the twelve articles of the faith, the seven petitions of the Lord's Prayer, the ten commandments, the seven deadly sins and the seven remedies for sin. This programme of instruction was an emancipation for the illiterate, and it also had a dramatic effect on the commoners who were not illiterate, and who wanted to develop their own mental and spiritual lives. For it gave rise to a growing body of homiletic literature, that is literature which gave moral instruction ('homilies'), written in Middle English for the clergy who were not fluent in Latin and for the literate laity. This genre of text became so popular as to make up the largest proportion of literary manuscripts in Middle English.

The commoners of the towns and larger villages who had more income, and greater aspirations to participation in local government, would have grasped at these educational opportunities. It is likely that it was this higher class of poor but literate commoners who became the new readers of homiletic texts in English, which enabled them to participate more fully in the Christian faith. It also seems that such participation made them hungry for even more independence, and led them to question the perfection and even the necessity of the clergy, who intruded between them and God. Such anti-clericism was promoted by John Wycliffe (1330–84), a polemical academic from Oxford, who instigated the tremendous project of translating the Bible into English so that the laity could read it for themselves. The first version of this was completed in about 1382 and he was probably personally responsible for the translation of the Gospels; some of his phrases survive into the Authorised Version. His sermons, tracts, books and this translation – which survives in more copies than any other Middle English text – set in motion a movement of religious dissent which became known as 'Lollardy', and which was associated with root-and-branch clerical reform and with violent social rebellion from 1381 until the end of the fifteenth century.

The first part of this chapter will briefly survey Homiletic and Confessional Literature, and I will then go on to discuss the developments in Sermon Writing, using as an Example Text, Wycliffe's *Of Servants and Lords*, a sermon on class relations. This will lead into a section on Lollard ideas and history, and to my second and third Example Texts: two Lollard poems, *Piers the Plowman's Crede* and *The Ploughman's Tale*. These, like the Wycliffite Bible, were the kind of texts for which a reader could be burned in the fifteenth century, but which laid the foundations for the Protestant Reformation in Europe.

(a) Homiletic and Confessional Literature

During the fourteenth century the clergy were encouraged to use all their teaching skills to impart the Christian faith to a largely illiterate laity, seizing their attention through anecdotes, dividing the complexities of the faith into manageable chunks and giving *aides mémoires* for the lists of sins and sacraments. The many texts which do this are known as 'homiletic' because they provide the kind of material used in sermons and homilies. The majority are in Latin, for the clergy to pass on to their parishioners in their own words, but English examples include the very popular *Northern Homily Cycle*, *Dives and Pauper*, *The Lay Folk's Catechism*, *Poor Caitif*, and Myrc's *Instructions for Parish Priests* (see Pantin 1955, for an accessible guide). This educational push seems to have had so much success in enabling the laity to participate in their faith that the *Prikke of Conscience*, a gloomy account of the end of the world, survives in over one hundred manuscripts, more than any other Middle English literary text. The Latin Bible was taught not just through the Drama, but through versified English paraphrases like the *Homily Cycles* and the *Speculum Christiani*. Such paraphrases could control the reader's response in a way that an unglossed translation could not, though Rolle's translation of the Psalms was an acceptable exception (see Chapter 5 below, p. 125).

The clergy were also instructed in how to hear confessions. Many Confessional Manuals were written throughout Europe, principally in Latin by Friars. The Friars had been founded in the thirteenth century to resist the spread of heresy by preaching and hearing confessions; the Dominicans were often the more academic and wrote the materials, while the Franciscans put the teaching into practice. During the fourteenth and fifteenth centuries Middle English translations of Confessional Manuals, or adaptations of their material, were made for priests to help them improve the spiritual health of the laity; texts such as the *Book of Vices and Virtues*, *Handling Sinne*, and the *Ayenbite of Inwit* (see Pantin 1955). An example of this kind of literature is Chaucer's *Parson's Tale*, based on a translation of a Latin Confessional Manual, and easily the most copied of all his *Canterbury Tales*. Through reading them the sinner (or more often, the sinner's priest) was instructed in how to cleanse the soul and restore it to the image of God. The laity were often helped in this exercise by the friars themselves, particularly the Franciscans who were licensed to hear confessions in the parishes, and who provided a more private and perhaps more sympathetic ear than the local parish priest. Chaucer's friar is notorious for abusing this position, and both *The Summoner's Tale* and *Piers Plowman* (e.g. B.3.35–73) satirise friars' way of asking for financial penances, which let the sinner off lightly while filling their convents' coffers. But in spite of the presence of false friars, this kind of instruction must have had a profound effect on the way writers perceived themselves. It conveyed a very particular view of the human psyche, waging a constant war against sin, supported by an armoury of saints and sacraments. The structure of sin, penance and forgiveness lies behind such didactic texts as *Everyman* and *Mankind*, where sin and penitence are structural (see above, p. 33), but it can also be seen to lie behind much less doctrinal texts, such as *Gawain and the Green Knight*, or even the *Canterbury Tales* itself (pp. 106, 258 below). And some knowledge of the confessional method of examining an individual's tendency to sin can enrich our understanding of a writer's way of analysing characters (see Braswell 1983).

(b) Sermons

Homiletic texts and confessional teaching were generally transmitted to the poor commons through sermons, so it was particularly important that these should be interesting and engaging. Once again it was the Friars who were in the instructional vanguard, giving very popular sermons both in their convents and in the country at large. The regular clergy could be very adept too, particularly if they used preaching manuals provided by the Friars, such as the *Fasciculi Morum*, a handbook arranged according to the Sins (see Wenzel 1989, *Fasciculi Morum*, ed. and trans. Wenzel).

One quality which makes these sermons memorable is their systematic structure; indeed this may have offered a model to other forms of literature. Of the Middle English sermons that have survived, most follow the Latin pattern of a complex structure, often comprising a statement of *Text* and *Theme*, a *Protheme* (introduction), a statement of the *Occasion* on which the sermon was preached, a *Process* or main discussion (in about three *Divisions* or *Questions*), and final *Summary* and *Prayers* (see O'Mara 2008, pp. 67–8). Rhetorical techniques such as striking language, the use of antitheses, and the grouping of ideas in threes (the *tricolon*) are employed to rivet the attention of the listener, and preachers liked to employ allegories and moral tales. The Friars are credited with enlarging this story-telling element by the inclusion of *exempla*, anecdotes taken not just from the Bible, but also from books of Tales, or even from personal experience. For example, one Middle English Sermon apparently addressed to a wealthy audience warns the listeners not to be rapacious towards their poor tenants, but to remember that once shot, birds of prey are generally *cast awey uppon the myddynges as no thynge of valew* (thrown on the rubbish heap as valueless) whereas the birds on whom they preyed are presented at the lords' tables (a slightly worrying image of heavenly bliss; see Ross, ed. 1838, p. 239). Preachers also learned from the Friars to allegorise their stories, and to incorporate such folk-tale features as common character types, magical happenings, humour and realism. Poetry was also used as a homiletic tool. The Friar John Grimestone made a collection in the 1370s of lyrics suitable for inclusion in sermons, no doubt to stimulate his listeners' imagination and memory:

> Gold and al this werdis win
> Is nought but Christis Rode
> I wolde be clad in Christis skin
> That ran so longe on blode (Davies, ed. 1963, p. 130)
>
> *win*: joy; *Is nought but Christis Rode*: is nothing but a Cross to Christ

Such lyrics, like the inscriptions and tags which met the eye everywhere in churches, in graveyards, on goblets and rings, even on cakes (see Gray 1972, p. 49, and see Chapter 5, p. 127) are sermons in little.

If we look in the sermon literature for a reflection of the life and character of the poor commons, we are given a contradictory picture. On the one hand the 'sermons on the estates' (a genre which lies behind the Estates Satire to be discussed in the next chapter) gives a pretty negative impression of their character and habits. The sermon-scholar Owst gives examples of establishment preachers, including the Friars Nicholas Bozon and John Bromyard, the Monk Robert Rypon, and the Bishop Thomas Brinton, all attacking servants and labourers for their offences to society, to the Church, and to God (Owst 1933, pp. 361–7; see also Spencer 1983, pp. 65–8). Not only do they fail to serve their masters properly, but they cheat each other (by such tricks as moving landmarks in the fields), and try to amass wealth by unfair dealings. Labourers are prone to the more animalistic vices of sloth and drunkenness, but are also subject to avarice; as one homilist says, *I can not see that Crist dwelleth in hem* (Owst 1933, p. 362). They disobey the Church by refusing to attend services or to pay tithes. We can find examples of these faults in Langland's Waster, who is reluctant to work and demands higher pay; in the recalcitrance of the Towneley Cain and in the laxity of Mankind. On the other hand, writers also remembered that Christ himself in the Sermon on the Mount reverses the value that the world puts upon the rich and poor. As Owst has demonstrated, in the most orthodox sermons of the fourteenth and fifteenth centuries there is 'the fiercest denunciation' (Owst 1933, p. 324) of all those who oppress the poor, be they lords, knights, lawyers, merchants or ecclesiastics. He quotes sermons from the whole spectrum of medieval clergy detailing the torments which will be incurred by oppressive lords.

This dual approach of criticism and support for the labouring poor can be seen in my Example Text, Wycliffe's late fourteenth-century *Of Servants and Lords*, in which the seditious potential of the Christian message is clearly visible in lines of thought we will soon come to see as 'Lollard'. This text give a clear impression of the part that sermon literature could play in the political and social changes of the time.

Example Text: The Sermon *Of Servants and Lords*

Of Servants and Lords (1380–90?) is published in a collection of *The Sermons of John Wycliffe*. It is an excellent example of medieval preaching polemic written in fairly accessible Middle English. At first sight it seems to be a sermon which maintains the traditional hierarchy, for his *theme* is the correct relation between servants and lords. The author is eager to insist that servants should not take the law into their own hands by withholding rents and tithes, or in other ways resisting the lawful authority of lords (even wicked ones) to whom they are *suget and underlout* (subject and submissive; ed. Matthew 1880, p. 228). He quotes the familiar text from Romans 13:1, 5 which bids us be *suget to princes ... not only for wrathe but also for conscience* (p. 229 apparently using a phrase from the Wycliffite Middle English Bible which persists in our Authorised Version). However, when, as a *division* of his argument, he lists the reciprocal obligations that kings have to their subjects and lords to their tenants, he does not suggest any ways of punishing those servants who (like the rebels of 1381) refuse to obey lords, but speaks only of punishing those lords who bully, mistreat and extort money from the poor and weak. His list of common offences done to poor men is a long one, and includes the receiving of high rents and taxes by the stewards of secular lords, who

> deuouren pore menus goodis in glotonye & wast & pride, & thei perischen for mischief, & hunger & thrist & colde, & there children also ... though thei be neuere so pore & nedi & ouerchargid with age, febilnesse & loos of catel & with many children. (p. 234)

Far from helping their cause, the law – in the persons of corrupt jurymen and lawyers – simply adds to their miseries by robbing them further of their goods.

The preacher may distance himself from accusations of fomenting revolt, but his complaints overlap with some of those of the rebels of 1381, and substantiate the claims of Walsingham and others that Wycliffite preachers were spreading the desire for rebellion (see Justice 1994, ch. 2).

The preacher's anticipation of the 'Lollard' programme becomes even more apparent as soon as, in the next *division*, he turns to the clergy's abuse of the poor (see the text-box on Lollards, p. 52). The preacher blames the clergy, and in particular the mendicant (i.e. begging) friars, for taking alms which rob the poor of the money they need. And although servants are not exempted from the general accusations of guile (for working hard only in the presence of their masters), their guilt is dwarfed by that of the prelates, who sell indulgences which purport to pay for sin, when as the preacher puts it, *ther cometh no pardon but of god for good lyuynge & endynge in charite, ... for who is in most charity is best herde of god, be he shepeherde or lewid man, or in the chirche or in the feld* (p. 238). Such a declaration of the powerlessness of the clergy, and the preacher's preference for a priesthood of all believers, proves that he was a Wycliffite, and makes it the more likely that he was Wycliffe himself. So rather than being a testament to traditional authority, this sermon takes Christ's reversal of the value of the poor and rich literally, at least as far as the moral authority of the poor is concerned. We will see this idea developed in my second Example Text, *Piers the Plowman's Crede*.

Questions on *Of Servants and Lords*

- Is the inclusiveness expressed by part of this sermon, particularly the notion of 'a priesthood of all believers', comparable with the inclusiveness of some of Julian of Norwich's writing, particularly her notion that no sinner can be alienated from God (see p. 138–40 below)?
- What rhetorical devices are used by the preacher to carry his points (e.g. repetition, patterning and balance, appeals to compassion, etc.)?

(c) The Lollards and their Literature

It is already clear then that this better-educated laity was less controllable than the illiterate poor, and, particularly in the towns, was beginning to develop reformist religious opinions. Sermons could be used not so much to uphold the established Church as to criticise it, and to demand both religious and political change. Wycliffe is credited with initiating a translation of the Bible into English in the 1390s – a remarkable collective literary feat which fed the appetite for personal devotion; there are 250 surviving manuscripts of the whole or a part of the three versions; these were condemned as heretical in 1408 by Archbishop Arundel (see Watson 1995, and p. 54 below). Wycliffe also inspired the new reformist movement known as 'Lollardy' from the late 1380s (see text-box below).

Lollard Principles

Lollards is the opprobrious name given from the late 1380s to the followers of Wycliffe. Their characteristic principles are expressed in a number of writings, including the *12 Conclusions* pinned to the door of Westminster Hall and St Paul's Cathedral in 1399, and the early fifteenth-century *16 Points on which the Bishops accuse Lollards*. Of course not all reformist Christians would have subscribed to all of these 'conclusions', but reading the following list will give a sense of the genuinely 'protestant' thrust of this early movement:

- The Bible and other important religious texts should be available in English to all believers. This belief prompted an impressive programme of translation centred on Oxford, which included the three Wycliffite Bible texts of 1382, 1388 and 1395. These enabled Lollards to read the Bible and the works of significant Church teachers, and use them to criticise the established Church.
- The riches, lordship and pride of the established Church make it in urgent need of 'reformation' including the removal of its temporal possessions. Tithes should therefore be abolished.
- The legal power of Pope and Bishops, and interference by the Church in temporal affairs, are also contrary to Christ's rule. The Pope and Bishops should not take part in battles against other Christians.
- The priesthood should be made up of poor and humble people who live a true Christian life; for 'euery good man is a prest and hath power to preche the worde of God' (*16 Points* no.7). For some, this included women.
- Priests should not be seen as having supernatural power; neither when saying Mass, administering the Sacraments (in particular the Sacrament of Penance) and praying for the dead; nor when cursing their fellow Christians.
- Images of the saints should also not be said to have miraculous powers.

Text of the *12 Conclusions* and the *16 Points* can be found in Hudson (ed.) (1978).

Demands for clerical reform had been made in England long before John Wycliffe began writing his inflammatory tracts in the 1370s. It was not only that the extravagance of a caste which was supposedly dedicated to poverty shocked the English Christians; they were also angry that the Church, which paid no taxes, was sending so much money to France in revenues and charitable payments, not only to monastic 'mother houses' but to the Pope, who between 1309 and 1376 was exiled in France, with whom England was at war. This 'Babylonian Captivity' was succeeded by the Great Schism (1378–1417) when two Popes were simultaneously claiming the Papal Seat. Bishop Despenser of Norwich even led a discreditable 'Crusade' in 1383 in Flanders against the rival Pope. Anti-Papal feeling in England in the later fourteenth century was widespread, but unfortunately the development of the Lollard movement was, from the first, so strongly associated with rebellion and a threat to property that loyalty to the Church began to seem a public duty. A tragic sign of the change is the condemnation to burning in 1423 of the Lollard William Taylor, for saying (among other things) that the Church's ownership of property was not in accordance with the ideal of Christian perfection (Aston 1984, p. 30), a claim made throughout church history including by Langland in the 1380s without him apparently being subject to any persecution.

It was indeed the case that some of the Lollard beliefs listed above undermined Church property law, and it might well be felt that they also undermined the secular hierarchy as well. Contemporary commentators on the Great Rising of 1381 (including the Commons of the Parliament of 1382) blamed it on the ideas of Wycliffe, supposedly disseminated throughout England by preachers like John Ball. Walsingham even claimed that John Ball had been preaching heresy and sedition for the previous twenty years (see Dunn 2002, pp. 69–6; Justice 1994, p. 102 and ch. 5). Walsingham's association of Lollardy and sedition seemed to be confirmed by the risings led by the Lollard Oldcastle in 1414, and by William Perkins in 1431. Both of these leaders wanted to strip the Church of its valuable possessions, though Oldcastle seems not to have gone as far as Perkins in his programme of redistributing the spoils. But this aim tainted the sect and meant that, like other proto-Protestant movements, such as that initiated by Hus (c. 1369–1415) in Bohemia, it was met by armed resistance. The Church was determined to rid itself of what it saw as a poison, even should this involve the suppression of the new religious confidence that religious education had brought about. The backlash was led by Archbishop Thomas Arundel acting in conjunction with the new king Henry IV; measures taken included getting rid of Lollard university fellows, licensing friars to preach against heresy throughout England, and persecuting all heretics in special Church courts. In 1401 the first English statute requiring the burning of heretics was passed, and the first Lollard was burned. In 1409 Arundel passed his *Constitutions against the Lollards*, which prohibited (among other things) lay preaching and the translation of Scriptures into English. The clergy wrote numerous tracts against heretical beliefs; Lydgate himself contributed a *Defence of Holy Church* urging Henry V to continue his father's persecutions against them (see Simpson 2009, p. 213). The more moderate writer Bishop Reginald Pecock (or Peacock) wrote several long tracts against their beliefs, hoping to convert them by argument, but his *Donet*, which attempted to find some common ground between their Creed and the Apostles' Creed, earned him only disgrace and the loss of his Bishopric.

Equally threatening to the Church was the Lollard attack on the clergy, and their assertions that the poor man or even the poor woman can be a truer priest than an ordained clergyman, for 'every good man is a priest and hath power to preach the word of God' (*16 Points*). The Lollards' encouragement of education for the laity and in particular for women had far-reaching consequences. Some learned examples of banned tracts by heart to disseminate them to others. Lollards increased in numbers in the south-east and eastern counties through the forteenth and fifteenth centuries, and there are many records of their 'poor preachers', often untrained but wearing russet cloth as a badge of office, speaking along high roads or in towns. Margery Kempe was several times accused in the bishop's court of being a Lollard because she preached, though she always managed to convince her accusers that she was a true daughter of the established Church. Julian of Norwich did not publish her *Revelations* during her lifetime, probably for the same reason (see pp. 138, 146). The conventionality of much fifteenth-century religious literature, with its many plays about saints and doctrine, and its didactic devotional poetry, is possibly a result of the Church's attempt to replace heresy by religious orthodoxy. Its efforts eventually failed, for the establishment of a Protestant Church in England in 1534, together with the disestablishment of Church property two years later, would not have been possible without the success of this movement in the country at large.

Lollards were particularly incensed by the power and success of the Friars. They saw them as a reformist movement whose members seemed to them to have lost much of the ideals of poverty and simplicity sought by their founders two hundred years before, and who were now coining money from the poor by administering Penance, a sacrament that many Lollards denied. I will now give as my Example Texts for this section the early fifteenth-century *Piers Ploughman's Creed* and the so-called *Ploughman's Tale*. These are examples of a group of Lollard tracts and poems which includes *Jack Upland and Friar Daw's Reply* (mid-fifteenth century), which, like the two I have chosen, directly honours the class with which these two chapters have been concerned – the poor commoners. They are therefore in the tradition of the sermon *Of Servants and Lords* looked at above, and make an appropriate end to this section of the Guide.

Example Texts: *Piers the Plowman's Crede* and *The Ploughman's Tale*

These texts are both apparently written by Lollards of the late fourteenth or early fifteenth centuries, and a claim is made in the *Ploughman's Tale* that they are by the same author. (The title and suggestion, in an added Frame Narrative, that this text is one of the *Canterbury Tales*, is a sixteenth-century addition, made possibly to improve sales.) They do in fact make a pair; the *Crede* is an attack on Friars, and the *Tale* on the monks and canons and the secular clergy, largely for their possessions, which are seen as anti-Christian. Such attacks are characteristically Lollard, as is the figure of the ploughman-preacher, though the author names him after Langland's popular and pre-Lollard hero.

He presents him as a genuinely poor man who is both charitable himself and able to instruct others in the charity of God:

> This man loked opon me and leet the plow stonden
> And seyde, 'Sely man, why syghest thou so harde?
> Yif thee lakke lijflode lene the ich wole.' (*Crede*, 443–5)
>
> *Yif thee lakke lijflode lene the ich wole*: if you lack livelihood I will lend you something

He is contrasted with the Friars, who preach but do not practise poverty, and whose pride and lordship go against the law both of St Francis and of Christ himself:

> For Crist seyde him-selfe to swiche as him folwede.
> 'Y-blessed mote thei ben that mene ben in soule'. (*Crede*, 519–20)
>
> '*Y-blessed mote thei ben that mene ben in soule*': blessed be the meek

The *Tale* is less obviously influenced by Langland, and is constructed as a debate between a Pelican (representing the way of Christ) and a Griffon (representing the clergy). It goes much further than the *Crede* in attacking clerical pride and lordship; indeed, it is from first to last a denunciation of the established Church hierarchy, as being counter to all Biblical teaching:

> Moyses lawe forbode it tho
> That preestes shuld no lordshippes welde
> Christes gospell byddeth also
> That they shulde no lordshippe helde ...
> But smeren her shepe and kepe her folde (*Tale*, 1533 edition, 702–7)
>
> *lordshippes welde*: priests should be lords (of property and land); *smeren*: anoint

The current shepherds of God's flock are exploiting their sheep, like the real-life shepherds of the time, by selling, fleecing, killing, and even cooking them:

> He culleth the sheepe as dothe the Cooke
> Of hem taken the woll to rende (*Tale*, 593–4)
>
> *culleth*: culls; *rende*: tear

With the legitimate shepherds (the clergy) proving to be such a danger to the flock, he, like the *Crede* author, seems to trust the ploughman's simple Christianity more:

> What knoweth a tyllour at the plowe
> The Pope's name and what he hate?
> His crede suffiyceth to him enowe (*Tale*, 453–5)

Priests should be poor (549–50), and epitomise the kind of non-hierarchical fellowship which goes directly to Christ:

> Christ is our heed that sytteth on hye
> Heddes ne ought we have no mo
> We ben his membres bothe also …
> All other maisters ben wicked and fals (*Tale*, 112–16)

The praise of the poor and lowly, and the condemnation of the rich and lordly in such texts as *Of Servants and Lords*, *Piers Plowman*, *Piers the Plowman's Crede* and *The Ploughman's Tale* demonstrate that the social changes occurring in England in the fourteenth and fifteenth centuries were having an effect on the hegemony of English society. These last two chapters have shown how those changes affected the literature available to the labouring poor, how they were themselves described in literature, and how the literature expressed their new religious aspirations. We will now turn to the upper level of commoners, the educated and professional 'middle class'. How is the emancipation of these more sophisticated commoners, who lived in the town rather than the country, reflected in the literature written about people like themselves? Here I will be turning from religious to secular literature, and leave religious literature, which this urban audience also enjoyed, to Chapters 6 and 7.

Questions on Lollard texts

- How do you characterise the attitude to poor people shown in these texts? Is poverty a state that the poet deplores, or only wishes to emulate? Compare the description of the ploughman

in the *Crede* with that of the peasants in Passus 6 of *Piers Plowman* (see above, pp. 18–25, and see Pearsall 1988, referenced in Chapter 1).
- The poet is building on assumptions about the Church that he feels are violated by the Friars and the established priesthood. How does his Piers appear both as an individual and as a complex symbol of the ideals of a 'true Church'?

Texts, Sources and Further Reading

Texts

(For texts and sources of *Piers Plowman*, see the Bibliography on p. 38.)
Barr, H. (ed.) (1993) *The Piers Plowman Tradition* (Everyman).
Blake, N. F. (ed.) (1972) *Middle English Religious Prose* (Arnold).
Bowers, J. M. (ed.) (1992) *The Ploughman's Tale* (http://d.lib.rochester.edu/teams/text/bowers-canterbury-tales-fifteenth-century-ploughmans-tale).
Davies R. T. (ed.) (1963) *Medieval English Lyrics: A Critical Anthology* (Faber & Faber).
Dean, J. M. (1991) *Piers the Plowman's Crede* (http://d.lib.rochester.edu/teams/text/dean-six-ecclesiastical-satires-piers-the-plowmans-crede). See also, W. W. Skeat (ed.) (1867) *Pierce the Ploughmans Crede* (Early English Text Society, EETS o.s. 30; repr. Greenwood Press, 1969).
Dean, J. M. (1991) *The Plowman's Tale* from *Six Ecclesiastical Satires* (http://d.lib.rochester.edu/teams/text/dean-six-ecclesiastical-satires-plowmans-tale).
Grisdale, M. (ed.) (1939) *Three Middle English Sermons from the Worcester MS* (Leeds School of English Texts and Monographs, 5).
Hudson, A. (ed.) (1978) *Selections from English Wycliffite Writings* (Cambridge University Press).
Matthew, F. D. (ed.) (1880; repr. 1902) 'Of servants and lords', in *The English Works of Wyclif hitherto unprinted* (Early English Text Society, EETS o.s. 74).
O'Mara, V. (ed.) (2008) *Four Middle English Sermons* (C. Winter).
Peacock, E. (ed.) (1902; repr. 1975) *Instructions for Parish Priests by John Myrc* (Early English Text Society, EETS o.s. 31).

Ross, W. O. (ed.) (1938; repr. 1960) *Middle English Sermons* (Early English Text Society, EETS o.s. 209) (also on TEAMS website).

Wenzel, S. (ed.) (1984) *Summa Virtutum de Remediis Anime* (Chaucer Library, University of California Press).

Wenzel, S. (ed. and transl.) (1989) *Fasciculus Morum: A Fourteenth-Century Preacher's Handbook* (Pennsylvania State University Press).

History of developments in lay devotion

Beckwith, S. (2003) *Learning and Literacy in Medieval England and Abroad* (Brepols).

Boyle, L. E. (1985) 'The fourth Lateran Council and Manuals of Popular Theology', in Heffernan, T. J. (ed.), *The Popular Literature of Medieval England* (Tennessee Studies in Literature, University of Tennessee Press).

Dunn, A. (2002) *The Great Rising: The Peasants' Revolt and England's Failed Revolution* (Tempus).

Finucane, R. C. (1977) *Miracles and Pilgrims: Popular Belief in Medieval England* (Dent).

Justice, S. (1994) *Writing and Rebellion: England in 1381* (University of California Press).

Orme, N. (1973) *English Schools in the Middle Ages* (Methuen).

Riches, S. (2006) 'Hagiography in context: images, miracles, shrines and festivals', in Salih, S. (ed.), *The Companion to Middle English Hagiography* (D. S. Brewer).

Homiletic literature, confessional manuals and sermons

Aers, D. (2003) 'John Wyclif: poverty and the poor', *Yearbook of Langland Studies*, 17, pp. 55–72.

Boitani, P. and Torti, A. (1990) *Religion in Poetry and Drama of the Late Middle Ages in England* (Boydell and Brewer).

Braswell, M. (1983) *The Medieval Sinner: Sin and Confession in the Literature of the English Middle Ages* (Associated University Presses).

Fitzgibbons, M. (2002) 'Disruptive simplicity: Gatrynge's translation of Archbishop Thoresby's *Injunctions*', in Blumenfeld-Kosinski, R. et al. (eds), *The Vernacular Spirit: Essays on Medieval Religious Literature* (Palgrave Macmillan).

Gray, D. (1972) *Themes and Images in the Medieval English Religious Lyric* (Routledge).

Grisdale, M. (1939) 'Introduction' to *Three Middle English Sermons from the Worcester MS* (Leeds School of English Texts and Monographs, 5).
Owst, G. R. (1933) *Literature and Pulpit in Medieval England* (Cambridge University Press).
Pantin, W. (1955) *The English Church in the Fourteenth Century* (Cambridge University Press).
Spencer, H. L. (1993) *English Preaching in the Later Middle Ages* (Oxford University Press).
Steele, F. J. (1995) *Towards a Spirituality for Layfolk: English Religious Literature from the Thirteenth Century to the Fifteenth* (Edwin Mellen Press).
Wenzel, S. (1990) 'Sermons', in Boitani, P. and Torti, A. (eds), *Religion in Poetry and Drama of the Late Middle Ages in England* (Boydell and Brewer).

The Lollards and their literature

(For Langland's relation to Lollardy, see *Yearbook of Langland Studies*, 17 (2003), which is devoted to this topic.)
Aston, M. (1984) *Lollards and Reformers: Images and Literacy in Late Medieval Religion* (Hambledon Press).
Bruschi, C. (2003) *Texts and the Repression of Medieval Heresy* (Boydell and Brewer).
Hornbeck, J. P. (2009) 'Theologies of sexuality in English Lollardy', *Journal of Ecclesiastical History*, 60, pp. 1–19.
Hudson, A. (1988) *The Premature Reformation: Wycliffite Texts and Lollard History* (Oxford University Press).
Justice, S. (1994) *Writing and Rebellion: England in 1381* (University of California Press).
McFarlane, K. B. (1972) *Wyclif and English Non-conformity* (Penguin).
Simpson, J. (2009) 'John Lydgate', in Scanlon, L. (ed.), *Cambridge Companion to Medieval English Literature 1100–1500* (Cambridge University Press; also available as Cambridge Companions Online).
Somerset, F., Havens, J. C. and Derrick, G. P. (eds) (2003) *Lollards and their Influence in Late Medieval England* (Boydell and Brewer).
Watson, N. (1995) 'Censorship and cultural change', *Speculum*, 70, 822–64.

Chapter 3

The Urban Middle Class: Satire, Debate and Political Advice

In the next two chapters we turn to the 'cream' of the estate of commoners, the wealthier and better-educated readers who lived principally in the towns. It was this audience who read the religious texts we were discussing in the last chapter, and who joined with their illiterate brothers and sisters to watch plays and listen to sermons, and even to attack Church and State. There are no walls to the reading choices of the literate; indeed it would have been quite natural to discuss drama in this chapter rather than in the first, and to look now at many of the genres I will be considering in Chapters 5 and 6. But those chapters are concerned with religious literature, and in these two chapters I want to consider secular genres and to see how these reflect the life of the towns and cities, in particular the cities of London and Westminster. So these two chapters will focus on literature that we might class as *bourgeois* and which was written neither in Latin for the clerics, nor in French for the nobility, but freshly in English by some of most significant authors of the period, Langland, Chaucer, Gower and Hoccleve. In the next chapter I will discuss Collections of Tales designed to entertain both the middle and the upper classes (and probably the clergy as well), and examine some of Chaucer's Tales about townsfolk. In this chapter I will look at genres which scrutinise the increasing variety and complexity of medieval society, and which are likely to have been read particularly by the urban literate laity. In my first group I will look at Estates Satire, which includes the *Prologues* to two of these Tale Collections (Gower's and Chaucer's), and which maps the increasing complexity and variety of medieval society. My Example

Texts here will be the *Prologues* to *Piers Plowman* and to the *Canterbury Tales*. I will then survey the Venality Satire and Debate Poetry which analysed social ills in terms of the misuse of money. Here my Example Texts will be the Vision of Lady Meed (also from *Piers Plowman*) and a poem which may well have influenced it, *Wynnere and Wastoure*. Finally I will look at the Political Prophecy and Advice addressed to the king and his lords, towards which, complaint and venality satire often tends, searching for political as well as moral or religious solutions to social problems. Most such Mirrors for Princes gave idealised advice, using mainly traditional material, and my Example Text for these will be Hoccleve's *Regement of Princes*. But political advice was given a compelling urgency in the later fourteenth century by the disastrous financial and political management of Richard II and his courtiers. Richard's misdeeds are the occasion for my Example Texts of this kind of personal political advice: *Richard Redeless* and *Mum and the Sothsegger*. I shall, however, begin this pair of chapters with a brief description of town life, which, in these texts, is often as much the foreground as are the vivid characters who live it. I will also give a brief account of the dramatic political events of the 1380s and 1390s, centring on London and culminating in the deposition of Richard II.

(a) Urban Communities and Political Crisis in the Reign of Richard II

The writing and reading communities in the towns and cities largely comprised men and women who lived by their skill and their minds rather than simply their manual labour. The members of the 'third estate' were increasingly literate; Orme calls the towns 'nurseries of literacy' (1973, p. 43). They included craftsmen and artisans, who were often taught to read by a Guild Chaplain, but also commoners of a higher class, merchants and business-people, lawyers, doctors, administrators and civil servants. This last group also included clerics, and there were many more representatives of the 'second' estate: priests, canons, friars and monks, summoners and the like, and of the 'first' estate, the gentry and nobility in their large town houses. Indeed it was often the clerics, and the more aristocratic Londoners, who wrote the literature that all classes might enjoy.

Small towns developed rapidly in the later middle ages, and cities expanded beyond their walls into suburbs. The poor were crowded into tenement-style buildings where diseases flourished, but these houses were often in close proximity to richer merchants' houses (Keene 1990). For although shops selling the same products often congregated in the same street, the different classes of citizens were not as geographically segregated as they are today, as can be seen from the records of the local parish guilds, which include all kinds and levels of people (Lindahl 1987, pp. 27–8). However, although living in close proximity, such people did not consider themselves to be equals, and indeed all kinds of distinctions were made in terms of dress and behaviour between the higher and the lower commoners and clergy. But together they formed communities not unlike that described by Chaucer in the *General Prologue* (see Strohm 1989, p. 153). The same is true to some extent of the noble households, where the different estates mixed together in their everyday life in a way much more reminiscent of modern than Victorian society. In several cases this wide social mix of people can be seen as a reading community, particularly in the reception of drama, tales, and sermons, though in other cases – such as the topical satire – the small number of surviving manuscripts suggests that their readership was smaller or more cautious about copying their manuscripts.

There is evidence from book ownership that the aspiring bourgeoisie was interested in the issues raised by their acquisition of more power and wealth; like the late medieval peasantry they were aware that times were changing, and that opportunities could be seized by the enterprising – and often literate – layman and laywomen. The individual towns generally had considerable independence; the larger ones had their own elected government of mayors and aldermen. They generated a community income, for they could collect considerable fees from the various markets and fairs, which they used for such purposes as maintaining the streets and walls, employing police (the 'watch'), and paying land rent for the town to the local overlord. They had their own borough courts and their own trade laws and customs. Women in particular enjoyed more economic and social power than in the feudal countryside, where they were generally excluded from the ownership of land; in the towns the saleable property was not the land but the houses, shops and stock, which were not covered by the feudal law. Indeed, Hanawalt has shown that it was generally the case in London that many widows owned property and transacted business, and a widow could expect any new suitor to join her trade guild before she would marry him (2007, ch. 3). It is not surprising that women's economic power (or absences of power) is thus a frequent issue in the *Canterbury Tales*.

The City of London had a particularly interesting mix of citizens because it was the largest city, the chief port, and close to Westminster, the seat of government. In the later fourteenth century both cities were involved in extraordinary political upheavals, as Richard II vied for power with his Parliamentary lords – a battle that was to end in his deposition and murder. His grandfather, Edward III, had been able to keep Parliament on his side, which was essential to pay for his wars in France. But towards the end of his fifty-year reign he increasingly lost his grip on power (which passed to nobles like his mistress Alice Perrers and his oldest surviving son John of Gaunt, patron of Chaucer). Corruption at court and in the City of London even spurred the 'Good Parliament' of 1376 to dismiss some of the worst perpetrators (including the mayor) from the court, an event commemorated in the B-text Prologue to *Piers Plowman*. Edward was succeeded in 1377 by Richard II, then just ten years old. Though at first he was governed by his uncles and other lords in Parliament, from the time of his marriage in 1382 he began to govern his own 'party' of courtiers and favourites, spending extravagantly on the arts and other luxuries (to the benefit of literature but not of his popularity). (He continued to patronise the arts throughout his troubled reign, and commissioned Chaucer to oversee the rebuilding of Westminster Hall in 1383.) In 1386 (the 'Wonderful Parliament') and 1388 (the 'Merciless Parliament', led by the 'Lords Appellant' Arundel, Gloucester, Warwick, Mowbray and Henry Bolingbroke), some of Richard's significant advisors at court were first warned and then executed. But Richard insisted on taking over government again in 1389 and tried to do without Parliament, raising money, by a variety of illegal methods, from rich nobility and from the important figures in the City of London, who thus became even more opposed to his rule. The long-standing antagonism between the chief citizens of London and the court party of

Westminster was not really allayed by the 'reconciliation pageant' of 1392 described on p. 36 above. The last straw came in 1397 when Richard forced the 'Revenge Parliament' to punish the Lords Appellant, executing Arundel and Warwick, and having Gloucester – his own uncle – murdered. He banished Mowbray and Henry Bolingbroke, and when Henry's father, John of Gaunt, died in 1399, he confiscated the enormous Duchy of Lancaster, with the result that Henry returned in 1399 at the head of an army and forced Richard to resign his crown. Henry was then crowned king, although not technically Richard's rightful heir. This allowed the 'Yorkist' cause to precipitate the Wars of the Roses in 1452; see pp. 242–3 below. These developments involved the citizens of London and Westminster at every level, including the very poets who were patronised by Richard's court.

The urban populations who witnessed these events made a reading community with a personal interest in the changes overtaking the social estates and empowering Parliament, and in the failings of the nobility and the king to respond to these changes. Contemporary writers provided social commentaries for this dynamic readership, and three major texts, *Piers Plowman*, the *Canterbury Tales*, and the *Confessio Amantis*, all begin with an extensive passage of estates satire in which the old Latin model of the 'sermon to the estates' (see above, pp. 48–9) is more or less transformed into contemporary social satire. I will look at the first two of these in some detail in the next section.

(b) Estates Satire

One of the favourite topics of the sermons and manuals of instruction for priests, discussed in the last chapter, was the failings of the different 'estates' or classes of society (see pp. 48–9). None was left out: from those who eat horse bread to those who only eat the finest white wheat-bread, all were attacked for the vices their way of life led to. This didactic material had parallels with more literary writing, generally in Latin and Old French, which also influenced the English secular tradition of Estates Satire. One example is the *Game of Chess Moralised*, by the early fourteenth-century Jacobus de Cessolis (see below, p. 85), in which the different chess-pieces represent different social 'estates' or classes. Jean de Meun's thirteenth-century continuation of the *Romance of the Rose* also has much material of this kind. Three notable English texts use this kind of material in the later fourteenth century: the Prologues to the *Confessio Amantis*, *Piers Plowman* and the *Canterbury Tales*. Gower never departs very far from his sources, principally the *Game of Chess*, so I will not look at it in detail. Langland was introduced in the first chapter (see pp. 19–20); as his text is essentially religious, his *Prologue* is closer to the 'sermon on the estates' tradition in its moral directing, but as it is a vivid and original description of medieval classes I will include it in this essentially secular chapter. Chaucer (as Mann has shown in 1973) develops the religious and secular material into accounts of realistic individuals and creates an extraordinary cast of characters. This is exactly the kind of satirical social analysis likely to appeal to the new self-confident urban classes. I will now look in more detail at Langland's and Chaucer's *Prologues*, for in such texts one can hear about the social changes and developments which were overtaking society.

Example Text: (i) Langland's *Prologue* to *Piers Plowman*

Langland's poem begins with a section of Estates Satire (B.Prol. 1–111) in which, although he does broadly divide the *fair feeld ful of folk* (17) into the commoners, clergy, and rulers, he also distinguishes individuals from one another by whether they are *wynners*, who actually contribute to society's well-being, or *wastours* who exploit others. It is therefore appropriate that he begins with the ploughmen, who work for all, and the clergy who actually 'win' spiritual benefits for others:

> Somme putten hem to the plough, pleiden ful selde …
> And wonnen that thise wastours wilth glotonye destruyeth.
> And somme putten hem to pride, apparailed hem therafter …
> In preieres and penaunce putten hem manye,
> Al for loue of Oure Lord lyueden ful streyte (B.Prol. 20–6)
>
> *pleiden ful selde*: enjoyed themselves little; *apparailed hem*: dressed themselves; *streyte*: narrowly, austerely

Among the 'winners' appear to be merchants and even poets:

> And somme chosen chaffare; they cheueden the bettre –
> As it semeth to oure sight that swiche men thryueth;
> And somme murthes to make as mynstralles konne
> (B.Prol. 27–9)
>
> *chaffare*: merchandise, business; *thryueth*: prosper; *murthes*: entertainments, songs

In the list of folk which follows, there seems to be a deliberate confusion of moral and economic productivity; for example, virtuous hermits and anchorites (itinerant or enclosed solitary religious men) are seen winning *heueneriche blisse* (27–8) for themselves and those they pray for, but are dismissed as wasters if they are *faitours* or hypocrites (53–7). The dreamer and poetic *persona*, Will, seems to be a *faitour* of the worst kind himself (a *heremite vnholy of werkes*, B.Prol. 3; see textbox on p. 19). Clerical hypocrites live off the poor, a flagrant example being the pardoner whom he catches using his spurious documents to rake in gifts:

> Ther preched a pardoner as he a preest were ...
> He bonched hem with his breuet and blered hire eighen,
> And raughte with his rageman rynges and broches.
> (B.Prol. 68–75)
>
> *bonched hem with his breuet and blered hire eighen*: he struck them with his (sealed) document and dimmed their eyes; *raughte with his rageman*: scooped in with his devilish bull

Some of this satire suggests the dissident literature we were looking at in the previous chapter, especially as Langland includes the cardinals and the Pope (100–11) in his attack, because they have failed to administer St Peter's power to *bynden* (bind) men to the discipline of the Church and so to *unbynden* them from punishment in Hell or Purgatory (101). The fabric of mutual responsibility in society is falling apart and it seems that the failings of the Church are the root cause.

However, in his (probably) first and second complete rewritings of the poem, Langland seems to offer a political solution to this disruptive society in terms of an idealised coronation scene – which briefly makes the poem an Advice for Princes text. This section (B.Prol. 112–38) was probably written shortly after Richard II's coronation in 1377 and it mimics that ceremony to some extent (see Donaldson 1949):

> The Kyng and the Commune and Kynde Wit the thridde
> Shopen lawe and leaute – ech lif to knowe his owene.
> (B.Prol. 121–2)
>
> *Kynde Wit*: Natural Reason; *leaute*: justice / loyalty; *knowe his owene*: know what belongs to him / know his duty

If '*Kynde Wit*' here refers to the clergy, the poet seems to be suggesting that all three estates – king and nobility, commoners, and clergy – join together in making the just state. *Leaute*, like the Middle English word *truthe*, means both loyalty and justice, concepts which were connected in medieval thought; the just man keeps the right and loyal relationship to those around him because he knows 'what is his own' (according to the Roman definition of justice). Passus 2–4 of the poem develop the possibility that the king can cure some of the problems in society, though in the C-text Langland allows himself a personal attack on the actual monarch, Richard II (see p. 81, below). But would political change really make a difference to the society we have glimpsed in the *Prologue*? The Estates Satire in the *Prologue* leaves the reader with a sense of a varied and lively but essentially dysfunctional community, which the rest of the poem will try to heal.

Example Text: (ii) Chaucer's *General Prologue to the Canterbury Tales*

By far the most significant London author is Chaucer, a well-connected writer who took part in the civic, commercial and governmental life of the city, and whose writing made English literature genuinely European. The *Canterbury Tales* was his last major work and it includes not only much learning, but much experience of the Londoners he encountered in his professional life (see text-box).

Geoffrey Chaucer

Chaucer was born in Thames Street in about 1343 to a wealthy vintner (wine merchant) family. He was sent as a page, when he was about 12, to the household of Elizabeth, Countess of Ulster, who was married to Lionel, Duke of Clarence, the second surviving son of King Edward III, and who kept a peripatetic household in England. This was a definite social advance, and here the young Geoffrey continued his reading of English and Latin, learned French and probably Italian, and acquired the life skills needed to serve at court. He also began to build what would later be known as the 'Chaucer circle', the aristocratic lords and the wealthy townsmen who were to be his friends and informal patrons in later life. Of these, probably the most significant was John of Gaunt, third son of the reigning King Edward III, who became Duke of Lancaster through his wife Blanche (and so the richest man in England) in 1362. When Blanche died in 1368, Chaucer wrote the elegiac *Book of the Duchess* about her loss, which seems to have won him Gaunt's faithful friendship. By 1366, Chaucer had married Philippa, one of Queen Philippa's ladies-in-waiting, who may have influenced his attitude to women's potential, for she had a career and an independent income from it, and often travelled with her mistress around England. Between 1367 and 1374, Chaucer himself lived at court, employed first as a *valetus* and then an *esquire*, and travelled in France, Flanders, Italy and Spain on the King's service (he was an excellent linguist and diplomat). He also took part in a couple of military campaigns, neither of them successful. But after the Queen's death in 1369 things began to deteriorate at court, the king becoming increasingly senile and in thrall to his mistress, Alice Perrers, and to the courtiers and city merchants who lent him money and who were embezzling state funds. In 1372, Philippa became the lady-in-waiting to Gaunt's new wife, Constanza, and it was probably Gaunt who helped Chaucer, too, to make a new career outside the court. For in 1374 he was offered the post of Controller of the Wool Custom (and related customs), and given a rent-free house above the portal of Aldgate. Although the proceeds of the customs went to the same rich merchants on whose wealth the king depended, Chaucer himself seems to have been scrupulously honest, collecting the customs dues and keeping records in his own hand. During the period in which he was controller (1374–86) he not only had ample opportunity to observe all kinds of Londoners, but also made several ambassadorial trips abroad, negotiating for the king in France and Italy. Towards the end of this period he bought property in Kent, where he became a

Justice of the Peace in 1384 and one of the two 'knights of the shire' (i.e. MPs) for a single session in the following year. In 1386 he resigned his post as controller of customs, and in 1388 all his other court annuities, but he did not give up his career in public service, holding the even more onerous post of Clerk of the King's (building) Works between 1389 and 1391, being partly responsible for the building of Westminster Hall. During this busy period he managed to compose the *Parliament of Fowles* and *Troilus and Criseyde*, among other significant works. In 1387 he began writing the *Canterbury Tales*, and his retirement to his Kent house in 1391 enabled him to work on it properly, putting into it, as with all his mature works, not only knowledge of European literature, but also his varied experience of practical life in both the city and the court. His was a remarkably successful career for a merchant's son, and Pearsall comments in the course of his detailed and fascinating *Life*, that 'he received patronage because his father was rich, because he was useful, and in some measure, also, because he was clever, funny, and inoffensive' (1994, p. 100). He was survived by two sons, one of whom, Thomas, became Speaker of the House of Commons. Chaucer's tomb is in a chapel of Westminster Abbey which became the location for 'Poet's Corner'.

Sources: Gray (2004); Pearsall (1994).

The Estates Satire in *The General Prologue* is even more innovative than Langland's, which Chaucer must surely have known (see Bennett 1969). It departs from the focus on the moral failings typical of the genre, and it develops Langland's naive narrator into an observer who seems to be on a moral holiday. This character (distinguished from Chaucer himself in a very illuminating essay by Donaldson in 1970) does not seem to know the estates hierarchy, but lists his pilgrims haphazardly, as if he was a fly-on-the-wall reporter, and seems also to have a policy of admiring his social superiors and believing everything they tell him about themselves; he is more discriminating about the middle-class townspeople. Both Langland and Chaucer were in fact working in the medieval tradition of the 'fallible first-person narrator' also used by Gower in the *Confessio Amantis*, and this narrative fiction prompts us to be aware of the moral failings of this *persona* and the people he describes so convincingly (see further discussion of Chaucer's narrators on pp. 105–6, below).

Two opposing lines of criticism are often applied to the *General Prologue*. One was initiated mainly by Jill Mann in 1973; she looks in detail at the long tradition of Estates Satire, and shows conclusively that moral and professional failings that we might think are the peculiarities of individual pilgrims, generally turn out to be highly traditional. Millers are cheats (*yet he hadde a thombe of gold, pardee*; by God he could make money! Fr.1, 563); friars are lascivious and need to marry off their victims (*He hadde maad ful many a mariage / Of yonge wommen at his owene cost*, Fr.1, 212); squires are dandies (*With lokkes crulle as they were leyd in presse*; locks as curly as if they had been pressed into shape, Fr.1, 81). But Chaucer again departs from tradition in making the work of each estate, as well as their moral failings, its distinguishing feature, giving us plenty of trade jargon and technical detail, often in the voice of the character (as loosely reported speech). For example, the Monk has clearly got Chaucer the pilgrim's ear for his defence of a life without manual labour (prescribed for monks by St Benedict and Augustine):

> He yaf nat of that text a pulled hen,
> That seith that hunters ben nat hooly men. . . .
> And I seyde his opinion was good.
> What, sholde he studie and make hymselven wood,
> Upon a book in cloystre alwey to poure,
> Or swynken with his handes, and laboure,
> As Austyn bit? How shal the world be served?
> Lat Austyn have his swynk to hym reserved!
> Therfore he was a prikasour aright (Fr.1, 177–8, 183–9)
>
> *pulled hen*: plucked hen; *wood*: mad; *poure*: pore (on a book); *swynken with his handes . . . As Austyn bit*: work with his hands as bidden by St Augustine (in his monastic Rule); *have his swynk to hym reserved!*: let him keep his labour!; *prikasour aright*: rightly a huntsman

Mann offers close parallels to this passage (1973, p. 28) from the Estates Satire in the *Romance of the Rose* and Gower's *Miroir de l'omme*, and gives many early and contemporary analogues for the rest of the Monk's portrait. But Chaucer's assumption both of the Monk's and of his 'own' voice makes these well-known criticisms personal, and even disarming. Do you, however, agree with Mann that the Monk's empathetic voice is undermined by a symbolic interpretation of his appearance? For example, do the lines:

> His eyen stepe, and rollynge in his heed,
> That stemed as a forneys of a leed (Fr.1, 201–2)
>
> *stepe*: bright, flashing; *stemed ... a leed*: glowed like the fire under a pot

suggest he will soon be burning in hell fire?

An alternative way of reading the *General Prologue* is to suggest that Chaucer was in fact moving away from types and traditions and towards a new realism which reflects the social realities of contemporary life. Critics like Wallace, Strohm and Turner place the pilgrims who appear in the *Prologue*, and the 'link passages' between the *Tales*, in the context of the medieval realities of socialisation. Lindahl (1987, pp. 1-4) demonstrates that many of them come from the upper level of the third estate, in other words, the middle class that was developing particularly in the towns and cities, and whose reading tastes are the focus of this chapter. Though the Cook and Manciple are from the lower part of this estate, and the Reeve, Miller and Ploughman from the country working class (the last two professions were also found in towns), Chaucer's pilgrim assembly of lesser nobility, clergy, traders, craftsmen, and women suggest the composition of the parish guilds that were flourishing in the towns before and during the rise of the craft guilds. This may even reflect the composition of Chaucer's audience, which, according to Strohm, comprised 'the most broadly conceived of his audiences', a 'shifting body of equals and near-equals' including the London intellectuals and prominent guildsmen (1989, p. 49). Townsmen were notoriously quarrelsome, and the antagonism between particular pairs of pilgrims, such as the Host and the Cook (rivals in the refreshment trade), or the Friar and the Wife of Bath, is the source of much of the dynamism of the Frame Narrative (discussed below, pp. 104–5). Turner (2006) has demonstrated how, as in the craft and parish guilds, this aggression and individualism is contained by the rituals that the pilgrims perform under the direction of Harry Bailey. They agree to form a 'felawship', which will follow his organisation of their pilgrimage, and they seal the oath – as guildsmen did – with a drink:

And we wol reuled been at his devys
In heigh and lough. And thus by oon assent
We been acorded to his juggement.
And therupon the wyn was fet anon.
We dronken, and to reste wente echon (Fr.1, 816–20)

devys: will; *heigh and lough*: in all respects; *therupon the wyn was fet anon*: the wine was fetched right away (to seal the agreement)

The individual antagonisms will thereafter be channelled into a story-telling competition.

Questions on Langland's and Chaucer's *Prologues*

- What details make the characters of Chaucer's and Langland's *Prologues* come to life? Do you feel that it is the literary traditions you can discover from reading Mann (1973) or Owst (1966), or the social realities you can learn from Strohm (1989) or Lindahl (1987), which are most helpful in your analysis?
- Compare the portrait of the Pardoner in Langland's *Prologue* (B.Prol. 68–73) with that in Chaucer's *Prologue* (Fr.4, 669–714).
- Do you find either Chaucer or Langland to be writing from an essentially moral standpoint? If Langland is, why does he move so quickly into advice for princes? If Chaucer is, why is his narrator so eager to accept the moral shortcomings of his fellow-pilgrims without criticism?

(c) Venality Satire on the Misuse of Money

Whereas Estates Satire celebrates as well as criticises the different classes of society, and allows that different professions and ways of life are constantly developing, Venality Satire – satire on the misuse of money – can be much darker, more critical, more expressive of the painful experience of the victim. English Venality Satire has its origins in attacks by clerical writers on Church abuse (see above, p. 53). But it was not only the Church which was seen as profiting from money that was not theirs, as sermons often made clear. The aristocracy's extravagance robbed the poor of their sustenance.

Lawyers came under constant attack for charging exorbitant fees for selling their God-given gifts of intelligence and learning, or for taking bribes to subvert justice. Tax and customs collectors, as we have seen in the biography of Chaucer himself, tended to 'farm' an area or a commodity (like wool), paying the king for the lucrative privilege of keeping all the income raised, which encouraged extortion and further corruption. Similar practices accompanied the raising of soldiers for the king's wars. Moreover, the economic envelopments of the period generated a demand for capital, and as usury was supposedly forbidden by Church and law, all kinds of ways were developed to allow creditors to charge interest, such as 'buying' a worthless product from a creditor and then selling it back again for more money. It seemed that everywhere one looked one saw evidence for St Paul's dictum that *the love of money is the root of all evil* (Timothy 6:10; see Owst 1966, for sermons addressed to the Estates).

'Literary' writers in Europe had been attacking such abuses for hundreds of years, in venality satires directed against both laymen and clergy, such as *Le Roman de Fauvel*, an allegory of the many kinds of people who groomed the horse of wealth (see Yunck 1963, pp. 221–6). The English poem known variously as *The Simonie*, *A Satire on the Consistory Courts* and *On the Evil Times of Edward II*, is a vivid example of traditional venality satire written in Middle English. It probably dates from shortly after Edward II's deposition for misrule in 1327, an event that provided a precedent and a procedure for Richard II's deposition seventy years later. The poet's gaze is directed first at the clergy – bishops, priests, monks and friars – who have so discredited their ideals of 'Peace and Love and Charity'. Then he ranges across the whole of society, from the Roman Papal court to the English shires, attacking all who profit at others' expense, and exposes the effect this has not only on the suffering poor, but on the middle and upper classes too:

> And if the king in the land makes a taxation
> And every man is set a certain ransom
> He shall be so for-pinched, for-toiled and to-twiht ...

> As if the king hit wiste, I trowe he wolde be wrothe
> How the pore are i-piled, and how the silver goth ... (301–14)
>
> *ransom*: sum to pay the tax; *for-pinched, for-toiled and to-twiht*: over-pinched, over-worked and despised; *wiste*: knew; *i-piled*: exploited

The king is politely seen as ignorant of the abuse because he too loses money to the corruption of others. The writer is adding to his moral condemnation an anxiety about over-taxation and economic collapse. This is also the theme of the (misnamed) *Song of the Husbandman*, which Kane (1986) sees as roughly contemporary. It is the misuse of money, not money in itself, which is under attack. Such poems also show the close link between venality satire and political advice.

I shall now briefly discuss two other examples of Venality Satire in Middle English, cast as 'Dream Visions': the secular *Wynnere and Wastoure*, and the more religious Vision of Lady Meed from *Piers Plowman*. Both texts move between anti-clerical material and a more general and even political consideration of the power of money. Indeed, *Wynnere and Wastoure* could claim to be an early treatise on economics, in which spending is not seen as wholly bad! The genre of secular Dream Vision goes back to the thirteenth century and will be introduced in Chapter 7 (see pp. 203–6). Religious Dream Visions are older (see text-box on p. 185). Both my examples are also Debate Poems (see text-box below). These two texts are therefore examples of Venality Satire, of Dream Visions, and of Debate Poetry.

Debate Poetry

The Debate is a Classical and originally dramatic form which was used in many genres in the European religious tradition, including the '*pro and contra*' form of scholastic debate, and dramas involving formal debates (such as those written by law students in the late fifteenth century). European poetic debates are often on standard topics such as debates between the Body and the Soul, or between the Devil and Christ, both of which have Middle English versions. The first surviving vernacular example in England, written in 'Early Middle English' at about 1200, is *The Owl and the Nightingale*, a lively and readable poetic debate. After a good deal of verbal abuse, it transpires that the Owl represents sacred, and the Nightingale secular song, and consequently the Owl must be the victor. Bird debates became a popular subject for Dream Visions about Love, and we will discuss Chaucer's *Parliament of Fowls* and Clanvowe's *Cuckoo and the Nightingale* in Chapter 7 (see pp. 212–16). Religious debates, such as that between the Four Daughters of God in *Piers Plowman* in B.18, or between Death and Life in a poem influenced by Langland, continued to be written. *Wynnere and Wastoure* is unusual both for its subject and for its early date.

It is characteristic of a Middle English Debate that the two contestants spend little time in putting forward their own particular points of view, but are engaged in attacking one another without responding to the attacks made by the other side. (The effect is reminiscent of a General Election campaign today.) The debate is often overseen by an umpire, who never seems to resolve the debate itself but instead introduces some new allegorical element.

Source: Conlee (1991).

Example Text: (i) *Wynnere and Wastoure*

If it was really written in 1352, as seems probable from internal evidence, then *Wynnere and Wastoure* is the first surviving Middle English poem from the Old English alliterative tradition, though its assured poetry and use of the idioms of Dream Vision and of Debate make it very contemporary (see Spiers 1957, p. 263, and the text-box on p. 25). Though its provenance is quite unclear, an emerging middle-class audience in London would have found it highly relevant to its concerns. The dreamer sees two armies ready to fight one another, one of Wynneres and one of Wastoures. Wynnere's army is weighed down by financial assets, and includes representatives of the international corporations of the fourteenth century – the Pope, the monks, canons and friars – a well as lawyers and merchants. The Wastoures are the knights and soldiers of the royal army, principally aristocrats who, we learn, are rich in valour and tradition but whose land can no longer support their lifestyles. Edward III is also present, and he prevents the battle and offers to judge between the armies, and so their representatives commence a lively and generally well-balanced debate. Just as nowadays both the bankers and big businesses which supposedly create wealth, and the National Health and Welfare systems which spend it, might each see themselves as of Britain, so do Wynnere and Wastoure each claim to serve the king. As is usual in such poems, the opposing armies concentrate on attacking their opponents, and rarely engage with the others' arguments, so it is quite unclear who should win. Moreover, the poet seems to includes different groupings and different preoccupations under the terms *Wynnere* and *Wastoure*, so that, as Barr puts it, 'the social roles of Wynnere and Wastoure are discontinuous and contradictory', embodying a 'social reconfiguration' (2001, pp. 21, 26).

The focus shifts at different points between the social, the moral and the economic. On one level the poet recalls the popular medieval theme of the opposition between different ages, as Wastoure seems much younger and more light-hearted than Wynnere:

> It lyes wele for a lede his lemman to fynde,
> Aftir hir faire chere to forthir hir herte (428–9)
>
> It is fitting for a man to provide for his mistress in a way appropriate to her good reception of him, so as to increase her love

This recalls the boast made by Youth to Middle-Elde in the contemporary *Parliament of Three Ages*, a Debate Poem possibly by the same author:

> And than kayre to the courte that I come fro,
> With ladys full lovely to lappyn in myn armes (*Parliament*, 246–7)
>
> *kayre*: go; *lappyn*: enfold

However, although it is easy to see how Youth might progress through Middle Elde to Elde (see *Parliament*, 652), it is less possible to see how Wastoure could turn into Wynnere; their differences are not simply a matter of changing tastes, but of personality and background. On another level we find that the terms of the debate are often reminiscent of the more moralistic Estates Satire, as it caricatures both the avarice of the wealthy middle class and the prodigality of the nobility. Indeed, Jacobs finds the theme of the poem to be class conflict, with the poet – who is writing in a pretty ornate and courtly style – sympathetic to the traditional feudal attitudes of the aristocratic Wastoure and hostile to the financial preoccupations of the urban merchant Wynnere (Jacobs 1985, p. 496).

But the poem also includes much shrewd analysis of the way people spend money, and the effect their attitudes have on the society they live in, and maybe we should read it as an experimental excursion into economic theory. Is the author saying, as Jacobs goes on to suggest, that 'some thrift and some expenditure are both necessary to a healthy economy, and that they are interdependent and need to exist in a proper reciprocal balance ... or they will degenerate into the contrasting vices of avarice and prodigality (1985, p. 486)? Such an inter-dependence has been stressed at more than one point, here by Wastoure:

> Whoso wele schal wyn, a wastour moste he fynde,
> For if it greves one gome, it gladdes another. (390; see also 495)
>
> *wele*: wealth; *gome*: man; *gladdes*: pleases

Wastoure even insists that his open extravagance benefits the poor, by giving them employment and the overflow from his feasts:

> With oure festes and oure fare we feden the pore (294)
>
> *festes ... fare*: feasts ... food

Not only do both Wynnere and Wastoure seem to be necessary to the kingdom, they also seem to be attributes of the king himself, for he says he will need them both in his wars. Nor does he appear to judge them, but rather to educate each in the ways of the other, sending Wastoure to the markets of Cheapside, and Wynnere to the luxurious palace of the Pope in Rome. Bestul points out that in the 1340s Edward III was closely involved with bankers and wool merchants in pursuit of his French war, and at the same time was an extravagant purchaser of food, clothes, jewels and all the other trappings of monarchy (Bestul 1974, pp. 49–50). Is the effect of the poem then to criticise or to celebrate the king as the supreme Wynnere and Wastoure? To deplore or praise the power of money? Or simply to recognise that in contemporary London it was not the old bonds of feudalism, but the new bond between production and consumption, which was shaping the future?

Questions on *Wynnere and Wastoure*

- To what extent is the poem a moral debate between two equally sinful approaches to the material goods and benefits that God has given to humankind? For example, Wynnere's army includes many of the traditional targets of venality satire, such as luxurious monks (255–161), and on his part Wynnere accuses Wastoure of pride, gluttony and prodigality (230).
- Compare Wastoure's feastings with the tavern-scene in *Piers Plowman* B.5.297–359. Despite the differences in class and situation, do you find any similarities in personality, in authorial attitude, or anything else in the two accounts of 'excess'? Is there any evidence that one might have influenced the other?

Example Text: (ii) The Vision of Lady Meed in *Piers Plowman* 2–4

We have already seen that the *Prologue* to *Piers Plowman* is structured as an Estates Satire, which keeps coming back to the opposition between the 'Wynnere', who *putten hem to the plough*, and the 'Wastoure', who *with glotonye destruyeth* (B.Prol. 20, 22) what Wynnere has produced. Like the poet of *Wynnere and Wastoure* Langland sees the opposition from a moral, economic and political perspective, and in the Vision of Lady Meed (B.2–4) he demonstrates how the misuse of money and power distorts the relation between man and God, between the producers and the consumers, and between the governors and the governed. 'Winning' in all three areas can be achieved in much quicker and more corrupt ways than honest toil, and Meed (which means reward of different kinds) represents many of these short cuts. Through the description of her appearance and followers which occupies Passus 2, Langland shows that her influence is corrosive on English justice, as she attempts to corrupt all the courts in England from the local manor court to Parliament itself (and even, through the friars, the Court of Heaven). Her influence on Church courts is also detailed, and is very reminiscent of *The Simonie* discussed above, p. 74. Meed's gender, rich attire and apparent complaisance suggests that she is an attractively easy conquest, for her reward does not represent proper earnings (which Langland calls *Mercede* in the C-text), but is offered falsely to buy justice, influence, power and further wealth. Meed's retinue of law-enforcers suggests her purchase of protection from crime, and her influence in high places suggests a corrupt government. She resembles one of those wealthy nobles who exercised so much influence in their localities that the members of their households could act, as the Commons described it in 1381, 'as Kings in the country, so that right and law are almost set at nothing' (*Rot. Parl.* 100b; see Baldwin 2007, p. 42). Her influence in government also suggests the power of the courtiers, particularly those who had no public position in the House of Lords, such as Edward III's extravagant mistress Alice Perrers who may even have provided Meed with a model (see Kennedy 2006, pp. 197–8).

The king in *Piers Plowman* seems ready to tackle the situation and summons Meed to London (B.2.203). However, as soon as she gets there she sets about corrupting those responsible for maintaining justice there, asking *Maires and maceres, that menes ben bitwene / The kyng and the comune to kepe le lawes* (3.78–9) to be lenient towards all kinds of illegal retailers and merchants. This section (B.3.76–100, expanded in C.3.77–114) has many fascinating insights into London life, investing the tricksters with verve but also cruelty. The central courts were located in Westminster, and Meed appears already to have corrupted the King's Bench 'before the King has even summons her there. He tries to solve the problems she is causing in his kingdom by giving her in marriage, as his ward, to one of his own knights, Conscience, suggesting that reward is acceptable if offered to the right people (B.3.101–19). The rest of the Passus is cast as a Debate between Conscience and Meed. Conscience begins it by firmly rejecting her and then explains to the king that she can corrupt the 'right people' as easily as the wrong ones. Indeed, the king's own misuse of money and rewards has harmed his relations with the law, with his army, and with his people. In the C-text, written possibly in the late 1380s, Langland ends this section with some Political Advice directed even more pointedly at Richard himself for his readiness to reward and protect unscrupulous followers:

> Ynsityng soffraunce, here suster, and heresulue
> Han almest mad, but Marye the helpe,
> That no lond ne loueth the – and yut leeste thyn owene.
> (Passus 3.207–9)
>
> *Ynsityng soffraunce*: inappropriate indulgence; *almest mad*: almost made it happen that

The events I described above (pp. 64–5) were to show that Langland was prescient in warning his monarch of the possible consequences of making corruption and extortion to be his method of government.

In all three texts the Vision leads in Passus 4 to a scene in Parliament which demonstrates the inevitable result of the government's failure in late fourteenth-century England to control the misuse of money and power: the breakdown in law and order and in the availability of justice. A new character, Peace (representing the 'King's Peace' cited in all criminal accusations), has been unable to receive justice against the criminal Wrong, and so has had to come directly to the king. He is like a petitioner in Chancery who complained in 1392 that his adversaries were 'so great in their county in kinsmen, alliances and friends, that the said supplicant cannot have any right against them by any suit at Common Law' (*Cases in Chancery*, p. 8; see Baldwin 2007, pp. 67–9):

> And thanne com Pees into parlement and putte vp a bille –
> How Wrong ayeins his wille hadde his wif taken,
> And how he rauysshede Rose, Reignaldes loue,
> And Margrete of hir maydenhede maugree hire chekes.
> 'Bohe my gees and my grys hise gadelynges feccheh;
> I dar noght for fere of hym fighte ne chide.
> He borwed of me bayard and brouste hym hom neuere,
> Ne no ferhyng herfore, for nought I koude plede ...
> I am noght hardy for hym vnnethe to loke!' (B.4.47–60)
>
> *bille*: petition; *maugree hire chekes*: in spite of her protests; *my grys hise gadelynges feccheth*: his fellows take my pigs; *chide*: complain; *bayard*: Dobbin; *noght hardy for hym vnnethe to loke*: scarcely bold enough to look out

Indeed, the Commons had been complaining to Richard II since the beginning of his reign, that criminals went unpunished, that armed bands were allowed to 'kill your liegemen, and ravish their daughters ...

and take their goods', and that wronged men 'dared not plead against them' (*Rot. Parl.*, pp. 42–3, for 1378; see Baldwin 2007, p. 68). Some of Wrong's crimes may even have been committed by the king's own 'purveyors' requisitioning goods and services for his peripatetic court. Wrong, the perpetrator of all these crimes, demonstrates his usual practice by asking Meed for protection, and she is prepared to 'maintain' (guard from justice) him even in this high court of Parliament. With the support of some wily judges Meed pleads for mercy for Wrong, *And profrede Pees a present al of pure golde* (B.4.95). It looks as though he will get away with it.

But as in the *Prologue*, Langland suddenly counters the problem he has been describing with a picture of an ideal monarch. The king refuses to allow the bribery and corruption to continue any more:

> 'Nay,' quod the Kyng tho, 'so me Crist helpe!
> Wrong wendeth noght so awey er I wite more.
> Lope he so lightly, laughen he wolde,
> And eft the boldere be to bete myne hewen.' (B.4.104–7)
>
> *er I wite more*: before I know more about this; *Lope he so lightly*: if he escaped so easily; *eft*: afterwards; *hewen*: servants

He calls for Reason to judge Wrong, and Reason condemns both Wrong and Meed with the support not only of the people present but also of the qualities of *Kynde Wit*, *Love* and *Leaute*, who helped found the ideal kingdom in the *Prologue* (B.4.161, Prol. 118–22). Wrong is put in irons and Meed is discredited – at least for the present – as a *mansed sherewe* (160), and the king dismisses the judges with the splendid assertion, *I wole haue leaute in lawe, and lete be al youre ianglyng* (I will have justice in my law in spite of all your chattering; B.4.179).

Questions on The Vision of Lady Meed

- What difference does it make to your interpretation of this section that Meed is a woman (see the discussion in Aers 1988, Kennedy 2006)?
- Compare the debate between Meed and Conscience in Passus 3 with the debate between Wynnere and Wastoure in *Wynnere and Wastoure*. To what extent does each present themselves as helpful

- to the king or the kingdom, and to what extent are other moral or political values invoked?
- Use the *Prologue* and the Vision of Lady Meed to discuss Langland's attitude to city life, and to the different classes of society.

(d) Complaint and Political Prophecy

Though I will not be looking at it here in any detail, there was a long tradition of vernacular complaint poetry in which the literate laity or clergy spoke on behalf of those suffering from the viciousness of the other classes. For example, in Robbins' *Historical Poems of the Fourteenth and Fifteenth Centuries* (1959), there are poems complaining of oppression by great lords (pp. 27–9), or by the king's tax collectors (such as the *Song of the Husbandman* (pp. 7–9, mentioned on p. 75, above), and songs concerning the civil wars of the fifteenth century (pp. 174–227). A more recent anthology is *Medieval English Political Writing* edited by James Dean in 1996, also available under individual titles on the TEAMS website. These and the other anthologies of political poems listed in the Further Reading section include a considerable proportion of texts describing the 'abuses of the age', many of which concern the misuse of money, and so are in the Venality Satire tradition discussed above. There are also general moral indictments, such as the early fourteenth-century *Sayings of the four philosophers*:

> ffor miht is right, the lond is laweless
> ffor niht is liht, the lond is loreless
>
> because might is now seen as right, there is no law; because darkness is seen as light, there is no faith

The oracular tone of this poem makes it an example of Political Prophecy, another way of commenting on the times, and one which protected the writer from the charge of sedition, as he could conceal his political complaints behind cryptic or visionary language and a famous and long-dead (supposed) writer. Robbins includes a prophecy attributed to the Scottish thirteenth-century prophet Thomas of Erceldoune, which gives a series of contemporary abuses as evidence of impending doom, and three (possibly) fifteenth-century prophecies attributed to Merlin:

> When lordes wille is londes law ...
> And robbery is helde no trespace ...
> Then schal the lond of Albyon
> Torne into confusion (ed. Robbins 1959, p. 121)

This prophecy is next to another in the same Dublin manuscript, which codes its utterances with pictures of dice (Robbins 1959, p. 120), for signs and riddles are often a feature of the genre. Another prophecy, beginning *Qwhen Rome is removyde into Inglande*, also gives a warning that the present corruption is a sign of an impending doom, but uses animal symbolism and a cryptic letter-code to convey its uncertain message:

> The Lyone, leder of bestis,
> Shall lowte to the Libert and long hume wytht ...
> Anon efter M*l*, evene to rewlle,
> Tre CCC in A sute semblyt to-gether (ed. Robbins 1959,
> pp. 119–20, lines 32–3, 61–2)
>
> *loute*: bow; *Libert*: leopard; *long hume wytht*: belong to him; *Ml evene to rewlle*: a thousand shall measure level; *Tre CCC in A sute semblyt to-gether*: 300 in a single livery assembled together

Here the leopard probably suggests Scotland, triumphant over the lion of England, but the numbers are more difficult to explain; do they refer to dates or to the soldiers in an army? Similar signs of a catastrophe to come are to be found in the Prologue to *Wynnere and Wastoure* (13–17), and Langland more than once incorporates riddles and prophecies into *Piers Plowman* (see Baldwin 2001). Like Estates satire and venality satire, then, political prophecy can often turn into advice to kings, the genre which I shall be discussing now.

(e) Political Advice

(i) Idealised and general advice

The genre of Political Advice includes the generalised and more specific warnings we have just been considering in Political Prophecies and *Piers Plowman*, and also the more theoretical advice literature of the European *Fürstenspiegel* (or Mirror for Princes) tradition. This tradition focuses in particular on the person of the king, head of the body politic, and ultimately stems from Aristotle's *Politics* via Aquinas' *De regno* and the Islamic *Secreta Secretorum* or *Secret of Secrets*, of which there are numerous manuscripts and translations into English. In the early fourteenth century the friars Jacob de Cessolis and Egidius Colonna (or Giles of Rome) wrote two significant *Fürstenspiegelen*, both of which were copied hundreds of times in Europe and translated into many languages. Jacobus' book was one of the first to be printed by Caxton in 1474, as *The Game and Play of Chess* (discussed briefly on p. 65). Trevisa translated the other book, by Giles of Rome, as *The Governance of Kings and Princes*, early in the fifteenth century for Lord Berkeley, a prominent supporter of Henry IV's accession. Texts in this tradition list various virtues, which the king should adopt. These were often four Cardinal Virtues of Justice – which included Faith-keeping, Prudence, Temperance, and Fortitude – with others such as Clemency and Largess. If he embodied these he should achieve what Aristotle called the 'common good' and bring peace, health, joy and even agricultural abundance to the kingdom (see Watts 1999).

As the English kings were indeed the effective as well as the nominal head of law and government (though liable to be deposed if they took this too literally, like Edward II and Richard II), it is not surprising that they should have been offered advice of this *Fürstenspiegel* type. Several important fourteenth- and fifteenth-century poets writing in English used these ancient principles to encourage responsive government or to imply criticism of the present government. Such texts were actually presented to the king, because they listed the ideals to which he should aspire, rather than pointing out too clearly how far he fell short of these ideals. An example of such a presentation text is Gower's *Confessio Amantis* (see the text-box on John Gower, p. 102). The first recension of this text (1390) is addressed to Richard II, but some three years later Gower changed the dedication to Henry Derby (later Henry IV), altered the Prologue and Epilogue, and added some new sections. These include a long passage added to Book 7 (1641ff.) in which Gower uses both Giles of Rome and the *Secreta*, among other authorities, and a section of Book 8 devoted to the sins of the different estates. This final version of the *Confessio* is clearly about good government in the macrocosm of the kingdom as well as the microcosm of the individual king and subject, what Peck calls 'a benevolent psychology of personal ethics' (2006, p. xxi). The speaker, Genius (meaning *natural production* rather than *brilliance*), offers five principal ideals: Truth, Liberality, Justice, Pity and Chastity, essentially personal qualities, and illustrates them by examples of good and bad rule. In many other parts of the *Confessio* Gower also discusses what makes for a contented kingdom: is it love, the theme of the entire work, or something closer to 'common profit'? Though the poem as a whole is moral rather than political, there is some scope for discussing contemporary political and constitutional issues (see Anstell 1999, pp. 73–7). Chaucer also ventured into this territory with his 'own' *Tale of Melibee* in the *Canterbury Tales*, which pertinently advised peace at a time when Richard II was acting with particular ferocity towards his political opponents. But perhaps the clearest example of an English *Fürstenspiegel* is Hoccleve's *Regement of Princes*, which I shall discuss now in a little more detail.

Thomas Hoccleve

Thomas Hoccleve (1367–1426) is interesting not only for his works, but for his autobiographical revelations in those works, which unlike Langland's self-revelations, seem literally rather than allegorically true. Like Chaucer, Hoccleve was a London civil servant for much of his life, and he describes his work in the office of the Privy Seal in fascinating detail in the *Prologue* to the *Regement of Princes* (2422), where he says he had already been in that office for nearly twenty-four years! We learn from a formulary of documents compiled by Hoccleve himself that this office issued notifications of the king's will to individuals, often by responding to complaints and petitions from individuals all over the country, notifying relevant officials of the need to remedy a wrong, take an action, issue a licence or the like. The dependence of the Crown upon personal supplication to initiate action helps to explain why so much political poetry is structured as complaint or petition. Hoccleve also describes the people he met as a senior civil servant, ranging from the humble cooks and taverners to the nobles and senior officials with whom he conducted official business. As a clerk in minor orders he probably lived, for nothing, in a London hostel with others like himself, travelling to work in Westminster by boat or on foot, though in his early forties he married, and lived very harmoniously with his wife. He was clearly a man who worried about money, and his poetry is full of petitions of his own that he be paid his arrears, suggesting that his audience included some of the most powerful men in the kingdom. By his own account he was also friendly with his fellow poets, Gower and Chaucer. His literary works include religious and courtly love pieces like the *Letter of Cupid* translated from Christine de Pisan, but he is best known for the autobiographical and political *Regement of Princes*.

Source: Knapp (2001).

Example Text: Hoccleve's *Regement of Princes*

The Regement of Princes is by Thomas Hoccleve, a civil servant writing in the first decades of the fifteenth century (see text-box on p. 86). He personalises his traditional material by giving an account of his own experience in the government of Henry IV, and by including some reflections on contemporary politics in the list of princely virtues which makes up the main part of the book. Thus the fact that his own wages are in arrears gives an edge to his praise of Largess, and his experience of Richard II's deposition also sharpens his praise of Faith-keeping. He even warns Henry not to break his coronation oath (as the articles of deposition claimed that Richard had done) but to exemplify *treuthe* or Faith-keeping:

> Tho oothes that at your creacioun
> Shul thurgh your tonge passe, hem wel observe. ...
> A kyng of trouthe, owith been exemplarie. (*Regement* 2192–3, 2198)

Hoccleve also involves his readers by insisting that the king should listen to counsel provided by ordinary citizens, who thereby 'serve the state and their fellow men' (see Wawn 1983, p. 281):

> And if that a man of symple degree,
> Or poore of birthe, or yong, thee wel conseille,
> Admitte his reson and take it in gree. (*Regement* 4874–6)
>
> *of symple degree*: humble class; *thee wel conseille*: counsel thee well; *reson*: argument; *in gree*: in good part

Like the author of *Richard Redeless*, to be discussed shortly, Hoccleve is also prejudiced against youthful counsellors: see 4936–42. However, being optimistic about Henry IV's character (or maybe just accepting the real-politique of the English constitution), Hoccleve then asserts that, having heard this counsel, the king should be free to perform his will.

> Also yee been at your eleccioun
> To do or leve it as yourselven leste (*Regement* 4890–1)
>
> *eleccioun*: choice; *as yourselven leste*: as you wish

The counsel offered by the poet is, however, disappointingly generalised, and the examples of rulership given are classical stories rather than contemporary anecdotes.

Questions on *The Regement of Princes*

- Compare the section on Largess, Prodigality and Avarice (4120ff.) with the dispute between Wynnere and Wastoure described above on pp. 76–9. Aquinas demonstrated that prodigality was better than avarice, as it does at least benefit someone (see Jacobs 1985, p. 485, referring to *S.T.* 2a 2ae q.129 a.3). Do both authors have an instinctive preference for the aristocratic 'fault' of prodigality over the middle-class 'virtue' of Prudence? (See, e.g., 4154–9.)
- What is the relation between the character of Hoccleve as a 'narrator' within his text, and Hoccleve the author who pieces together the text from old authorities?

(ii) Personal Political Advice

Some advice addressed to kings, however, does not so much suggest that it is the king's general moral reformation which is the key to political change, but rather urges him to accept specific good counsel and reform corruption. As we have seen (p. 81), Langland adds a passage to the C-text of Passus 3 (late 1380s) in which he warns

Richard II directly of the consequences of his own involvement with Lady Meed. In the problematic nineties, when Richard posted spies to report opposition, and after Henry IV's coup in 1399, when loyalty to the earlier monarch suddenly became disloyalty to the current one, it was much more difficult to speak out so directly about what was wrong with government. One political poet, whose early fifteenth-century work survives in a single manuscript (Digby MS 102; and also containing part of the C-text of *Piers Plowman*), comments directly on the dangers of speaking out. Their first editor argues (Kail 1904, pp. xiii–xiv) that the poem *Lerne say wele, say litel or say nought* arises from the parliamentary conditions of 1404, where the Commons warned the king not to listen to tale-bearers and slanderers who advised him to imprison innocent people without trial:

> Sum man dar not be thef for drede;
> His trouthe is vice, and no vertue.
> In heuene he nys not worthi mede,
> that clothes trouthe in falsed hewe. (ed. Kail 1904, p. 15, lines 9–12)
>
> *Sum man dar not be thef for drede*: Some people dare not show their wickedness openly for fear; *worthi mede*: honourable reward; *falsed hewe*: false colours

Wawn demonstrates (1983) that in the early fifteenth century the fear expressed in the proverb *whoso seyth the truth he shall be shent* is the subject of many poems. After all, although it may appear safer to attack the counsellors than the king himself, it is clear to any discerning subject that the responsibility of encouraging truth-tellers must lie with the king, who should not surround himself with flatterers, as the Digby Manuscript poet says a little later:

> Gloseres maken mony lesynges –
> Al to sone men hem leue –
> Bothe to lordys and to kynges,
> That bothe partye ofte greue (ed. Kail 1904, p. 17, lines 73–6)
>
> *Gloseres maken mony lesynges*: commentators tell lies; *hem leue*: believe them; *that bothe partye ofte greue*: both groups often do harm

The issue of truth-telling becomes even more personal when the poet not only condemns 'prince-pleasers' but takes it upon himself to act as *Sothsegger* or Truth-teller. A remarkably fresh and topical account of the problem of good counsel can be found in the early fifteenth-century alliterative poem *Richard Redeless* and its sequel, *Mum and the Sothsegger*, probably written by the same author about ten years later. They are alliterative poems in the tradition inspired by *Piers Plowman* which also includes the Lollard poems we looked at in Chapter 2 (see pp. 55–8). Both poems reflect on the prevalence of deceit and flattery at court and in government, and the elusiveness of real truth-telling. I will now discuss both poems, as fascinating examples of personal political advice – advice which crackles with danger for the writer. Both are critically edited and discussed by H. Barr in *The Piers Plowman Tradition* (1993).

Example Texts: *Richard Redeless* and *Mum and the Sothsegger*

Richard Redeless dates from shortly after Henry IV's accession, and is firmly focused on the urgent need for good political advice. After an introduction claiming his genuine loyalty, the poem proper begins by blaming Richard's deposition on his moral failings:

> Now, Richard the redeles, reweth on you-self,
> That lawelesse leddyn youre lyf and youre peple bothe.
> For thoru the wyles and wronge and wast in youre tyme,
> Ye were lyghtlich ylyfte from that you leef thoughte. (*Richard* 1–4)
>
> *redeles*: ill-advised; *reweth*: take pity; *wyles*: deceits; *lyghtlich ylyfte from that you leef thoughte*: quickly taken from what you thought dear

However, as soon as the author begins to detail the problems which led to the catastrophe of the deposition, we realise that he is seeking political rather than moral change:

> Of alegeaunce now lerneth a lesson other tweyne
> Wherby it standith and stablithe moste –
> By dride, or be dyntis, or domes untrewe ...
> By pillynge of youre peple, youre prynces to plese ...
> Or be ledinge of lawe with love well ytemprid. (*Richard* 9–13, 19)
>
> Allegiance is not confirmed by blows, or untrue judgements, or pillage of your people to please your nobles, but by leadership tempered by mercy.

The poet blames these disastrous policies on the king's counsellors who have managed to *usurpe* the *governaunce of grete and of good age ... myghthffull men, of the mydill age*, men who would *laboure on the lawe, as lewde men on plowes* (labour on the law as unlearned men labour with their ploughs – an image from *Piers Plowman*; 3.250, 252, 267). Instead his counsellors are youths who can scarcely read, and how can *yonge men of yistirday ... geve good redis* (261)? They are like dangerous versions of Wastoure in *Wynnere and Wastoure*, or of Youth in the *Parliament of Three Ages*, wielding their power over the helpless commoners with the unscrupulousness of a Lady Meed. Their youthful folly implies that the king should empower his own older relatives and the established Lords of his Parliament rather than these members of a personal 'court party'. Characterising Richard's subjects as a herd of frightened wild deer, the poet describes how they are starved and flayed, and how their children are neglected. These sufferings were inflicted by another group of much more ferocious deer, those who wore Richard's livery of the White Hart, and were backed by Richard's private army of Cheshire archers. In 1397 Richard had built up enough power to avenge himself on the Lords Appellant, and executed Warwick, Gloucester and Arundel (named cryptically by the poet at 3.27–9; see above, p. 64):

> For tho that had hertis on hie on her brestis, (2.36)
> They ... busshid with her brestis and bare adoun the pouere ...
> For on that ye merkyd, ye myssed ten schore
> Of homeliche hertis that the harme hente. (*Richard* 2.39, 42–3)
>
> Those that bore the White Hart badge beat down the poor with their breasts.
> For one *hart* that you marked on a badge, you lost ten score of faithful *hearts*.

This word-play on the false *hearts / harts* advances the modern notion that counsellors should represent the interests of the whole community, not just a palace minority.

In the course of the next Passus the poet introduces the figure of the true counsellor, personified as Wit. Here the poet seems to invoke the proverb that *whoso seyth the truth he shall be shent*, for he sees Witt / Wisdom ousted from Richard's court:

> But als sone as they wiste that Witt was his name,
> And that the kyng knewe him not, ne non of his knyghtis,

> He was halowid and yhuntid and yhotte trusse. ...
> 'Lete sle him!' quod the sleves that slode uppon the erthe ...
> And schorned him, for his slaveyn was of the olde schappe.
> Thus Malaperte was myghtffull and maister of hous
> And evere wandrid Wisdom without the gatis.
> (*Richard* 3.226–8, 234–8)
>
> *wiste*: knew; *halowid and yhuntid and yhotte trusse*: hollered at and sent packing; *'Lete sle him!' quod the sleves that slode*: 'Let him be killed' cried the sliding sleeves; *Malaperte*: Impudence; *without*: outside

The youthful courtiers are seen as no more than their own long empty sleeves, and they condemn Wit as much for his clothes as his counsel; like all good satire the poem is funny as well as incisive. The kingdom is, however, saved by Henry Bolingbroke (characterised as a royal eagle, or a loving father, or the emissary of Christ himself). Is the poet himself becoming a flatterer of the new regime? However, in the last Passus the poet moves even further towards demanding real political change, by describing the failure of Members of Parliament to use this forum for informed counsel; unfortunately this section is incomplete in the only surviving manuscript.

Mum and the Sothsegger is usually seen as a somewhat later sequel to *Richard Redeless*. The poet takes up his predecessor's contrast between Wisdom and the flattering courtier, now characterised as the Sothsegger (Truth-teller) and Mum. He describes himself in London searching for sothseggers among the establishment – members of the Universities, Church and State – but finding that such people do not want to hear the truth, and that very few will try to tell them what it is. They prefer to exercise their power without restraint, to promote the interests of their own group, not of the population at large. Consequently he finally spots the Sothsegger hiding in a workshop and licking his wounds:

> I sawe a sothesigger, in sothe as me thought,
> Sitte in a shoppe and salwyn his woundes (*Mum* 846–7)
>
> *shoppe*: workshop; *salwyn*: anoint

The poet then falls asleep and dreams of a Bee-keeper, who explains the workings of the kingdom in an allegory similar to the allegory of the deer in *Richard Redeless*, but using natural details from the encyclopaedist Bartholomeus Anglicus. A contrast is drawn between the true worker bees and the unproductive and greedy drones, which the beekeeper must kill before they destroy the little kingdom of the hive. The poet turns back to his consideration of England and claims that:

> al the mischief and myssereule that in the royaulme groweth
> Mum hath be maker alle thees many yeres (*Mum* 1115–16)

Once again the poet is seeking for genuinely political reform, for he argues that the House of Commons has been emasculated by Mum – by the dread of speaking out, and in consequence the king never learns the grievances of the people, and so is in danger of another catastrophic coup like that of 1399:

> Thay wollen not parle of thoo poyntz for peril that might falle,
> But hiden alle the hevynes and halten echone
> And maken Mum thaire messaigier thaire mote to determine
> (*Mum* 1136–8)
>
> *parle of thoo poyntz*: speak of those sufferings; *halten*: stop speaking; *thaire mote to determine*: to conclude their discussion

At this point the poet begins to ascribe *all wronge on this world* (1150) to the power of Mum; we feel his focus shifting to a more social and moral analysis, and the Lollard implications of his earlier attacks on the Church become increasingly overt (see Barr 2001, pp. 165ff. and Yeager 2010 for recent considerations of this). But the poem remains a fascinating insight into how the middle-class city-dweller might have viewed the problems of government. If counsel was better, more reflective of the truth and of public opinion, and if the ruling class was forced to take account of it, then self-interest and ignorance might not so dominate the government of England. But what is to make the governors take this good advice?

Questions

- Why do these poems make the problem of counsel so crucial to their discussion of government? (See Ferguson 1955.) How do the battles between the Lords of Parliament and Richard II's courtiers relate to the poet's concerns?

- To what extent does the poet cast himself as Sothsegger, and what implications does this have for his position as narrator in the text?

In a time when social change was often precipitated by violent events, the old language of sin and judgement used by the Church was often inadequate to explain what was happening. Literature could suggest other ways of seeing things, or at least use the old language in new ways, and it could above all describe the changes themselves in vivid and enduring poetry. I will now look at what literature reveals about the ways that these social and economic developments were affecting people in their own homes, and in their marriages, for here too, literature was forging a new language, and even a new morality.

Texts, Sources and Further Reading

(For Chaucer and Gower Texts, see Chapter 4. For *Piers Plowman* texts, see Chapter 1.)

Anthologies
Dean, J. M. (ed.) (1996) *Medieval English Political Writings* (Medieval Institute Publications, Western Michigan University, for TEAMS).
See, under names of individual poems, TEAMS Middle English Texts Online.
Ginsburg, W. (ed.) (1992) *Parliament of Three Ages* (TEAMS) (http://d.lib.rochester.edu/teams/text/ginsberg-parlement-of-the-three-ages).
Kail, J. (ed.) (1904; repr. 1973) *Twenty-six Political and other Poems* (Early English Text Society, EETS o.s. 124).
Robbins, R. H. (ed.) (1959) *Historical Poems of the XIVth and XVth Centuries* (Columbia University Press).
Wright, T. (1839) *The Political Songs of England, from the Reign of John to that of Edward II* (ed. and transl. Coss, P.) (Cambridge University Press).

Hoccleve
Furnivall, F. J. (ed.) (1897; repr. 1978) *Hoccleve's Works: The Regement of Princes and Fourteen Minor Poems* (Early English Text Society, EETS e.s. 72).
Jacobus de Cessolis, *The Game and Play of Chess*, translated by Caxton (http://www.gutenberg.org/files/10672/10672-h/10672-h.htm).

Richard Redeless **and** *Mum and the Sothsegger*
Barr, H. (ed.) (1993) *The Piers Plowman Tradition* (Everyman).
Day, M. and Steele, R. (eds) (1934; repr. 1971) *Mum and the Sothsegger* (Early English Text Society, EETS o.s. 199).
Dean, J. (ed.) (2000) *Richard Redeless, Mum and the Sothsegger* (http://d.lib.rochester.edu/teams/text/dean-richard-the-redeless-and-mum-and-the-sothsegger-richard-the-redeless), (http://d.lib.rochester.edu/teams/text/dean-richard-the-redeless-and-mum-and-the-sothsegger-mum-and-the-sothsegger).These are the texts used for quotation.

The Simonie
Dean, J. M. (1996) *The Simonie* (TEAMS Middle English Texts, http://d.lib.rochester.edu/teams/text/dean-medieval-english-political-writings-simonie).
Embree, D. and Urquhart, E. (1991) *The Simonie: A Parallel Text Edition* (C. Winter).

Wynnere and Wastoure **and** *Parliament of Three Ages*
Burrow, J. (ed.) (1977) *English Verse 1300–1500* (Longman). Translations are from this text.
Trigg, S. (ed.) 1990) *Wynnere and Wastoure* (Early English Text Society, EETS, o.s. 297; Oxford University Press, http://d.lib.rochester.edu/teams/text/ginsberg-wynnere-and-wastoure).

History of the urban community
Dyer, C. (1989) *Standards of Living in the Later Middle Ages: Social Change in England 1200–1520* (Cambridge University Press).
Hanawalt, B. (2007) *The Wealth of Wives* (Oxford University Press).
Keene, D. (1990) 'Suburban growth', in Holt, R. and Rosser, G. (eds), *The English Medieval Town 1200–1540* (Longman).

Lindahl, C. (1987) *Earnest Games: Folkloric Patterns in the Canterbury Tales* (Indiana University Press).
Miller, E. and Hatcher, J. (1995) *Medieval England: Towns, Commerce and Crafts* (Longman).
Orme, N. (1973) *English Schools in the Middle Ages* (Methuen).

Estates Satire: Chaucer and Langland (includes Lady Meed)
Baldwin, A. (1981) *The Theme of Government in* Piers Plowman (Boydell and Brewer).
Baldwin, A. (2007) *A Guidebook to Piers Plowman* (Palgrave Macmillan).
Bennett, J. A .W. (1969) 'Chaucer's contemporary', in Hussey, S. (ed.), *Piers Plowman: Critical Approaches* (Methuen).
Bowden, M. (1967) *A Commentary on the General Prologue to the Canterbury Tales* (Macmillan).
Burrow, J. A. (2005) 'Lady Meed and the Power of Money', *Medium Aevum*, 74, pp. 113–18.
Donaldson, E. T. (1949) *Piers Plowman: The C-text and its Poet* (Yale University Press).
Donaldson, E. T. (1970) 'Chaucer the pilgrim', in *Speaking of Chaucer* (Athlone); this article is reprinted in the Norton edition of the *Canterbury Tales*.
George, J-A. (ed.) (2000) *Geoffrey Chaucer: The General Prologue to the Canterbury Tales: A Reader's Guide to Essential Criticism* (Icon Books).
Gray, D. (2004) 'Geoffrey Chaucer', in *The Oxford Dictionary of National Biography* (Oxford University Press).
Lindahl, C. (1987) *Earnest Games: Folkloric Patterns in the Canterbury Tales* (Indiana University Press).
Mann, J. (1973) *Chaucer and Medieval Estates Satire* (Cambridge University Press).
Morgan, G. (2010) 'The Status and Meaning of Meed in the First Vision of *Piers Plowman*', in Morgan, G. (ed.), *The Shaping of English Poetry*(Peter Lang).
Owst, G. R. (1966) *Literature and Pulpit in Medieval England* (Oxford University Press).
Pearsall, D. (1994) *Life of Geoffrey Chaucer: A Critical Biography* (Blackwell Critical Biographies, Blackwell).

Strohm, P. (1989) *Social Chaucer* (Harvard University Press).
Turner, M. (2006) *Chaucerian Conflict: Languages of Antagonism in Late Fourteenth-century London* (Oxford University Press).

Venality Satire, *Wynnere and Wastoure* and *The Simonie*
Aers, D. (1988) *Community and Individual Identity: Writing, 1360–1430* (Routledge).
Barr, H. (2001) 'Constructing social realities: *Wynnere and Wastoure*, Hoccleve, and Chaucer', in *Socioliterary Practice in Late Medieval England* (Oxford University Press).
Bestul, T. (1974) *Satire and Allegory in Wynnere and Wastoure* (University of Nebraska Press).
Conlee, J. W. (1991) *Middle English Debate Poetry: A Critical Anthology* (Colleagues Press).
Finlayson, J. (1989) '*The Simonie*: two authors?', *Archiv für das Studium der neueren Sprachen und Literaturen*, 226, pp. 39–51.
Jacobs, N. (1985) 'Typology of debate and the interpretation of *Wynnere and Wastoure*', *Review of English Studies*, 36, pp. 481–500.
Kane, G. (1986) 'Some fourteenth-century political poems', in Kratzmann, G. and *Simpson*, J. (eds), *Medieval* English *Religious and Ethical Literature* (Boydell and Brewer).
Kennedy, K. E. (2006) 'Retaining men (and a retaining woman) in *Piers Plowman*', *Yearbook of Langland Studies*, 20, pp. 191–214.
Owst, G. R. (1966) *Literature and Pulpit in Medieval England* (Oxford University Press).
Roney, L. (1994) '*Wynnere and Wastoure*'s 'wyse wordes': teaching economics and nationalism in fourteenth-century England', *Speculum*, 69, pp. 1070–1100.
Scattergood, J. (2000) *The Lost Tradition: Essays on Middle English Alliterative Poetry* (Four Courts Press).
Spiers, J. (1957) *Medieval English Poetry: The Non-Chaucerian Tradition* (Faber and Faber).
Tavormina, M. T. (1995) *Kindly Similitude: Marriage and Family in Piers Plowman* (D. S. Brewer).
Turville-Petre, T. (1977) *The Alliterative Revival* (D. S. Brewer).
Yunck, J. A. (1963) *The Lineage of Lady Meed* (Notre Dame University Press).

Complaint, Prophecy and Political Advice

Anstell, A. W. (1999) *Political Allegory in Late Medieval England* (Cornell University Press).

Baldwin, A. (2001) 'Patient politics in *Piers Plowman*', *Yearbook of Langland Studies*, 15, pp. 99–108.

Barr, H. (2001) *Socioliterary Practice in Late Medieval England* (Oxford University Press).

Boffey, J. and Edwards, A. (2013) *A Companion to Fifteenth-Century Poetry* (D. S. Brewer).

Facinelli, D. A. (1989) 'Treasonous criticisms of Henry IV: the loyal poet of *Richard the Redeless* and *Mum and the Sothsegger*', *Journal of the Rocky Mountain Medieval and Renaissance Association*, 10, pp. 51–62.

Ferguson, A. B. (1955) 'The problem of counsel in *Mum and the Sothsegger*', *Studies in the Renaissance*, 2, pp. 67–83.

Firth Green, R. (1980) *Poets and Princepleasers: Literature and the English Court in the Late Middle Ages* (University of Toronto Press).

Grassnick, U. (2006) '"O prince, desyre to be honourable": the deposition of Richard II and *Mirrors for Princes*', in Hamilton, J. S. (ed.), *Fourteenth-Century England*, Vol. IV (Boydell Press).

Hanrahan, M. (2002) 'Speaking of sodomy: Gower's advice to princes in the *Confessio Amantis*', *Exemplaria*, 14, pp. 423–46.

Horobin, S. (2004) 'The dialect and authorship of *Richard Redeless* and *Mum and the Sothsegger*', *Yearbook of Langland Studies*, 18, pp. 133–52.

Kennedy, K. (2006) 'Hoccleve's dangerous game of draughts', *Notes and Queries*, 53, pp. 410–14.

Knapp, E. (2001) *The Bureaucratic Muse: Thomas Hoccleve and the Literature of Late Medieval England* (Pennsylvania State University Press).

Krug, I. (2012) 'Complaint literature: the voice of the people or literary formula?', *Medieval Perspectives*, 27, pp. 125–35.

Matthews, D. (2010) *Writing to the King: Nation, Kingship and Literature in England 1260–1350* (Cambridge University Press).

Miller, B. (1998) '*Richard Redeless* and the concept of advice', *Reading Medieval Studies*, 24, pp. 53–77.

Peck, R. (2006) 'Introduction', in Gower, J., *Confessio Amantis* (Medieval Institute Publications).

Scattergood, J. (1971) *Politics amd Poetry in the Fifteenth Century* (Barnes and Noble).

Scattergood, J. (2000) *The Lost Tradition: Essays on Middle English Alliterative Poetry* (Four Courts Press).

Simpson, J. (1990) 'The constraints of Satire in *Piers Plowman* and *Mum and the Sothsegger*', in Phillips, H. (ed.), *Langland, the Mystics, and the Medieval English Religious Tradition: Essays in Honour of S. S. Hussey* (D. S. Brewer).

Taylor, R. (1911; repr. 1965) *The Political Prophecy in England* (Columbia University Press).

Watts, J. (1999) *Henry VI and the Politics of Kingship*, 2nd edn (Cambridge University Press).

Wawn, A. (1983) '*Truth-telling and the Tradition of Mum and the Sothsegger*', *Yearbook of English Studies*, 13, pp. 270–87.

Yeager, S. (2010) 'Lollardy in *Mum and the Sothsegge:* a reconsideration', *Yearbook of Langland Studies*, 24, pp. 161–88.

Chapter 4

The Urban Middle Class: Tales of Women and Marriage

The urban readership we were looking at in the last chapter included townspeople from most of the different classes, at least to judge by fifteenth-century wills. Such readers were not just interested in social comment, however; they also enjoyed recreational reading, particularly of stories, a genre which will be the subject of three chapters in this Guide, and which included readers from every estate in countryside and town. The nobility had a long tradition of public story-telling, and there are several records of them enjoying convivial evenings hearing oral tales, and readings from written Romances (see the Introduction, p. 7); I will be looking at these 'high-life' stories in detail in the final chapter. Gatherings of clergy or of pious laymen and women were more interested in Religious Tales, and I will consider this important genre in Chapter 6. But here I want to consider a more 'modern' kind of story – the realistic and secular tales which are so much part of Chaucer's accomplishment. It is a convenience to use them here to illustrate the tastes of the emerging and largely urban middle class, but it is the case that Chaucer's and Gower's story collections became best-sellers in London in the fifteenth century. I will begin therefore by looking at the genre of Story Collections, which mix Romances, Religious Tales and Realistic Stories together as Boccaccio had done in his *Decameron*, discussing Gower's and Chaucer's contributions to it in more detail. For the rest of the chapter I will focus first on the statements about women and marriage made by some of Chaucer's most vividly realised pilgrims, setting up a theme with enormous potential for realistic, moral and comic treatment in their Tales. I will look at the Prologues and link passages where such statements are made, using the *Wife of Bath's Prologue*, and the opening of the *Merchant's Tale* and the *Franklyn's Tale*, as my Example Texts. Finally I will look at two contrasting tales which exploit another theme: 'town against gown', in the *Miller's Tale* and the *Reeve's Tale*, set in (or near) Oxford and Cambridge. These tales will fill out the commentary on urban life which was introduced in the previous chapter. (I will return briefly to the *Franklyn's Tale*, and discuss in detail Chaucer's moral *exemplum* about women and marriage, the *Clerk's Tale*, in Chapter 6.)

(a) Story Collections

English tales have their origins in different parts of the literary culture, and often derive from European collections of tales and comic fables or *fabliaux*. Others derive more from a native folk-tale tradition, such as the *Rhymes of Robin Hood*. And as there was a close link between the religious and the secular in the Middle Ages, English story collections were also modelled on their homiletic counterparts. Thus a rich source of secular stories was the collections of *exempla* or moral anecdotes, often written by Friars for use in sermons (see Chapter 2, p. 47). One popular collection was the French *Manuel des Péchés* (late thirteenth century), which has a large number of Tales arranged under the headings of the different sins. It was translated by Robert Mannyng of Brunne as *Handlynge Synne* (1303), which modified the original to place an even greater emphasis on the stories, and added several more, making a total of 67. This is clearly a model for Gower's *Confessio Amantis* – the confessions not of a sinner, but of a lover. A closely related collection of tales read by the aristocracy in French (though twice translated into English in the fifteenth century) was the *Book of the Knight of La Tour-Landry* (1371), a collection of stories about the deeds of good and evil women, taken from a variety of sources including his own experience – a text which interestingly illuminates the expectations placed on medieval women. I will now look in more detail at Chaucer's and Gower's collections of tales.

John Gower

Chaucer's contemporary and friend John Gower retired from a successful career (probably as a lawyer or perhaps as a merchant) in about 1378. He had inherited or bought good estates in Norfolk and Suffolk and used some of the income he received from them to be accommodated in a 'half-house' within the precinct of the Augustinian priory of St Mary Overy. The priory was in Southwark, just south of London Bridge and near to the Tabard Inn, at which Chaucer's pilgrims are supposed to assemble. Apparently a confirmed bachelor, Gower could now devote himself to his writing, chiefly using his books and the priory library, but also his observation of this rather rackety but bustling part of the metropolis of London. He had already written one of his three great works, the French-language *Miroir de l'omme* (1378?), and now set to work to complete the Latin *Vox Clamantis*, adding to it a new first Book alluding with horror to the Great Rising of 1381. By his own account he fled the rebels who passed through Southwark (breaking open the two prisons there), and hid for several days in the nearby fields (see *Vox Clamantis* 1.16). Both the *Miroir* and the *Vox* use political and social ideals, as well as religious ones, in their moral criticism of mankind. He wrote the *Confessio Amantis* in English during the late 1380s and 1390s, dedicating a revised edition to Henry Derby in 1393, and, on his accession six years later, offering him his other main English poem, *In Praise of Peace* (1399–1400) – he was rewarded by an annual grant of two barrels or pipes of wine). When he was nearly seventy he married Agnes Groundolf, perhaps to look after him as by then he was blind, or perhaps because, like the elderly Amans of the *Confessio Amantis*, he had fallen in love. He died in 1408, aged nearly eighty.

Source: Allen (1995).

(i) Gower's *Confessio Amantis*

In the last two decades of the fourteenth century, in which his great friend Chaucer was composing his *Canterbury Tales*, John Gower (supposedly at the king's request) put together a collection of stories, the *Confessio Amantis* or *The Confession of a Lover*. This is, apart from the later *In Praise of Peace*, his only work in English, and that for which he is best known; indeed, about forty manuscripts of it survive from the Middle Ages, putting it in the 'best-seller' category. It follows Robert Mannyng's model of a confession (see p. 46), with Venus' priest, Genius, questioning a Lover (Gower himself, under the *persona* of Amans) about whether he has committed the seven Deadly Sins in pursuit of his beloved. For each of the sins, Genius tells a series of illustrative stories. That Gower understood sin to be both personal and social, a loss of self-government leading to social disruption, is argued convincingly by Peck (1978), who sees Amans as needing serious education by Genius to understand his place in the wider community:

> Without knowledge of the dimensions of his [inner] kingdom no man can rule himself adequately. Nor can he contribute to the larger community without such knowledge. ... In his love-fantasy [Amans] has overturned Reason and set himself wilfully apart. (p. 29)

Gower dedicated the first version of the *Confessio* to his friend Chaucer and to the young Richard II, who, he claims, had encouraged him to write it (1390). However he became increasingly disillusioned with Richard and, having added a long section of political advice and illustrative stories to the text, he dedicated a new version to Henry Derby (the future Henry IV) in 1393 (see above, p. 102). The Frame Narrative is an interesting mixture of the personal and the didactic. As is usual in religious story collections, the tales are all narrated by a single voice, that of Genius, though he is characterised well and develops a convincing relationship with Amans. The stories themselves are of very different lengths, the longest and probably the most famous being the *Tale of Apollonius of Tyre*, used by Shakespeare in *Pericles*, which occupies much of Book 8, and which illustrates Lechery defined as 'unnatural love'. There are several analogues to the *Canterbury Tales*, such as the *Tale of Florent* in Book 1, which is well worth comparing with the *Wife of Bath's Tale* to illumine Chaucer's distinctive style and interests. At the end of the series Amans confesses that he is Gower himself, and that he is an old man. Venus appears and assures Gower his love is pretty futile. Cupid then removes his dart and so cures his love. Should we make a comparison here with Chaucer's Merchant, who in his *Prologue* and the first section of his *Tale*, warns older men against marrying young wives? Or should we see

Gower warning himself against the temptation to marry, and maybe also see as self-reflective the mismatched marriage in the concluding story of Apollonius? But there is a great deal more to this mighty work than the theme of the 'old lover', and Gower's emotional/political theme, and his combination of psychological and political insight, make this far more than a mere collection of tales.

(ii) Chaucer's *Canterbury Tales*

Chaucer wrote his *Canterbury Tales* some time in the 1390s and it is filled with his experience of courts and the countryside, but above all of city life. Strohm has argued in *Social Chaucer* (1989) that it was written for a city audience, consisting of the wealthier merchants and gentry, significant churchmen, and members of the royal court; this is not quite the same social mix as that represented by the pilgrims themselves, which includes a higher proportion of middle-class professionals, traders and minor clerics (or as that of England as a whole, with its high proportion of peasant workers). Chaucer had written a story collection of this kind for a court audience some ten years earlier, the *Legend of Good Women*, tales of virtuous women recounted by a contrite *persona* of the author in response to a demand by Alceste or the Queen. The *Canterbury Tales* are very different, much more eclectic and experimental, and as we saw in the discussion of the *General Prologue* (Chapter 3, pp. 68–73), they mix the estates and personalities of his pilgrims into a brilliant cross-section of city society.

One of the most attractive features of the *Canterbury Tales* is its 'Frame Narrative', which connects the stories and suggests a 'reality' from which the stories themselves depart as fictions. Here Chaucer was bringing European narrative to England, by following the example of the *Decameron*, which had been written by Boccaccio in Italian in 1350–3. Boccaccio's stories are recounted by a group of young men and women waiting out the plague in a villa near Florence. The Frame Narrative of Chaucer's great story collection, written in the 1380s and 1390s, is too well known to need much recapitulation here: a group of pilgrims on their way to Canterbury are coerced by their first Host into taking part in a story competition in which each pilgrim will tell four tales. This ambitious programme is not carried out, though 21 of the 29 pilgrims do tell a tale, and three more tales are abandoned for one reason or another. Was the whole text left unfinished at Chaucer's death in 1400? If so, it would explain why the different sections in the Frame Narrative do not join up. Instead they remain as a series of 'Fragments' or 'Parts', which appear in a different order in different manuscripts but are generally used to provide a universal line-numbering system (see Pearsall's *Canterbury Tales*, 1985, and Cooper's *Structure of the Canterbury Tales*, 1983, for excellent discussions of this structure and of the *Tales* themselves). Within each Fragment there are links between the tales which reveal intriguing conflicts between the different pilgrims, and several of the tales are introduced by self-revelatory prologues. Indeed, Chaucer's use of this Frame Narrative is one of his most significant achievements. Comparing the *Canterbury Tales* with *The Decameron* or with the *Confessio Amantis* simply highlights, as Pearsall argues, Chaucer's naturalism, dramatic characterisation and wide social range, and demonstrates 'the inimitable explosive drama of the frame-narrative' (1985, p. 38).

The Frame also demonstrates Chaucer's great interest in the narrative forms he was pioneering, and in particular the role of the narrator. Narrative studies have brought this aspect of Chaucer's work into particular prominence. Some studies are very specific, focusing on just one individual tale teller in great depth (e.g. Klitgard 1995); others look at the *Canterbury Tales* as a whole, or look at the theoretical framework for Chaucer's narrative experiments (e.g. Harding 2003; Davenport 2004). Although Gower takes on the *persona* of Amans (see Burrow 2012), the stories are told in the authoritative voice of Genius, and so cannot avoid the didacticism of religious literature. Chaucer's use of multiple narrators gives him much greater freedom than Gower, not only to voice attitudes in which he as author does not participate, but also to colour the tales themselves in a way that the single voice of Genius cannot. This gives the storytelling a dramatic quality which must have been particularly effective when so much reading was done in social groups (see Introduction p. 7). The frontispiece of a fifteenth-century manuscript of *Troilus and Criseyde* (Corpus Christi 61) shows Chaucer reciting – without a book – to an attentive audience, and so demonstrates how he could have assumed the voice and *persona* of a dramatic narrator (see Pearsall 1977; Strohm 1989; Kolve 1984, pp. 13–14). The period was, after all, dominated by oral forms, such as drama and sermon; indeed, the thirteenth-century chronicler and classicist Nicholas Trivet, in his commentary on Seneca's plays, asserts that the poet reciting his own text is the first kind of dramatic performance (see Norton-Smith 1974, p. 167). In modern critical terms, this translates into Chaucer's use of a narrative *persona*, either the easily-impressed 'Chaucer the pilgrim' or his own humorously ironic voice, to mediate the story and characters to the reader (see Donaldson 1970). On the other hand, it is often equally possible to see the narration as the silent voice of January or another character, using what in modern novel analysis is known as *free indirect speech*. Chaucer's subtle and changing use of narrative will suggest other ways or combinations of ways for us to read the *Tales*.

These different ways of seeing the narrator lead to different ways of relating each *Tale* to its individual teller. If even a solitary reader had dramatic delivery in mind, he might well have thought of the narrator as the assumed voice of the pilgrim telling the tale, sometimes directly addressing the audience, commenting on the action or even making a personal 'confession' in a prologue, and always colouring the tale with his or her personality and social situation. Aers (1986) likes to read the tale through its teller in this way, and for example, finds that the Merchant reveals his innate prejudices against women as well as his own narrow-mindedness in the story he tells. However, Benson (1986) argues that the pronouns at the beginning of the *Shipman's Tale* suggest it was originally intended for the Wife of Bath, and that the churlish Miller seems an inappropriate spokesman for the complex story he produces. These two approaches to the teller/tale issue can even be combined in a single tale; for example, in the same article on the *Merchant's Tale*, Aers also argues that the 'critical perspective, subtlety, imagistic resonance and overall organisation, cannot meaningfully be attributed to the perverse shallowness of the misogynistic merchant who is the nominal pilgrim-teller' (1986, p. 71; see also Mehl 1986).

To open up some of the issues raised by the confessional and narrative voices of Chaucer's pilgrims, and the relationship of the tales to their tellers, I will now look at some parts of the Frame Narrative which focus on the issue of Women and Marriage. I will then look in more detail at two of Chaucer's *fabliaux*, a genre of realistic low-life comic tale that Chaucer had encountered on the continent.

(b) Statements about Women and Marriage in the Frame Narrative of the *Canterbury Tales*

In a famous essay first published in 1912 (reprinted in the Norton edition of the *Tales*), Kittridge grouped together the *Wife of Bath's Prologue and Tale* (Fragment 3), the *Clerk's Tale* and *Merchant's Tale* (Fragment 4), and the *Franklyn's Tale* (Fragment 5). (As is usual, I have given the Ellesmere MS order of the Fragments, which is not maintained in all the manuscripts, but which makes sense of the fact that both the Clerk and the Merchant allude to the Wife of Bath's 'Envoy' or conclusion; see p. 111, below.) Although it seems likely that the *Franklyn's Tale* (Fragment 5) comes after the *Clerk's Tale* and the *Merchant's Tale*, few now would go as far as Kittredge in saying not only that these four tales are meant to be read as a group, but also that the Franklyn offers a solution to the marriage debate 'which Geoffrey Chaucer the man accepted for his own part'. Indeed, most critics now deny the existence of such a group, seeing sexual and marital relations as simply a theme to which Chaucer constantly returns. Blamires, for example, places Chaucer's discussion of gender as part of his wider portrayal of the conflict between secular virtues, 'because Chaucer's creative energy goes into expressing how moral ideas conflict with numerous emotional or pragmatic or social or egocentric impulses that pull away from those ideals' (2006, p. 2). Simpson sees the significant theme in the tales being one of class, and argues for the moral triumph of ordinary people over the nobility (2006, p. 82). However, for the purposes of this Introduction a single area of conflict is a good place to start an exploration of Chaucer's methods. So I will now look more closely at the Prologue of the *Wife of Bath's Tale*, and the opening sections – where the pilgrim-narrators still seem to be speaking for themselves – of the *Merchant's Tale* and the *Franklyn's Tale*. Analysing this group of texts not only demonstrates Chaucer's sophisticated use of narrators, but also introduces a subject which was a preoccupation of the period: the role of women in marriage. (The *Clerk's Tale*, which is also about marriage, will be discussed in Chapter 6.)

Example Text: (i) The *Wife of Bath's Prologue*

Chaucer was by no means the first author to reveal a character through an improbably frank confession; and the *Wife of Bath's Prologue*, like the *Pardoner's Prologue*, is considerably influenced by one of the best known writers of such confessions, Jean de Meun in his thirteenth-century continuation of the *Romance of the Rose*. Chaucer's raunchy Wife, like Jean de Meun's Duenna, boasts about her own past sexual success, and it is worth reading a translation of the French text (provided in the Norton edition of the *Tales*) to see how Chaucer has intensified the realism and comic reversal in his version. Instead of having hundreds of lovers, his protagonist has five husbands, yet in these legitimate relationships she is even more domineering than the Duenna in her extra-marital ones, proving that *the wo that is in marriage* (Fr.3, 3) is experienced by the husbands and not by herself, for *myself have been the whippe* (Fr.3, 175). Realistic again, she shows that a key aspect of this dominance is her economic independence:

> They had me yeven hir lond and hir tresoor;
> Me neded nat do lenger diligence
> To wynne hir love, or doon hem reverence (Fr.3, 204–6)
>
> *diligence*: trouble; *reverence*: honour

This independence is due to her being a townswoman, able to hold property (buildings and weaving equipment) in her own right, unlike a countrywoman denied ownership of land under feudal law. Widows of craftsmen, as explained in Chapter 3 (p. 64), could even insist that a future husband join the relevant craft guild. Thus Chaucer has transformed a narrative device (the fictional confession) into a vehicle for presenting the 'real' situation of a realistic and representative citizen. She even uses her wits to plan her own future in the eventuality that her present husband might die (*Yet was I nevere withouten purveiance / Of marriage* (Fr.3, 570–1). See Brown and Butcher (1991, pp. 43ff.) for an interpretation of the Wife's excursion into the fields with Jankyn and her gossip Alis as a 'marriage ritual' (564–71), and see Rowland (1986) for an interpretation which slots her into history. As in the *Shipman's Tale* (which may have been originally intended for her), the Wife uses St Paul's image of a 'marital debt' (I Corinthians 7:3) to claim that her husband should be in debt to her; both sexually and financially he *shal be bothe my detour and my thral* (slave; Fr.3, 155). The Wife's appropriation of St Paul is only part of her general attack on the Church's teaching on marriage. God's controlling edict to Eve that her husband *shall rule over thee* (Genesis 3:16) was only the first in a series of Biblical restrictions, meaning that St Paul's model of marriage was taught as the ideal to which all should conform. It can be found largely in 1 Corinthians 7, and (with more emphasis on a loving relationship) in Ephesians 5. Ultimately derived from the Bible and from Classical biology was an immense body of Church teaching on women and marriage, designed not only to help the laity in their relationships, but also to put off the clergy from losing their virginity by a denigration of both women and sex. (For a useful anthology of anti-feminist texts, see the Norton edition of *The Canterbury Tales*, pp. 311–58).

The Prologue is in four parts, each beginning with the word *Now*. In the first part (Fr.3, 1–192) the Wife first takes issue with the Church's position on sex and marriage, targeting St Paul, St Jerome and Theophrastus. In the second part (Fr.3, 193–451) she describes the verbal attacks made on her by her first three husbands and her ripostes to these; in the third part (Fr.3, 452–563) she describes her adulterous revenge on her fourth husband; and in the fourth part (Fr.3, 564–856) she describes the verbal attacks made by her fifth husband and her response to these. Her technique of paraphrasing all these authoritative attacks before giving her own responses means that, paradoxically, 'she voices the longest and most vehement body of traditionally anti-feminist commonplace in the whole of the *Canterbury Tales*' (Mann 1991, p. 70). Does this make the text essentially an anti-feminist one? When she then describes her own behaviour as a wife, she seems to be conforming very closely to the anti-feminist stereotype in not staying at home, but visiting whom she likes when she likes (including lovers), by spending freely and often competitively with other wives, and by her disobedience and garrulousness. We hear more of her personal emotional experience when she describes her life with her last two husbands, although the denouement (the fight that made her deaf) again includes much quotation of anti-feminist material.

The Wife's strategies for attacking all this body of authority further suggest her dominance and her desire for personal autonomy, something we might view rather differently from how a male medieval audience would have seen it. In the first place, like the Duenna in the *Romance of the Rose*, she claims to prefer the wisdom born of 'experience', which of course allows her to prove what she likes:

> Experience, though noon auctoritee
> Were in this world, is right ynogh for me (Fr.3, 1–2)
>
> *Experience, though noon auctoritee*: personal experience, even without written authority

Indeed, as Josopovici points out in *The Word and the Book* (quoted in Saunders 2001, p. 42), her long citations and arguments are clinched by a bit of raw experience when she describes her final row with her fifth husband. Secondly, she rejects St Paul's and St Jerome's strictures on the grounds that they are addressed to those who would be perfect, and she herself is a woman living in the real world and so entitled to the freedoms of imperfection. St Jerome had suggested that marriage was very much a third best to virginity, as bread made from barley flour is much poorer eating than wheat-flour bread. But the Wife uses the Biblical example of the Feeding of the Five Thousand to assert the usefulness of barley-bread:

> And yet with barley-breed, mark telle kan,
> Oure lord jhesu refresshed many a man. (Fr.3, 141–6)
>
> *mark telle kan*: as St Mark can tell us (in fact it is John 6:9 who mentions barley loaves)

Indeed, in championing the imperfect, the socially inferior (and barley bread is definitely low class), and making a bid for experience as against precedent, the Wife seems to embrace Chaucer's own literary values. For the Tale he gives her, though not as funny as the Shipman's, does explore the idea that real worth may be found somewhere different from where medieval society expects it to be. For the old wife in the Tale demonstrates that the old, the poor and the ugly – and the female – may have a better right to *maistrie* (mastery) than the rich, young and handsome males who are represented by the knight who learns to obey her.

Questions on the *Wife of Bath's Prologue*

- Has Chaucer reversed the usual marital paradigm to demonstrate that in a modern marriage a woman should have some of the privileges traditionally monopolised by men? Or does the reversal simply provide opportunities for Chaucer to satirise both women and men?
- To what extent do you think that the *Wife of Bath's Tale* is an attack on *maistrie* rather than a recommendation to reposition it with the woman?
- How far are the Wife's methods of dealing with her husbands simply the result of having such a weak place in the relationship, not entitled by society to an equal share in either her husband's property, or his economic decisions?

Example Text: (ii) The *Merchant's Prologue* and opening of his *Tale*

The next tales which directly address the issue of dominance in marriage are the two tales in Fragment 4, told by the Clerk and the Merchant. Both refer directly to the *Wife of Bath's Prologue*: in the *Merchant's Tale* a character, Justinius, actually breaks the narrative fiction to mention *the wyf of bethe* (Fr.4, 1685), and at the end of his *Tale* the Clerk (in the ambiguously named 'Lenvoy de Chaucer') advises wives to follow her methods and make their husbands *wepe, and wrynge, and waille* (wring their hands; Fr.4, 1212). It is with these words that the Merchant begins his *Prologue*, assuming, as the Wife of Bath did, that it is the husband who is the greater sufferer:

> Wepyng and waylyng, care and oother sorwe
> I knowe ynogh ... and so doon other mo
> That wedded been. (Fr.4, 1213–16)
>
> *other mo*: many others

In this *Prologue*, which Chaucer may have added as an afterthought as it exists in fewer than half the manuscripts, we hear again the 'assumed voice' of the pilgrim-narrator speaking directly of his own experience:

> She is a shrewe at al.
> Ther is a long and large difference
> Bitwix grisildis grete pacience
> And of my wyf the passyng crueltee. (Fr.4, 1222–5)
>
> *at al:* in every circumstance; *passing*: surpassing

This establishes the Merchant as someone whose later praise of marriage and even of women should not be taken at face value. When in lines 1267–92 of the *Merchant's Tale* we are presented with a protracted 'aside' to the audience in praise of wives, we should probably read it as also in the 'assumed dramatic voice' of an embittered Merchant, and I can imagine Chaucer himself comically exaggerating the sarcasm in such lines as:

> And certeinly, as sooth as God is kyng,
> To take a wyf it is a glorious thyng (Fr.4, 1267–8)
>
> *sooth*: truly

The speaker's praise of wives for their obedience, their care of the husband's property, and above all their faithfulness (71–80) therefore seems to be ironic: indeed, this passage has been called 'Chaucer's most daring – or most rash – use of irony' (Donaldson 1970, p. 37; see also Mann 1991, pp. 61–4). The Merchant then paraphrases authorities on women and marriage in rather the same way as the Wife of Bath did in her *Prologue*, but whereas the Wife – ostensibly at least – argued against Theophrastus and Jerome, the Merchant seems to suggest agreement with them while actually telling us to defy them, in 'a sort of double-talk' (Mann 1991, p. 61):

> Deffie Theofraste, and herke me.
> A wyf is goddes yifte verraily …
> She seith nat ones nay, whan he seith ye
> 'Do this,' seith he; 'al redy, sire,' seith she. (Fr.4, 1310-11, 1345–6)

This opening section makes the *Merchant's Tale* a key one for considering the role of the narrative voice in the *Canterbury Tales*. For example, the viewpoint put forward so sarcastically by the Merchant in his *Prologue* is expressed apparently without irony by January at Fr.4, 231–56 and

421–43 of the *Tale*. Are we then to assume that this idealisation of women and marriage is part of January's *Heigh fantasye*, and that Chaucer is therefore suggesting that women can never in practice be the ideal wives described by the encyclopaedist Bartholomaeus Anglicus (see the Norton edition of *Tales*)? Persephone, when she appears at 1052, insists that there are many women who are *ful trewe, ful goode, and virtuous*. Both Laskaya (1995) and David (1976) point out that January's fantasy is opposed by an equally mistaken fantasy of the evil of women and of marriage suggested by the Merchant himself in his *Prologue*. So if what we have called the Merchant's 'assumed narrative voice' is responsible for this misogynistic *Tale*, then we do not need to accept that it promotes any valid view of marriage at all. Instead we could see the Merchant as using January to express his own self-contempt for having married unwisely, and criticising the wilful blindness of the egocentric and hypocritical January more than the faithlessness of his cold and scheming wife. However, Pearsall argues that we do feel sympathy both for May at the beginning of the *Tale* and for January, increasing towards the end (indeed Pearsall calls him 'the warmest and most idealistic figure in the Tale' (1977, p. 207). Does this sympathy nudge us towards a larger and more humane view of relationships in marriage?

Questions on the *Merchant's Prologue* and *Tale*

- Who or what is responsible for the 'woe that is in this marriage'? Is it the personal defects of husbands and wives, which at least suggests that they enjoy personal autonomy? Or is Chaucer blaming an economic necessity in contemporary society which legitimates old husbands demanding young flesh, and prevents young women from resisting the sexual demands of either husbands or lovers? Helpful discussions are to be found in Pearsall (1985), Mann (1991), and Laskaya (1995).
- What is the effect of Chaucer's presentation of two equally partial and one-sided views of marriage in the *Wife of Bath's Prologue* and *Merchant's Prologue*? Should we simply see them as comic extremes? Should we search for an authorial judgement on these views, through analysing Chaucer's use of realism and irony? How important is the role of different narrators here?

Example Text: (iii) The *Franklyn's Tale* Fr.5, 761–86

In contrast to the individuality of the Merchant's and the Wife of Bath's voices, the Franklyn's does not seem so obviously distinct from Chaucer's own voice. This may tempt us, like Kitteridge, to give authorial authority to the Franklyn's view of marriage, though as Olson suggests, this view can also be seen as an unrealistic ideal of delight without pain, exactly what we might expect from a pilgrim described as *epicurus owene sone* (Fr.1, 336). The Franklyn expresses these views in a long 'aside' (761–86) which contrasts dramatically with the views of both the Wife of Bath and the Merchant:

> For o thyng, sires, saufly dar I seye,
> That freendes everych oother moot obeye,
> If they wol longe holden compaignye.
> Love wol nat been constreyned by maistrye.
> Whan maistrie comth, the God of love anon
> Beteth his wynges, and farewel, he is gon!
> Love is a thyng as any spirit free.
> Wommen, of kynde, desiren liberte,
> And nat to been constreyned as a thral;
> And so doon men, if I sooth seyen shal.
> Looke who that is moost pacient in love,
> He is at his avantage al above. (Fr.5, 761–72)
> ...
> Lerneth to suffre, or elles, so moot I goon,
> Ye shul it lerne, wher so ye wole or noon (Fr.5, 777–78)

constreyned as a thral: forced like a slave; *Lerneth to suffre*: learn to endure; *so moot I goon*: on my life

The tone is practical and pragmatic, founded on experience rather than ideals, and it seems a direct answer to the Wife of Bath. While the Wife had conveyed her own desire for autonomy and indeed domination, the effect of her *Prologue* – and indeed her *Tale* – is to show the danger of either gender appropriating dominance or 'maistrie'. The Franklyn here suggests sharing authority in order to achieve the mutual choice more characteristic of *fin amour* or courtly love than of medieval marriage (see Chapter 7, below). However, Aers (1980) argues that this is still the language of authority, and that the husband in the *Franklyn's Tale* retains his dominance while supposedly giving it up to his wife. Hansen applies a similar line of thought to the *Tale*, showing that it frustrates the Franklyn's apparent claim that 'Men and women are alike in their desire for liberty' because 'only men can truly achieve and use freedom' (1992, p. 270). However, both these readings see the learning of 'souffraunce' as something negative and constraining, whereas, as we shall see, Chaucer elevates this virtue in other tales as a positive and necessary exercise of free will in the face of adversity (see Chapter 6, pp. 170–3, 180–4, below). The *Prologue* can be seen therefore to lead the reader away from a narrow consideration of *maistrie* in marriage towards a demonstration of patience in love, which can be relevant to all human and even human/divine relations.

Questions on the Franklyn's Introduction to his *Tale*

- Are you persuaded that there is such a thing as a 'Marriage Debate' in the *Canterbury Tales*, and that this is its conclusion, as Kittredge claimed in 1911?
- What does Chaucer really mean by *Lerneth to suffre* (Fr.5, 777)? *Sufferance* and *patience* mean endurance, but what does this imply in the context of the speech, or the Tale, or the 'Marriage Debate'? (See Mann 1991, pp. 163–4, for some leads.)

(c) Chaucer's *Fabliaux*

There is not room in this Guide to discuss all Chaucer's tales, though I will also look in some detail at a sentimental Romance and a moral *Exemplum* in Chapter 6. In this chapter, focused as it is on realism and 'low life' stories, I will consider the tales which reflect some of the characteristics of the urban society which has been the probable milieu of the genres discussed in the last two chapters. These tales belong to a genre also represented by the *Merchant's Tale*: the *fabliau* or comic tale in verse. Such tales appeared in Europe along with the *novella* (comic tales in prose; see Brewer 1985, p. 131), and there are several surviving Anglo-Norman examples in England, though only one in Middle English. This is the thirteenth-century *Dame Sirith*, in which a wily bawd convinces a merchant's wife that if she does not sleep with a clerk he will turn her into a weeping bitch (see Davenport 2004, p. 157; the stereotype of a wizard-clerk certainly survived long enough for Chaucer to use it in his *Miller's Tale*). *Fabliaux* characteristically laugh at the folly of ordinary 'low-life' people, through exaggerating them into stock types such as the bossy woman, the stupid labourer and the cunning clerk. The viewpoint of the narrator is generally worldly or cynical, in welcome contrast to the overriding moralising of so much medieval literature. The time and setting are usually contemporary and often quite realistic, in spite of the burlesque or bawdy nature of the plots.

Five of the *Canterbury Tales* are definitely *fabliaux* of this European type. At the beginning of the collection, after the opening Romance of the *Knight's Tale*, come the notorious *Miller's Tale* and *Reeve's Tale*, which form a pair (the *Miller's Tale* being also a riposte to the *Knight's Tale*; see Cooper 1983, p. 92–4). Another closely connected pair comes in Fragment 3, the *Friar's Tale* and *Summoner's Tale* (though the *Friar's Tale* should properly be classed as an *exemplum*), both satirising the other's way of life. Finally the *Merchant's Tale* and *Shipman's Tale*, in Fragments 4 and 7, are firmly focused on the relationship between husbands and wives (another *fabliau*, the 'litel jape' offered by the Cook, after the Reeve has finished, is abandoned after some 40 lines). Like their antecedents, these tales are in verse, and show how common people trap each other into ridiculous physical humiliations, generally centred on sex. The heroes and heroines of *fabliaux* are cunning and unscrupulous, but they often suffer a comic fall just when they think they have got the better of their stupider rivals. What Chaucer has done with this rather slight material is, however, quite remarkably innovative, anticipating many of the techniques associated with modern farce. His settings are realistic and believable, he is concerned to suggest appropriate costume and lighting, and details of scenery and props are consistently maintained and used for dramatic effect. The tales are also very literary: his imagery and language-choice reflect key themes and issues, and he alters the plots of his sources not only to make the stories more plausible and less extreme, but also to drive them to a comic climax which reverses the original situation. Above all, the characters themselves are brought to vivid life by the detail Chaucer gives us of their clothes, their possessions, their way of speaking and relating to others – and the plots are shown to arise from this characterisation and to punish them in ways that comically reveal and reverse all their private loves and hates. And, of course, there is the constant interplay between the narrative and the narrator, who may or may not be usefully identified with the pilgrim as he appears in the *General Prologue*. These qualities have been discussed by many critics (see above, p. 106, on narration; Pearsall 1985, on characterisation; Kolve 1984, on imagery). I do not have space to look at all these characteristics in the following Example Texts, and so will focus upon the situation and plot in two tales which return us to the urban setting of these last two chapters.

Example Texts: The *Miller's Tale* and *Reeve's Tale*

In both of these tales, literate clever students (technically clerks, but in no way holy) get the better of uneducated working men. Chaucer sets each tale in or near one of the two University towns, whose demands for carpentry or milling are served by two urban artisans, a carpenter and a miller, their antagonism demonstrating some of the urban conflicts of the time. The tales also pit age against youth, for the carpenter (John in the *Miller's Tale*) and the Miller (Smikin in the *Reeve's Tale*) begin by despising the pretensions of the young *learnd* scholars who intrude into their society. For example, the miller boasts that he has stolen some of the scholars' flour *for al the sleighte in hir philosophye* (Fr.1, 196), and the carpenter remarks patronisingly:

> Ye blessed be alwey a lewed man
> That nought but onley his bileve kan (Fr.1, 3455–6)
> *lewed*: ignorant; *onley his bileve kan*: only knows his creed

(In Chapter 2 we saw how praise of ignorant men who only knew their Creed was offered quite seriously in *Piers the Ploughman's Crede*.) It is ironic that in the *Miller's Tale* it is the Miller's reliance on his own ignorant learning which makes him vulnerable to Nicholas's tall stories. And Nicholas relies on John having the kind of illiterate pious knowledge of Noah we were discussing in the last chapter, learned not from the Bible but from Mystery Plays. John has taken literally such dramatic features as the quickness of the scene-change, which transforms the world *in lasse than an hour* (3519) into a lake. Because John believes that the 'real' Noah had *sorwe* before he could *gete his wyf to shipe* (3539–40 – a scene which appears in all the Mystery Plays), he agrees to provide Alison with a separate boat, thus facilitating her exit with Nicholas to her bedroom while the Miller sleeps in his boat, and enabling the comic reversal in both his own and Nicholas's fortunes.

The ignorant and self-satisfied older peasant is also outdone by the clever boys in the *Reeve's Tale*. Here John the scholar shrewdly moves the cradle to the bottom of his own bed, so confusing the Miller's wife, who gets into bed with him instead of her husband, allows him to *swyve* (Fr.1, 4178) her and so he avenges the Miller's theft of the scholars' corn. And in so doing, this second John, as Helen Cooper points out (1983, pp. 116–17), also avenges the insult on the carpenter John in the Miller's own Tale, to the satisfaction of the Reeve, who was himself a carpenter. Thus as well as depicting an underlying class-war, Chaucer is again energising his story collection by a series of conflicts between rich and poor, nobleman and poor peasant, between town and country, learned and ignorant, clerk and layman, and so forth. The frequent antagonism between men and women which has been an underlying theme of this chapter is therefore only part of a whole pattern of conflict in the *Canterbury Tales*.

Questions about Chaucer's *Fabliaux*

- Muscatine (1957) describes Chaucer's realistic methods as giving the Tales an 'overpowering substantiality', and yet such details also contribute to abstract themes and more general social satire. Discuss the interplay between the more particular and the more general in these two *fabliaux* (see Kolve 1984, pp. 152–256, for specific uses of imagery, and Mann 1973, on social satire).
- To what extent are particular pilgrims appropriate narrators of their Tales? Does Chaucer use the 'assumed narrator's voice' we discussed in the *Merchant's Tale*, or is the narrator 'absorbed in the narrative', as Pearsall puts it (1985, p. 73)?

- Chaucer's handling of structure, both within each tale and within the *Canterbury Tales* as a whole, is innovative and impressive. By comparing a tale with its analogue (printed, for example, in Kolve 1989), discuss Chaucer's plot changes and suggest their rationale (see Davenport 1998, or Cooper 1983, on Chaucer's structuring).
- Does Chaucer 'erase traditional gender boundaries and dissolve the power structures on which they rest', as Mann argues in her feminist reading in Chaucer (1991, p. 186)? Or should we see women in these tales as mere pawns in the revenge of men on men, as Laskaya suggests (1995)?

Texts, Sources and Further Reading

Texts: Chaucer
Fisher, J. (1989) *The Complete Poetry and Prose of Geoffrey Chaucer*, 2nd edn (Holt, Rinehart and Winston). Glossaries often taken from this text.
Kolve, V. A. (ed.) (1989) *Geoffrey Chaucer: The Canterbury Tales: Nine Tales and the General Prologue* (Norton Critical Editions, Norton).
Robinson, F. N. (ed.) (1993) *Chaucer: The Canterbury Tales* (Oxford Text Archive; http://www.hti.umich.edu/c/cme/). This is the text used for quotation.

Chaucer analogues
Anderson, L. D. and Benson, D. (1971) *The Literary Context of the Canterbury Tales: Texts and Translations* (Bobbs-Merrill).
See also Kolve (1989) above.

Gower
Gower, J. (2006) *Confessio Amantis*, ed. R. A. Peck, with Latin translations by S. Galloway (Medieval Institute Publications).

Story Collections
Aers, D. (1986) *Chaucer* (Harvester New Readings, Harvester).
Allen, R. S. (1995) 'John Gower and Southwark: the Paradox of the Social Self', in Boffey, J. and King, P. (eds), *London and Europe in*

the Later Middle Ages (Centre for Medieval and Renaissance Studies QMU, University of London).

Benson, L. D. (1986) 'The *Canterbury Tales*: personal drama or experiments in poetic variety', in Boitani, P. and Mann, J. (eds), *The Cambridge Chaucer Companion* (Cambridge University Press).

Burrow, J. (2012) 'The portrayal of Amans', in Minnis, A. (ed.), *English Poets in the Late Middle Ages: Chaucer, Langland and Others* (Ashgate).

Cooper, H. (1989) *The Canterbury Tales* (Oxford Guides to Chaucer, Oxford University Press), ch. 1.

Donaldson, T. (1970) 'Chaucer the pilgrim', in *Speaking of Chaucer* (Melbourne University Press); reprinted in the Norton edition of *The Canterbury Tales*.

Echard, Sian (2004) *A Companion to Gower* (D. S. Brewer).

Leff, A. (1998) 'Writing, gender and power in Gower's *Confessio Amantis*', *Exemplaria*, 20, pp. 28–47.

Mehl, D. (1986) 'Chaucer's narrator: *Troilus and Crisseyde* and the *Canterbury Tales*', in Boitani, P. and Mann, J. (eds), *The Cambridge Chaucer Companion* (Cambridge University Press).

Minnis, A. J. (ed.) (1983) *Gower's Confessio Amantis: Responses and Reassessments* (D. S. Brewer).

Norton-Smith, J. (1974) *Geoffrey Chaucer* (Routledge).

Pearsall, D. A. (1977) 'The Troilus Frontispiece and Chaucer's audience', *Yearbook of English Studies*, 7, pp. 68–77.

Peck, R. A. (1978) *Kingship and Common Profit in Gower's Confessio Amantis* (Southern Illinois University Press).

Saunders, C. (ed.) (2001) *Chaucer* (Blackwell Guides to Criticism, Blackwell).

Strohm, P. (1989) *Social Chaucer* (Harvard University Press).

Urban, M. (ed.) (2009) *John Gower: Manuscripts, Readers, Contexts* (Brepols).

Watt, S. (2009) 'John Gower', in Scanlon, L. (ed.), *The Cambridge Companion to Medieval English Literature 1100–1500* (Cambridge University Press).

Chaucer's Frame Narrative and discussion of marriage
(For general discussions of Chaucer's *Canterbury Tales*, see also the 'General Guides to Middle English literature' listed at the end of the Introduction.)

Blamires, A. (2006) *Chaucer, Ethics and Gender* (Oxford University Press).
Boitani, P. and Mann, J. (1996) *The Cambridge Chaucer Companion* (Cambridge University Press).
Burnley, J. A. (1970) *Chaucer's Language and the Philosophers' Tradition* (D. S. Brewer).
Carruthers, M. (1979) 'The Wife of Bath and the Painting of Lions', *PMLA*, 94, pp. 209–22.
Cooper, H. (1983) *The Structure of the Canterbury Tales* (Duckworth).
Cooper, H. (2002) 'The Frame', in Correale, R. M. and Hamel, M. (eds), *Sources and Analogues of the Canterbury Tales* (D. S. Brewer).
Davenport, W. A. (1998) *Chaucer and his English Contemporaries* (Macmillan).
Davenport, W. A. (2004) *Medieval Narrative: An Introduction* (Oxford University Press).
David, A. (1976) *The Strumpet Muse: Art and Morals in Chaucer's Poetry* (Indiana University Press).
Davis, C. R. (2002) 'A perfect marriage on the rocks: Geoffrey and Philippa Chaucer, and the *Franklin's Tale*', *Chaucer Review*, 37, pp. 129–44.
Dinshaw, C. (1989) *Chaucer's Sexual Poetics* (University of Wisconsin Press).
Erler, M. and Kowalski, M. (1988) *Women and Power in the Middle Ages* (University of Georgia Press).
Hansen, E. T. (1992) *Chaucer and the Fictions of Gender* (University of California Press).
Harding, W. (ed.) (2003) *Drama, Narrative and Poetry in the Canterbury Tales* (Presses Universitaires du Mirail).
Hume, C. (2008) 'The name of Soveraynetee: the private and public faces of marriage in *The Franklin's Tale*', *Studies in Philology*, 105, pp. 284–303.
Josopovici, G. (1971) *The Word and the Book: A Study of Modern Fiction* (Macmillan).
Klitgard, E. (1995) *Chaucer's Narrative Voice in the Knight's Tale* (Museum Tusculanum Press).
Kittredge, G. L. (1911–12) 'Chaucer's discussion of marriage', *Modern Philology*, 9, pp. 435–67; repr. in Kolve, V. A. (ed.) (2005), *Geoffrey Chaucer: The Canterbury Tales: Nine Tales and the General Prologue* (Norton Critical Editions, Norton).

Kolve, V. A. (1984) *Chaucer and the Imagery of Narrative* (Arnold).
Laskaya, A. (1995) *Chaucer's Approach to Gender in the Canterbury Tales* (D. S. Brewer).
Lewis, C. M. (2003) 'Framing fiction with death: Chaucer's *Canterbury Tales* and the Plague', in Benson, R. G. and Ridyard, S. G. (eds), *New Readings of Chaucer's Poetry* (Boydell and Brewer).
Mann, J. (1991) *Geoffrey Chaucer* (Feminist Readings, Harvester Wheatsheaf).
Olson, P. (1986) *The Canterbury Tales and the Good Society* (Princeton University Press).
Pakkala-Weckström, M. (2004) 'Discourse strategies in the marriage dialogue of Chaucer's *Canterbury Tales*', *Neuphilologische Mitteilungen*, 105, pp. 153–75.
Parsons, B. (2012) 'No laughing matter: Fraud, the *Fabliau*, and Chaucer's *Franklin's Tale*', *Neophilologus*, 96, pp. 121–36.
Pearsall, D. (1985) *The Canterbury Tales* (Unwin Critical Library, Allen and Unwin).
Rowland, B. (1986) 'Chaucer's working wyf', in Blanch, R. J. and Wasserman, J. N. (eds), *Chaucer in the Eighties* (Syracuse University Press).
Simpson, J. (2006) 'Chaucer as European writer', in Lehrer, S. (ed.), *The Yale Companion to Chaucer* (Yale University Press).
Smith, W. S. (2005) 'The Wife of Bath and Dorigen debate Jerome', in Smith, W. S. (ed.), *Satiric Advice on Women and Marriage: From Plautus to Chaucer* (University of Michigan Press).
Tinkle, T. (2010) 'Contested authority: Jerome and the Wife of Bath on 1 Timothy 2', *Chaucer Review*, 44, pp. 268–93.
Turner, M. (2007) *Chaucerian Conflict: Languages of Antagonism in Late Fourteenth-Century London* (Oxford University Press).

Miller's Tale and *Reeve's Tale*

Aers, D. (1986) *Chaucer* (Harvester New Readings, Harvester).
Beichner, P. E. (1952) 'Chaucer's Hende Nicholas', *Medieval Studies*, 14, pp. 151–3.
Blamires, A. (2007) 'Philosophical sleaze: The 'strok of thought' in the *Miller's Tale* and Chaucer's *Fabliaux*', *Modern Language Review*, 102, pp. 621–40.

Brewer, D. (1985) 'The international Medieval popular comic tale in England', in Heffernan, T. J. (ed.), *The Popular Literature of Medieval England* (University of Tennessee Press).
Brown, P. and Butcher, A. (1991) *The Age of Satire: Literature and History in the Canterbury Tales* (Blackwell).
Cooke, T. (1978) *The Old French and Chaucerian Fabliaux* (University of Missouri Press).
Hardwick, P. (ed.) (2010) *The Playful Middle Ages: Meanings of Play and Plays of Meaning* (Brepols).
Heffernan, C. F. (2004) 'Chaucer's *Miller's Tale* and *Reeve's Tale*, Boccaccio's *Decameron*, and the French *Fabliaux*', *Italica*, 81, pp. 311–24.
Knight, S. (2010) 'Toward the Fen: Church and churl in Chaucer's *Fabliaux*', in Phillips, H. (ed.), *Chaucer and Religion* (D. S. Brewer), pp. 41–51.
Mann, J. (1973) *Chaucer and Medieval Estates Satire* (Cambridge University Press).
Muscatine, C. (1957) *Chaucer and the French Tradition* (University of California Press).
Richardson, J. (1970) *Blameth Nat Me: A Study of Imagery in Chaucer's Fabliaux* (Mouton).
Rowland, B. (ed.) (1985) *Essays on Chaucerian Irony* (University of Toronto Press).

Chapter 5

The Community of the Church: Religious Lyrics and the English Mystics

The next two chapters are about religious literature. In this chapter I will look at some of the most expressive and sophisticated of all medieval writing in English: the texts in which religious men and women describe their inner lives and encourage others to try their own spiritual journeys. Here I am not talking about the homiletic texts, and the dramatisations of Bible stories written to educate the laity, which I discussed in Chapters 1 and 2. The largest community of writers and readers in fourteenth- and fifteenth-century England lived in religious houses: the monks, canons, friars and nuns, who spent some of every day in reading, prayer and meditation. Most of these could read Latin, and so had access to more than a thousand years of European religious teaching – or at least to those texts which were available in their community's library. Some developed into very sophisticated writers themselves, whose Latin ranged from the technical and academic, to the personal and imaginative. But not all those in religious communities were proficient in Latin, particularly if they were only on the verge of joining an Order, and it was for new and apprentice (novice) monks and nuns that the male English mystics I will be discussing wrote texts in English, perhaps to encourage their vocations.

However, the 'Church community' also includes the laity, and some of this literature, particularly Rolle's English poems and treatises, became immediately popular with the growing readership of devout people who lived in the world. This included the 'secular' clergy, from high status bishops to poor and relatively uneducated parish priests and even priests without parishes. And as we saw in Chapter 2, there was a growing readership of laity who wanted to be reminded of an eternal world, and be helped to glimpse that world for themselves. In the developing individualism of the fourteenth century, readers were becoming dissatisfied with simple homiletic texts that constantly focused upon sin and insisted on clerical intercession through the sacraments and the confessional. It was Rolle, above all, who responded to this need with his treatises and poems, which described a direct and emotional devotion to Jesus, Mary and God and encouraged the reader to follow this path. The prestige and popularity of Rolle's translation of the Psalms (the first book of the Bible to be readable in English) made it an acceptable text even in the fifteenth century, when Wycliffe's English Bible was forcibly suppressed and independent lay devotion was viewed with suspicion. It must have been this curtailing of religious freedom which inhibited any followers from copying out either of our two women mystics' accounts of their individual devotion.

I will begin this chapter by giving an account of the Affective Devotional method, and use this to illuminate some (largely anonymous) medieval English lyrics and Rolle's English writing. I will then look at another meditative technique, the Negative Way, and two of the English mystics who used this approach to God, Walter Hilton (d. 1396) and his probable contemporary, the anonymous author of *The Cloud of Unknowing*. Finally I will return to the devotional approach, to look at the two women mystics, in fact the only known Middle English women writers: Julian of Norwich (died c. 1416) and Margery Kempe (died c. 1438). Mystical texts are pioneering in other ways as well; they are among the very first to be written in English prose, and they cover a wide diversity of styles, ranging from the rhapsodic to the confessional. Indeed, *The Book of Margery Kempe* can claim to be the first English autobiography. Rolle also wrote some of the most personal of medieval religious lyrics, which will be included in the discussion of devotional poetry (p. 129). It is perhaps not surprising therefore, that musical and lyrical writing – particularly Julian's *Revelations* and some of the songs and carols – are still read today in modern versions by people who are moved by their content rather than interested in their literary history; only the drama, and perhaps some of Chaucer, has also crossed the centuries in this way. Students are always interested in the gender of Julian and Margery and in their biographical revelations, but you do not need to be either Christian or at all spiritual in your outlook to find all these religious writers fascinating. They show courage in finding their individual ways to God, and eloquence in articulating their emotions and expressing the inexpressible.

(a) Affective Devotion to God

By far the most popular mystical or contemplative method used in the fourteenth century in England was that of affective devotion, developed by European Cistercian monks and by Friars in the twelfth and thirteenth centuries. In England the most widely read devotional text was probably the thirteenth-century *Meditations on the Life of Christ*, attributed to the Franciscan St Bonaventura. A widely-read English translation was made by Nicholas Love in about 1400 as *The Mirror of the Blessed Life of Jesus Christ*. Texts in this tradition focus upon stimulating a love for and empathy with Jesus by such spiritual exercises as imagining – as an eye-witness – his Nativity or Passion. Devotion could be stimulated by repeating his holy name. English writers in Latin in this tradition included Ailred of Rievaulx (who praised human love and is seen by some today as an early defender of homosexual friendship), and St Edmund Rich of Canterbury, each of whom used this method to inspire novice monks (see Colledge 1962, for description and selections). A closely-related Cistercian tradition used the love language of the *Song of Songs* in the Old Testament to express the love between Christ and the human soul, in such physical metaphors as sweetness, music and embracing. An extremely widely-read text of this kind was the Sermons on the *Song of Songs* by St Bernard of Clairvaux, the founder of the Cistercian Order, which had much power and prestige in England in the fourteenth century. Latin texts such as these inspired many writers of English religious poetry, to which I shall now turn, and both the lyrics and prose treatises of Richard Rolle, whom I shall discuss after that.

(i) The devotional lyric

Most of the short religious poems found scattered through the varieties of Middle English writing, or jotted down in the blank spaces of Latin texts, can be described as didactic, teaching their readers doctrine or the details of Christ's life and death, or making unfamiliar images memorable. They take many forms, ranging from the song lyrics (often carols with a refrain) and *chansons d'aventure* (poems which begin as a story, like the *Corpus Christi Carol*), to longer stanzaic *chansons* and meditations with prayers. A considerable proportion of these *chansons* and meditations use the methods of affective devotion, as many Latin poems, like the *Stabat Mater*, had done. They place the readers within a scene from Jesus' or Mary's life, and invite them both to wonder at and to involve themselves in it. Good examples of this method can be found in the lyrics that Friar John Grimestone included in his collection (see Chapter 2, p. 48; and Brown 1924, pp. 69–92). For example, in a stanzaic meditational poem beginning *Man rent me on Rode* (Brown 1924, p. 67; Davies 1963, p. 116), Jesus reveals his pain to the reader in order to disrupt their tendency to sin:

> Under my gore
> Ben wundes selcouthe sore.
> Ler, man, my lore
> For my love sinne no more (17–20)
>
> *under my gore*: under my clothes (skirt); *selcouthe*: extremely; *Ler*: learn

A more evocative example of this kind of Passion devotion is *Jesu that hast me dere ibought*, which is a version of a Latin poem by John of Howden (Brown 1924, p. 114; Davies 1963, p. 120; discussed in Gray 1972, pp. 127–8). The poet asks – or demands – that Jesus write the events of the Passion, which he details, upon the reader's heart, using the nails and spear as a pen and his own blood as ink.

> Jesu, yit write in my hert
> How bloode out of thy woundes stert;
> And with that blode write thou so ofte
> Mine hard hert, til it be softe. (49–52)
>
> *stert*: sprang

This poem is very vivid; these lines, for example, enact the contrast between Jesus' vulnerability to pain (*blode*, *woundes*), and man's imperviousness to it (*hard hert*), so explaining why the poet is dependent on Jesus to convert him in spite of himself. Later the poet imagines the self-reversal he could achieve through this meditation:

> Whan I am lowe for thy love
> Than am I moste at mine above:
> Fastinge is feest, murninge is blis;
> For thy love, povert is richesse. (p. 123, lines 113–16)
>
> *at mine above*: exalted

It is therefore no surprise to discover that as many as ten manuscripts of this poem survive, one of which includes crosses to mark where the reader should stop and think. Passion lyrics of this kind, sometimes illustrated by a picture, were extensively used by laypeople for private devotion.

Poems about Mary had been popular in Latin and then English from earliest times, but in the fifteenth century they seem particularly abundant. Often addressing her as the beloved, the poets pile up her attributes and the images traditionally associated with her – star of the sea, the bush that burns and is not consumed, the dew on Gideon's fleece, the flowering rod of Aaron. For example, the later fifteenth-century Scottish poet William Dunbar (born 1459; see Chapter 7, p. 219), addresses her with:

> Haile! sterne superne. Haile! in eterne,
> In Godis sicht to shine. (Davies 1963, p. 247, lines 1–2)
>
> *sterne*: star; *superne*: on high

A slightly earlier carol affirms

> Ther is no rose of swych vertu
> As is the rose that bare Jesu. (Saupe, ed. 1997, No. 20)
>
> *swych vertu*: such power (see Ecclesiastes 24:28)

Many such carols – originally sacred dances – celebrate the paradoxes and mystery of her role in Jesus' birth:

> Moder and maiden
> Was never non but she:
> Well may swich a lady
> Godes moder be. (Davies 1963, p. 155, lines 17–20)
>
> *maiden*: virgin; *swich*: such

Some of this praise can seem rather abstract and formulaic; more personal and painful are the poems addressed to the mourning Virgin, either at the Cross or with her Christ dead on her lap; in one example of this she contrasts herself with the happy mothers who kiss and dandle their living child:

> O! wemen, loketh to me ageine
> That playe and kisse youre childer pappis.
> To see my sone I have grete peine,
> In his breste so grete a gappe is. (Davies 1963, p. 210, lines 25–8)
>
> *pappis*: breasts; *gappe*: wound

The homeliness of the rhyme here conveys the simplicity of the Virgin, and perhaps of the poet, who might herself have been a woman.

Such lyrics are, however, not always as personal as this, and it is in the writing of the mystics that we can find a more personal expression of religious feeling. Indeed, Rolle's own lyrics (ed. Allen 1931) stand out as being often in the first person, and revealing his own experience of the love of Jesus rather than directing the reader in how to feel:

> My sange es in syhtyng, my lyfe es in langynge,
> Til I the se, my keyng (Allen 1931, p. 70, lines 313–14)
>
> *syhtyng*: sighing; *langynge*: longing

This poem, which is quite extensive, is embedded in *Ego Dormio*, one of the three English epistles that Rolle addressed to Margaret on her enclosure as a nun, and which, as we shall now see, were an inspiration to the English mystics.

(ii) Richard Rolle's mystical prose

The new lay readers' hunger for religious self-expression and spiritual guidance on their own journeys towards God was partially met by English versions of Latin texts, such as the *Stimulus Amoris* and Bonaventura's *Meditations on the Life of Christ* (discussed above, p. 126). These texts generally used Franciscan devotional techniques to deepen the readers' emotional response to Jesus, Mary and God, and religious writers trained in these techniques were also writing their own treatises and poems in English, both for the growing lay readership and for other clerics. Foremost and earliest among these was Richard Rolle, whose popularity grew so rapidly that he became the most widely-read named English writer of the later Middle Ages throughout Europe. His works demonstrate the intermixing of the reading communities, for they include both Latin texts and English treatises, meditations and lyrics, as well as a translation of the Psalms. This was the first complete book of the Bible to be translated from Latin into English. Its immense popularity indicates a significant contrast between the earlier and later parts of the period; Wycliffe's English Bible was to be suppressed from the 1380s and independent lay devotion became tainted by association with the rebellious Lollards.

Richard Rolle

Richard Rolle was born around 1300 and died in the first terrible visitation of the Black Death in 1348–9. A large number of manuscripts of his works survive – over 450 in Latin and 50 in English – often in much-used copies found in lay households, all over Europe, as well as religious institutions. Most of his works are in Latin, but his English works include his pioneering translation of the Psalms, a *Meditation on the Passion* (I will use the longer version of this), and a series of religious lyrics. Most interesting for us is a group of prose texts probably all written for Margaret of Kirkby, a nun at Hampole who was preparing to become an anchoress and to whom he addressed *The Form of Living*, written a few months before his death; the other two tracts are *Ego Dormio*, and *The Commandment*. All these texts inspire the reader with confidence that she too can live a life focused on the Divine. His often rhapsodic and metaphor-rich style expresses his own happiness in such a life.

Richard Rolle took the techniques of Affective Devotion to a wider audience both inside and outside religious institutions. He taught the affective devotional exercises which would lead his readers to experience what he himself had experienced, the love for Jesus, which he felt quite literally as burning, as sweetness, and as melody. So in *The Form of Living* (Allen 1931) he suggests his reader should repeat the holy name of Jesus like a mantra to stimulate her love of him – but he also trusts her to find some other word if she prefers:

> And when thou spekes til hym, and says 'Jhesu' thurgh custom, it sal be in thi ere joy, in thi mouth hony, and in thi hert melody ... it removes anger, and dose away slawnes; it woundes in lufe, and fulfilles of charite. (*Form of Living*, Ch. 9; Allen 1931, p. 108, lines 4–6, 10–12)
> Or if thou have other thoghtes that thou has mare swetnes in and devocion than in thase that I lere the, thou may thynk tham.
> (*Form of Living*, Ch. 7; Allen 1931, p. 104, lines 41–3)
>
> *lere the*: teach you

Note the number of physical sensations Rolle offers here. And there is a wonderfully relaxed mingling of the conversational and the rhapsodic in Rolle's style which empowers the reader to believe he or she can achieve a state of grace:

> Now may thou ask me, and say: 'thou spekes sa mykel of lufe, tel me, what es lufe? ... And I answer: Love es a byrnand yernyng in God, with a wonderfull delyte and sykernes ... lufe makes us ane with God. (*Form of Living*, Ch. 10; Allen 1931, pp. 108–9, lines 1–2, 10–12, 17)
>
> *sa mykel*: so much; *sykernes*: security

In his *Mediations on the Passion* (Allen 1931) Rolle uses the love-language of the *Song of Songs*, a book on which he had written a commentary, to express the vision of Christ's wounds:

> Efte, swet Jhesu, thy body is like to a dufhouse. For a dufhouse is ful of holys, so is thy body ful of woundes. (Allen 1931, p. 35, lines 265–7)

> And yit, swet Jhesu, thy body is lyk to a medow ful of swete flours and holsome herbes; so is thy body fulle of woundes. (Allen 1931, p. 36, lines 298–300)

Do you find such language deliberately feminised, or do you feel Rolle is simply focusing on physical metaphors so as to involve his reader's whole personality in the search for God? See the discussion of the implied reader in McIlroy (2004), and of the metaphorical language of the *Song of Songs* in Riehle (1981).

(b) The Negative Way

The affective tradition continued to be very popular throughout the fourteenth century, and we will return to it when discussing the female mystics Julian of Norwich and Margery Kempe. Another tradition, often called the Negative Way, was usually directed to the enclosed professional religious, though Hilton's work at least was also popular with the increasing audience of devout laity. The mystic is encouraged to move beyond the affective affirmative understanding of God to reach towards a new level, which acknowledges the unknowability of God. The mystic develops exercises which cut him off from his previous knowledge, gained through the reading of Scripture or through intellectual thought. Instead he learns to empty his mind through the reciting of a mantra or through focusing on a single image, and reaches out to God with a single impulse of love which might begin to realise God as he is in Himself. This essentially Eastern kind of mysticism was associated in the West with the works of the fifth-century neo-Platonist known as the pseudo-Dionysius. The two English authors whose English writing we will briefly consider here are Walter Hilton (d. 1395) and his contemporary and admirer, the anonymous author of the *Cloud of Unknowing*, both of whom lived monastic lives. The *Cloud* author in particular translated Dionysius' *Mystical Theology* as *Deonise Hid Divinity*, and used the terminology developed by Dionysius' twelfth- and thirteenth-century monastic followers (Richard of St Victor and Thomas Gallius, discussed by Glasscoe 1993, pp. 73–5) to describe the mystic's experience of darkness and illumination. Unlike the mystics who worked in the tradition of Affective Devotion, the followers of the Negative Way tried to strip their love of God of all its emotional and imaginative power, and to use it as a *nakid entent unto God* (*Cloud*, Chapter 3) to search not for the humanity but the divinity of God.

(i) Walter Hilton, *The Scale of Perfection*

Hilton was an Augustinian Canon from Thurgarten in Nottinghamshire, and as such would have worked in the town community with his fellow canons as well as living a monastic life. The *Scale of Perfection* is his best-known work, but he also wrote a popular treatise on the *Mixed Life*, addressed to would-be contemplatives who live in the world. Book 1 of the *Scale* seems to be addressed to the same kind of reader, and to contain discussion of sin as well as mystical techniques such as devotion to the Holy Name. Book 2, however, seems to be addressed to those more dedicated to the spiritual life. Both parts are in the second person, and so are more handbooks of the method of contemplating than descriptions, such as those found in Rolle's writings, of the wonderful spiritual rewards experienced by the successful contemplative. Large numbers of manuscripts of Hilton's works survive, and suggest a readership beyond the cloister which includes merchants and noblemen; indeed the Scale was printed in 1494 at the request of Margaret Tudor, mother of Henry VII.

In Book 2 of the *Scale* Hilton follows St Augustine's interpretation of Genesis (in *De Trinitate*) in seeing human nature made in the image of the Divine Trinity but damaged by sin. Christ restored our potential to reform the soul, and the mystic can promote this through a reformation in Faith (mirroring the power of the Father), in Feeling, particularly Love (mirroring the Son), and in Understanding (mirroring the Holy Spirit); Julian of Norwich was to use a similar Augustinian pattern. Hilton distances this gradual abandoning of intellect and emotion from Rolle's affective method and imaginative feelings:

> Other manner feelings that are like to bodily, as hearing of delectable song or feeling of comfortable heat in the body. ... These are not ghostly feelings, for ghostly feelings are felt ... principally in

understanding and love and little in imagination. (Book 2, Ch. 30; Underhill 1923, pp. 363–4)

Hilton then introduces the idea of a Negative Way through an extended allegory of a journey to Jerusalem, the Heavenly City located in the centre of the psyche as the real Jerusalem was in the centre of the medieval map (see Glasscoe 1993). The pilgrim mystic should at once be dead to any desire suggested by the world or the body, and focus himself entirely upon his desire for Jesus, and entering a darkness that is lit only by his growing awareness:

> Now then, since thou art in the sure way, if thou wilt speed in thy going and make good journeys thee behoveth to hold these two things often in thy mind: meekness and love. ... Meekness saith I am nought, I have nought. Love saith, I covet nought but one, and that is Jhesu. (Book 2. Ch. 21; Underhill 1923, pp. 305–6)
>
> *behoveth*: is appropriate, necessary

In doing this, the mystic enters a kind of darkness in which he might – through grace – catch some glimpses of the true light of Jesus:

> if thou wilt be a ghostly pilgrim, thou shalt make thyself naked from all that thou hast, that are both good deeds and bad, and cast them all behind thee, that thou be so poor in thine own feeling that there be nothing of thine own working that thou wilt lean upon restingly, but aye desiring more grace of love and aye seeking the ghostly presence of Jhesu. (Book 2, Ch. 21; Underhill 1923, pp. 307–8)

This difficult search is in marked contrast to Rolle's encouragement of the mystic's own personality, but it made a strong impression on the *Cloud* author, to whom we will now turn.

(ii) The *Cloud* Author

The anonymous author of *The Cloud of Unknowing* is even closer to Dionysian tradition than *The Scale of Perfection*; since Dionysius' works are generally recorded as being in Carthusian libraries, it seems likely that he was a member of the Carthusian Order of enclosed and largely silent contemplative monks. He wrote seven or eight English works, including three translations of Latin texts in the Negative Way tradition (see above, p. 132). Like Hilton's *Scale*, the *Cloud of Unknowing* is a handbook for would-be mystics, and is addressed in the second person to a lay brother in the Order (that is to say, a brother who works for the monastery but has not taken vows).

Example Text: *The Cloud of Unknowing*: the explanation of the *Cloud*

The author begins by explaining that he wants to develop in his reader the ability to worship God as He really is, without using either his reason or his emotions, but instead waiting inside a 'cloud of unknowing':

> For at the first time when thou dost it, thou fyndest bot a derknes, and as it were a cloude of unknowyng, thou wost never what, savyng that thou felist in thi wille a nakid entent unto God. This derknes and this cloude is, howsoever thou dost, bitwix thee and thi God, and letteth thee that thou maist not see Him cleerly by light of understonding in thi reson, ne fele Him in swetnes of love in thin affeccion. (Ch. 3; ed. Gallacher, lines 289–92)
>
> *thou wost never what*: you don't know what it is; *nakid entent unto God*: a desire for God stripped of all images

Like Hilton, he sees this 'work' as an ascent from the intellectual reading and discussion, and from the devotional exercises which have helped his reader in the past and prepared him for this next stage of contemplation. Now these should be hidden with all worldly thoughts under 'a cloud of forgetting':

> And yif ever thou schalt come to this cloude, and wone and worche therin as I bid thee ... put a cloude of forgetyng bineth thee, bitwix thee and alle the cretures that ever ben maad. (Ch. 5; ed. Gallacher, lines 421–4)
>
> *wone and worche therin as I bid thee*: live in and work in as I tell thee

Thoughts, however sweet, of *the Passion, the kyndenes and the grete goodnes and the worthynes of God*, however helpful they have been in the past, will only result in a *scateryng* of his soul away from his purpose (Chapter 7), which is to get closer to God as He really is:

> Lift than up thin herte unto God with a meek steryng of love. And mene God love That maad thee, and bought thee, and That graciousli hath clepid thee to this werk; and resseive none other thought of God. For it suffiseth inough a naked entent directe unto God, withouten any other cause then Himself. (Ch. 7; ed. Gallacher, lines 494–8)

meek steryng of love: humble impulse of love

It is very difficult to remain focused like this, balanced between these two clouds, and silencing all thoughts and feelings apart from an impulse of love. The author suggests he use a mantra to help him, *a litil worde of o silable* such as 'God' or 'love' (Chapter 7). But eventually, and not through any forcing of his will, a patient and steadfast love, beating constantly on the cloud, may be rewarded by God:

> Than will He sumtyme paraventure seend oute a beme of goostly light, peersyng this cloude of unknowing that is bitwix thee and Hym, and schewe thee sum of His priveté, the whiche man may not, ne kan not, speke. Than schalt thou fele thine affeccion enflaumid with the fiire of His love, fer more then I kan telle thee, or may, or wile, at this tyme. (Chapter 26; ed. Galacher, lines 1140–2)

paraventure: perhaps; *priveté*: secrets

The author is at pains to keep this reticence, and like Hilton to dissociate himself from the sensations of burning or sweetness or the sounds *that comen in by the wyndowes of thi witte* (Chapter 48), promised to the contemplative by Richard Rolle and his followers. Yet, as Glasscoe argues (1993, pp. 176–80), he too has to rely on metaphor to convey his experience, and indeed it is the evocative quality of his language which makes him so compelling to read.

Questions on *The Cloud of Unknowing*

- This text is both a handbook and a description of the Negative Way. Do you find that these rather different textual functions lead to contradictions, for example in the employment of metaphor?
- Compare *The Cloud of Unknowing* with Rolle's *Form of Living*. To what extent is the later author in dialogue with the earlier, and how do you, as a reader, respond to their different approaches?

(c) The Women Mystics

(i) Julian of Norwich

With Julian of Norwich we return to the tradition of affective devotion popularised by Richard Rolle, and encounter the first authentic voice of a female author. And what a voice! Although she claims in the first version of her *Revelations* (written some time after 1373) to be *a simple creature that cowde no letter* (*Short Text*, Chapter 2), by the time she had completed the revised or *Long Text* in about 1394, she was clearly able to read the important Latin theologians and mystics, and to write complex, expressive and vivid prose. She can therefore be seen as the equal of the male mystics we have been surveying, though there are several aspects of her work which mark it as different and possibly characteristically female. For example, unlike the male authors of poems and prose treatises we have been analysing, she does not address the reader in the second person, directing his or her response, but uses the non-authoritative and more personal first person as if she is writing a journal. Moreover, her ideas, although developed from her reading, are strikingly original in their use of 'homely' metaphors, including her development of the old theological comparison of Christ to a mother. Her belief that God's love is at the centre of all that he does, and that judgement and condemnation are alien to His nature, could also be seen as characteristic of 'Mother Julian'. Is it possible to read this without thinking of Julian's gender? Do you think she gives a genuinely female view of God's relation to herself and her fellow Christians? If you read no other mystic, try her.

Julian of Norwich

Julian's visions took place on 8 May 1373 when she says she was 30, so she must have been born in 1342–3. She wrote a short version (now kown as the *Short Text*) of them and then may have become a nun in Carrow Benedictine convent just outside Norwich, learning to read and then using the library to develop her ideas, for she says she did not write the final version of her Visions (the *Long Text*) until twenty years had passed. But she may still have been living 'in the world' during these twenty years, fulfilling the roles of daughter, wife and mother, and developing her ideas through practical experience. She had two additional visions in 1388 and 1393. In about 1394, probably after she had finished writing her book, she was enclosed as an anchoress in St Julian's Church in Norwich, from which she took her name. Margery Kempe visited her there in 1413 and Julian probably died a year or so after this. Her close association with Norwich citizens, who came to consult her on both religious and personal matters, would have alerted her to the abuses and hypocrisy of the Church in Norwich. In 1380 the local Bishop, Despenser, led a cynical 'crusade' against the followers of the rival Pope in the Low Countries, and from 1407 he burned the Lollards who objected to such abuses, in the 'Lollard pit' around the corner from her anchorhold. Although her *Revelations* include several protestations of obedience to the Church, and avoid dangerous topics, their insistence on God's love for all, and her refusal to condemn sinners, seem at striking variance with the orthodoxy of the times, focused as it was on the suppression of heresy. It is perhaps for this reason that her writings, like those of Margery Kempe, seem not to have been known during the Middle Ages; indeed, she herself may have kept her *Long Text* hidden from the world. Only a single medieval manuscript of her work – that of the *Short Text* – survives from the mid-fifteenth century. Three seventeenth-century manuscripts of the *Long Text* were produced in Northern France by recusant nuns escaping from persecution in England.

Julian reveals her conviction of God's love in ways that become deeper and more layered as we read her *Long Text*. The first ten *Revelations* are directly inspired by the Passion, and so are in the tradition of Affective Devotion we have already discussed in the religious lyrics and in Rolle's Treatises. However, not only are these written in the first person as discussed above, but her use of surreal imagery suggests her own experience of a vision on a sickbed:

> The grete dropis of blode fel downe from under the garland like pellots semand as it had cum out of the veynis. The plentioushede is like to the dropys of water that fallen of the evys after a greate showre of reyne ... And for the roundhede, it were like to the scale of heryng ... This shewing was quick and lively, and hidouse and dredfull, swete and lovely. (Ch. 7; ed. Glasscoe 1976, p. 8)
>
> *pellots*: pellets, globes; *plentioushede*: plenitude, plenteousness; *roundhead*: roundness

Other parts of the *Revelations* do, however, focus more sharply on Jesus' pain as a manifestation of his love:

> Than seyd Iesus, our kinde lord: 'If thou art payde, I am payde. It is a ioy, a blis, an endles lekyng to me that ever suffrid I passion for the; and if I myht suffre more, I wold suffre more' (Ch. 22; ed. Glasscoe 1976, p. 24)
>
> *payde*: satisfied; *lekyng*: liking, enjoying

Such visions raise for Julian the problem of sin – both the Actual Sins of the crucifiers, and the Original Sin for which Jesus pays by his Crucifixion. Since Julian increasingly interprets her *Revelations* and parables to suggest that our human nature is good, she wrestles with the orthodox teaching of sin and judgement. In her third *Revelation*, an intellectual epiphany revealing that God exists in a point, she looks for sin but does not find it, experiencing instead the reassuring care and continuing responsibility of God for His creation:

> And after this I saw God in a poynte, that is to sey, in myn vnderstondyng, be which sight I saw that he is in al things ... and thought: 'What is synne?' ... And here I saw sothly that synne is no dede, for in al this was not synne shewid. ... And al this shewid he ful blissfully,

> meneng thus: 'Se I am God. Se I am in althing. Se I doe althyng. Se I left never myne hands of myn werks.' (Ch. 11; ed. Glasscoe 1976, pp. 13–14)
>
> *sothly*: truly; *althing*: everything

As Nuth argues (1991, p. 48–9), God encloses all human weaknesses and conflicts within His own goodness, thus neutralising them by His love. Julian continues to argue with herself about the existence of sin, and implicitly with the doctrines of the Church, in spite of her reliance on Jesus' words given her in her *Thirteenth Revelation* that:

> Synne is behovabil, but al shal be wel, and al shal be wel, and al manner of thyng shal be wele. (Ch. 27; ed. Glasscoe 1976, p. 28)
>
> *behovabil*: expedient, appropriate

It is not until she has worked out an interpretation of another epiphany, that of the wonderful 'example' of a lord and his servant (Ch. 51), that she feels she has resolved the problem of human sinfulness:

> The lord sittith solemnly in rest and in peace, the servant standyth by, aforn his lord reverently, redy to don his lords will. The lord lookyth upon his servant ful lovely and swetely, and mekely he sendyth hym to a certain place to don his will. The servant, not only he goeth, but suddenly he stirtith and rynnith in grete haste for love to don his lords will. And anon he fallith in a slade and takith grete sore ... but he ne may rysen ne helpyn hymself be no manner wey ... And I beheld ... if I cowth perceyve in hym any defaute, or if the lord shuld assigne in hym any blame, and sothly ther was non seen; for only his good will and his grete desire was cause of his fallyng ... (Ch. 51; ed. Glasscoe 1976, pp. 54, 55)
>
> *slade*: valley, a boggy place

Julian writes that it took her all of the twenty years which separate the two texts, to interpret this parable, though the process was probably helped by a new vision in 1388, and maybe also by reading the Tree of Charity episode in *Piers Plowman* (B.16). The servant, like Piers, is a gardener, and like Piers can be interpreted both as falling Adam, and as the Christ who falls to earth to redeem him:

> The lord is the Fadir, God. The servant is the Son, Christ Iesus. The Holy Gost is even love which is in them both. Whan Adam fell, God Son fell ... by Adam I understand all man. Adam fell fro lif to deth into the slade of this wretchid world and after that into hell. Gods Son fell with Adam into the slade of the mayden wombe ... And mytyly he fetchid him out of hell. (Ch. 5; ed. Glasscoe 1976, pp. 58, 59)
>
> *even*: equal, alike

If the servant's sin (in taking the fruit of the Tree of Knowledge) was really a mistake, showing his excess of love, then the lord's rescue (by taking the penalty of death on himself) is also a revelation of love; sin really has no place in this story. Indeed, from this point on, Julian insists that God does not blame sin, but only forgives and encloses it in Himself. Such an interpretation of human nature as essentially unfallen allows Julian to see God within us, indeed ruling the Universe from his seat in the human soul (*Our soule is made to be Gods wonyng place, and the wonyng place of the soule is God, which is onmade* (dwelling place; Ch. 54; ed. Glasscoe 1976, p. 65). Just as Jesus' enclosure in the womb led to His birth and growth and so to our redemption, and just as the tiny hazelnut (Ch. 5) encloses the seed which will become the tree, so God both encloses us and is enclosed by us. McInerney (1996, pp. 147–82) even sees Julian deliberately linking the notion of a womb enclosure with the anchorhold which would eventually become her tomb: 'Julian develops the concept of enclosure into an imagistic system which plays upon the related images of anchorhold and womb' (quoted in McAvoy 2004, p. 82). It may indeed be the womb images which lead Julian to develop, at the end of the 'lord and his servant' analogy, her famous metaphor of Jesus as the Mother, which I shall now discuss as an Example Text.

Example Text: Julian's Metaphor of Jesus the Mother

In these Chapters (58–61, *Long Text*) of her *Revelations*, Julian develops her conviction that God is our father, Jesus our mother, the Holy Spirit our 'lord' or husband, and that we are enclosed within all of them. Her inspiration for seeing the Trinity in terms of a family group comes from St Augustine's treatise *On the Trinity* (Bk 15), which also describes the parallels between the Trinity and the human psyche supposedly made in his image. Julian's version of this idea is, however, much more personal and affectionate:

> And thus in our makeyng God almigty is our kindely fader; and God al wisdam is our kindly moder, with the love and the goodnes of the Holy Gost; which is al one God, on lord. And in the knittyng and in the onyng he is our very trew spouse, and we his lovid wif and his fair maiden, with which wif he is never displesid; for he seith: 'I love the and thou lovist me, and our love shal never be departid on to.' (Ch. 58; ed. Glasscoe 1976, p. 70)
>
> *kindly*: natural; *knittyng and in the onyng*: joinng and uniting

Julian then develops the metaphor of Jesus as mother to express the forgiving and undemanding love she feels is characteristic of him:

> All the fair werkyng and all the swete kindly office of dere-worthy moderhede is impropried to the second person; for in him we have this godly will hole and save without ende, both in kinde and grace, of his owne proper goodnes. (Ch. 59; ed. Glasscoe 1976, p. 72)
>
> *dere-worthy*: worthy to be dear; *impropried*: approriated

She goes even further in implying that the mother is closer than the father in imitating the uncritical care of Jesus for us:

> The moders service is nerest, redyest and sekirest, for it is most of trueth. (Ch. 60; ed. Glasscoe 1976, p. 73)
>
> *redyest and sekirest*: most immediate and most sure; *trueth*: faithfulness, honesty

We may think of the Marian poem discussed above (see p. 129) in which Mary appeals to other mothers to understand fully her grief and pain. Beth Robertson sees Julian in such passages as 'a subtle strategist who sought to undo assumptions about women and to provide ... a new celebration of femininity through contemplation of Christ's "feminine" attributes' (1993, p. 161). However, Caroline Walker Bynham gives extensive evidence that male authors had also spoken of Jesus the mother who suckles us at his breast; she quotes passages from eleventh- and twelfth-century theologians, including Anselm, Bernard of Clairvaux, and Wiliam of Thierry:

> The Church turns to your bosom and... puts her mouth to your breasts instead of solid food. (Thierry, quoted Bynum 1982, p. 199)

Though it is likely that Julian will have been influenced by at least one of these authorities, her use of the analogy seems very different from theirs. As McAvoy puts it, Julian

> has become confident enough to extend simile to metaphor, which she then develops into her unique assertion that, rather than being like our mother, in fact Christ *is* our mother. In so doing, Julian surpasses the traditional (and primarily male) use of the motherhood similitude and transforms it into something which is entirely her own. (McAvoy 2004, p. 85)

Julian can indeed see other attributes of motherhood as relevant besides those which her predecessors garnered from the Bible (the hen gathering her brood in Matthew 23, the breasts filled with milk of Isaiah 66, and so on). For example, she sees the mother reacting to her child's progress, and Jesus also changing his treatment of us as we grow and develop:

> The kynde, love and moder that wote and knowith the need of hir child, she kepith it ful tenderly as the kind and condition of moderhede will. And as it wexith in age she chongith hir werking but not hir love. ... This werkyng, with al that be fair and good, our lord doith it in hem be whom it is done. (Ch. 60; ed. Glasscoe 1976, p. 74)

And she sees Jesus, even more than a human mother, rejoicing in the opportunity to help the child even if it is through her own pain.

> We wetyn that all our moders beryng is us to peyne and to deyeng; and what is that but our very moder Iesus, he, al love, beryth us to loye and to endles lyving; blissid mot he be! (Ch. 60; ed. Glasscoe 1976, p. 73)
>
> *wetyn*: know; *beryth us... endles lyving*: gives us birth into a world of love and eternal life

In such ways, Julian further confirms her belief in a reciprocal relationship between God and mankind, which informs her whole work. The passage on the motherhood of Jesus brings *The Revelations* to an affirmative conclusion:

> ... love was his mening. Who shewid it the? Love. What shewid he the? Love. Wherfore shewid it he? For love. (Ch. 86; ed. Glasscoe 1976, p. 102)

Questions about Julian's *Revelations*

- What evidence can you find in the text to suggest that it was written by a woman? Is the way she compares Jesus to earthly mothers more 'inward' than the similar comparison with Mary made in the poem discussed on p. 129, above?
- Do you agree with Robertson (2008) that Julian is supporting femininity by celebrating Christ's 'feminine' attributes, or do you find that Bynum's research detailed in 1982 indicates that this is in fact a masculine strategy?
- How subversive do you think the *Revelations* really are? Do they disrupt established thinking on sin, for example? Or avoid accepted social hierarchies ('Female power is identified with a positive creative force outside hierarchical structures', as Seikorska puts it in *Voices against silence*)?

(ii) Margery Kempe

Margery Kempe has attracted more modern readers than the other mystics I have been introducing. This is largely because, in the course of detailing her mystical (or at least devotional) experiences, she offers an astonishingly frank and revealing account of her life in early fifteenth-century Lynn, and her travels around England to Jerusalem and Rome. She writes in the third person, describing herself as 'this creature', probably because she saw her *Book* as a saint's life (albeit one 'dictated by the would-be saint' herself; see Windeatt 2004, p. 12). I will first consider it as such, and then as possibly the first English autobiography, and finally as a mystical treatise.

Margery Kempe

Margery is an outstanding example of the development of lay piety in the later Middle Ages, always involved in the world, and living an 'active' rather than a 'contemplative' or an enclosed life. She was born about 1373, a daughter of the then mayor of Lynn (now King's Lynn), and she never forgot her high status in this bustling bourgeois community, though her own business enterprises failed to thrive. She was married at the age of 20 and bore eleven children, but was constantly impelled by religious experience to give up this worldly life, and eventually persuaded her husband to allow her to be chaste and to leave his house in order to travel (at the cost of paying his debts). She then visited the important pilgrimage centres in England, including Norwich, where she was encouraged by Julian (*Book*, Ch. 18). She made the arduous journey to Jerusalem and Rome without any escort apart from other – often hostile – pilgrims. She displayed her devotion on all these jaunts, as she had in Lynn, talking incessantly about her 'visions' or meditations, weeping and crying out in reaction to the shrines, the historic places and the people she encountered (she discusses her weeping in Ch. 28). This apparently attention-seeking and even hypocritical behaviour tended to antagonise those who encountered it, and could provoke persecution and violence. Indeed, she was clearly an unstable, neurotic character, and she even admits she had a bout of near insanity after the birth of her first child. Yet her *Book* seems utterly sincere, and her determination and passionate enthusiasm for the life she was living and the validation she felt God was giving to her, make reading her testimony an energising as well as a startling experience. She died sometime after 1348.

Example Text: The *Book of Margery Kempe* seen from three viewpoints

Margery as saint (or heretic)?

If we see Margery through her own eyes as a saint – or a woman with saintly pretensions – then much of her oddity can be justified. Her evidence for her own sanctity includes her account of long dialogues with God and Jesus (for example, in Chs 17–21), her claim to prophesy and to work minor miracles (see Ch. 9), and her devout and chaste life, despite having borne eleven children. In Chapter 5 she describes how Jesus forgave her all her sins and called her to be his beloved:

> Dowtyr, why wepyst thow so sor? I am comyn to the, Jhesu Cryst. ... I, the same God, forgefe the thi synnes to the utterest poynt. And thow schalt nevyr com in helle ne in purgatorye. ... Therfor I bydde the and comawnd the, boldly clepe me Jhesus, thi love, for I am thi love. (Ch. 5; see also Ch. 22; ed. Staley, lines 368–75)
>
> *clepe me Jhesus*: call me Jesus

In Chapter 35 she goes further and imagines a mystic marriage with God the Father, who uses the English marriage vow:

> I take the, Margery, for my weddyd wyfe, for fayrar, for fowelar, for richar, for powerar, so that thu be buxom and bonyr to do what I byd the do. (Ch. 35; ed. Staley, lines 2031–2)
>
> *buxom and bonyr*: good and obedient (words from the marriage vow)

Such statements read as homely liberalisations of the *Revelations* of St Bridget of Sweden (d. 1373), which she claims in Chapter 17 to have read; Bridget also had many children before she saw herself as a bride of Christ and went on Pilgrimage. Indeed, Margery's knowledge of famous mystics' lives provide her with models of female sanctity to which to aspire.

However, far from being revered as a saint by her own contemporaries, she was brought before the church courts seven times on the charge of being a Lollard, including before Archbishop Arundel in Lambeth in 1413 (Ch. 16), and in Leicester, Hull and Hassle in 1417 (Chs 46–9, 53; see Arnold 2004). Pious women who moved around independently often attracted such accusations, particularly in the period just after Oldcastle's Revolt of 1414 (see above, p. 53), and her outspoken monologues were often seen as dangerous unlicensed 'preaching'. Margery's vocal insistence that she had a direct line of communication with God and Jesus through her 'visions' could indeed have led her to the heretical position that she did not need the guidance of Church ministers. But this she never said, and she was at pains to profess herself an obedient daughter of the Church, taking the sacrament more, rather than less, than her fellow-Christians, and honouring all the saints – points on which genuine Lollards refused to conform. Her orthodoxy was always eventually accepted by the Church authorities, and her excessive weeping and testifying seen as proofs of piety rather than heresy, though she was never recommended for the sainthood, which she craved.

The autobiography of an empowered woman?

Even if we are unconvinced of Margery's sanctity, we will surely admire the woman who emerges from the autobiographical revelation of the book. In contrast to so many women of the period, her life seems to be empowered on several different levels. Even when she was living in Lynn she seems to have made her own decisions about her activities with little consideration of her husband's opinion, and while on her travels was prepared to fulfil her ambitions alone. When rebuked by secular or ecclesiastical authorities she stood her ground, and in many cases persuaded important figures like Thomas Arundel the Archbishop of Canterbury to defend her and even promote her wishes. Her imagined conversations with Divine beings are themselves empowering, legitimating her desire to think and act as she chooses, and giving her an importance and prestige above not only the crowds of people who abuse or jeer at her, but even above acknowledged saints. Even the writing of the *Book*, which had to be dictated as she was illiterate, and then re-dictated because her first scribe could only write in unintelligible Dutch, demonstrates her determination to seize the power of the pen. Even today she is a significant figure in her world.

Margery as an English mystic?

If, finally, we attempt to read Margery as a genuine mystic, then we should see her *Book* centring not on her personality and activities, but on her 'visions' or meditations, her conversations with God, Jesus, the

Virgin Mary and some other saints. She testifies that she was commanded by Jesus to make these a daily exercise:

> I schal gevyn the leve to byddyn tyl sex of the cloke to sey what thow wyld. Than schalt thow ly stylle and speke to me be thowt, and I schal gefe to the hey medytacyon and very contemplacyon. (Ch. 5; ed. Staley, lines 390–2)

byddyn: pray; *very contemplacyon*: true contemplation

She gives as an example a meditation on the Nativity which is entirely in the tradition of Affective Devotion, and close to Bonaventura's recently-translated *Meditations on the Blessed Life of Jesus Christ* (see above, p. 126) in imagining the homely detail of the scene. Where Love's translation suggests that Mary lacked swaddling clothes for Jesus, as

> a pore womans son, that skarsly hade eft to wrappe him irme, & a craeche as for a credile to lay him (*Nicholas Love: Mirrour*, ed. Powell, p. 39)

Margery imagines herself remedying the situation:

> And than went the creatur forth wyth owyr Lady to Bedlem... and beggyd for owyr Lady fayr whyte clothys and kerchys for to swathyn in hir sone whan he wer born. (*Book of Margery Kempe*, Ch. 6; ed. Staley, lines 428–30)

swathyn: swaddle

When she visits Jerusalem and is brought to Calvary, her imagining of Christ's wounds actually uses Rolle's comparison with a dove-house (see ed. Allen, p. 35, quoted above, p. 131):

> And, whan thorw dispensacyon of the hy mercy of owyr sovereyn savyowr Crist Jhesu it was grawntd this creatur to beholdyn so verily hys precyows tendyr body, alto rent and toryn wyth scorgys, mor ful of wowndys than evyr was duffehows of holys, hangyng upon the cros... than sche fel down and cryed wyth lowde voys. (*Book*, Ch. 28; ed. Staley, lines 615–18)

thorw dispensacyon: dispensation, allowance; *duffehows of holys*: pigeon-holes in a dove-house

On her return to Lynn she found it increasingly difficult to retain her way of life in the face of increasing criticism and hostility, so that, as Windeatt showed in 2004, her meditations were forced to confront the reality of her various humiliations, and her God seemed to contradict his earlier promises.

Questions on Margery Kempe

- Which of the three ways of reading the text – as a saint's life, as an autobiography, or as a mystical treatise – do you find most helpful?
- Do you see Margery as a striking example of the development of female lay devotion, or as a marginalised and idiosyncratic individual (see Parker 2004, and Davis 2004)?
- Do you find the text interesting mainly for the light it throws on Margery's personality and historical context, or does it offer any spiritual insights or literary qualities (for example, in the vividness of the writing)?
- Can you distinguish any of Margery's meditations as characteristically feminine? For example, does she use the word 'homely' in the same way that Julian does to express her relationship with God, and if so, are the domestic associations of the word wholly feminine?

Margery wanted to be thought a saint, and I will now turn to genuine saints' lives, and to other exemplary stories generally told by writers in Holy Orders to inspire laymen and women to devotion. These are probably the most popular written genres of the period, and here, too, women play a significant part both as subjects and as readers.

Texts, Sources and Further Reading

Texts

Allen, H. E. (ed. and transl.) (1931) *The English Writings of Richard Rolle, Hermit of Hampole* (Oxford University Press). Includes *Meditations on the Passion, Ego Dormio* and *The Form of Living*. This is the text used for quotation.

Allen, R. S. (ed. and transl.) (1988) *Richard Rolle: The English Writings* (Classics of Western Spirituality, Paulist Press).

Brook, G. L. (1956) *The Harley Lyrics* (Manchester University Press).

Brown, C. (ed., rev. Smithers, G. 1924) *Religious Lyrics of the Fourteenth Century* (Clarendon). This is the text used for quotation.

Butler-Bowdon, W. and Allen, H. E. (eds) (1949; repr. 1961) *The Book of Margery Kempe* (Early English Text Society, EETS o.s. 212).

Crampton, G. R. (ed.) (1994) *The Shewings of Julian of Norwich* (TEAMS Middle English Text Series, http://d.lib.rochester.edu/teams/text/the-shewings-of-julian-of-norwich). This is the text used for quotation.

Davies, R. (ed.) (1963) *Medieval English Lyrics: A Critical Anthology* (Faber and Faber). This is the text used for quotation.

Duncan, G. T. (1995) *Medieval English Lyrics 1200–1400* (Penguin Books).

Gallacher, P. J. (ed.) (1997) *The Cloud of Unknowing* (TEAMS Middle English Text Series, http://d.lib.rochester.edu/teams/text/gallacher-cloud-of-unknowing). This is the text used for quotation.

Glasscoe, M. (ed.) (1976) *Julian of Norwich: A Revelation of Love* (University of Exeter Press). This is the text used for quotation.

Hodgson, P. (ed.) (1953; repr. 1978) *The Cloud of Unknowing with the Book of Privy Counselling* (Early English Text Society, EETS o.s. 218).

Powell, L. F. (ed.) (1908) *Nicholas Love: The Mirrour of the Blessyd Lyf of Jesu Crist* (Clarendon Press). This is the text used for quotation.

St Augustine, *On the Trinity* (Fathers of the Church, http://www.newadvent.org/fathers/1301.htm).

Sargent, M. (ed.) (2004) *Nicholas Love: The Mirror of the Blessed Life of our Lord Jesus Christ* (University of Exeter Press).

Saupe, K. (ed.) (1997) *English Marian Lyrics* (Robbins Library Digital Projects, http://d.lib.rochester.edu/teams/text/saupe-middle-english-marian-lyrics-nativity#six).

Staly, L. (ed.) (1995) *The Book of Margery Kempe* (TEAMS Middle English Text Series, http://d.lib.rochester.edu/teams/text/staley-book-of-margery-kempe-book). This is the text used for quotation.

Underhill, E. (1923) *Walter Hilton: The Scale of Pefection* (modernised spelling) (John M. Watkins). This is the text used for quotation.
Walsh, J. (transl.) (1961) *The Revelations of Divine Love* (Burns and Oates).
Windeatt, B. (transl). (1985) *The Book of Margery Kempe* (Penguin).
Windeatt, B. (ed. and transl.) (2007) *The English Mystics of the Middle Ages* (Cambridge English Prose Texts, Cambridge University Press).

Devotional Lyrics and Richard Rolle

Beckwith, S. (1996) *Christ's Body: Identity, Culture and Society in Late Medieval Writing* (Routledge).
Colledge, E. (ed.) (1962) *The Medieval Mystics of England, edited with an Introduction* (Murray).
Glasscoe, M. (1993) *English Medieval Mystics: Games of Faith* (Longman).
Glasscoe, M. (ed.) (1999) *The Medieval Mystical Tradition in England, Ireland and Wales* (D. S. Brewer).
Gray, D. (1972) *Themes and Images in the Medieval English Religious Lyric* (Routledge).
Greer, F. (1998) *Moral Love Songs and Laments* (Cambridge University Press).
Gustafson, K. (2002) 'Richard Rolle's English Psalter and the making of a Lollard text', *Viator*, 33, pp. 294–309.
MacDonald, A. A. et al. (eds) (1998) *The Broken Body: Passion and Devotion in Late Medieval Culture* (Egbert Forsten).
Manter, L. (2002) 'Rolle playing "And the word became flesh"', in Blumenfeld-Kosinski, R. et al. (eds), *The Vernacular Spirit: Essays on Medieval Religious Literature* (Palgrave Macmillan).
McIlroy, C. E. (2004) *The English Prose Treatises of Richard Rolle* (Boydell and Brewer).
Pantin, W. (1955) *The English Church in the Fourteenth Century* (Cambridge University Press).
Riehle, W. (transl. Standring, B.) (1981) *The Middle English Mystics* (Routledge and Kegan Paul).
Whitehead, C. (2005) 'Middle English Religious Lyrics', in Duncan, T. G. (ed.), *A Companion to the Middle English Lyric* (D. S. Brewer).

The Negative Way, Hilton and the *Cloud* author

Colledge, E. (ed.) (1962) *The Medieval Mystics of England, edited with an Introduction* (Murray).
Glasscoe, M. (1993) *English Medieval Mystics: Games of Faith* (Longman).
Glasscoe, M. (ed.) (1999) *The Medieval Mystical Tradition in England, Ireland and Wales* (D. S.Brewer).
Louth, A. (1994) 'Platonism in the Middle English mystics', in Baldwin, A. and Hutton, S. (eds) *Platonism and the English Imagination* (Cambridge University Press).
Riehle, W. (transl. Standring, B.) (1981) *The Middle English Mystics* (Routledge and Kegan Paul).
Ross, E. (1996) 'Ethical mysticism: Walter Hilton and the *Scale of Perfection*', *Studia Mystica*, n.s. 2, pp. 160–84.
Watson, N. (2002) 'Idols and images in Walter Hilton', in Dimmick, J. et al. (eds), *Images, Idolatry, and Iconoclasm in Late Medieval England* (Oxford University Press).

Julian of Norwich and Margery Kempe

Arnold, J. and Lewis, K. (eds) (2004) *A Companion to the Book of Margery Kempe* (D. S. Brewer).
Beckwith, S. (1996) *Christ's Body: Identity, Culture and Society in Late Medieval Writing* (Routledge).
Bynum, C. W. (1982) *Jesus as Mother: Studies in the Spirituality of the High Middle Ages* (University of California Press).
Davis, I. (2004) 'Men and Margery: negotiating medieval patriarchy', in Arnold, J. H. and Lewis, K. J. (eds), *A Companion to the Book of Margery Kempe* (D. S. Brewer).
Dinshaw, C. and Wallace, D. (eds.) (2003) *The Cambridge Companion to Medieval Women's Writing* (Cambridge University Press).
Dyas, D. et al. (eds) (2005) *Approaching Medieval English Anchoritic and Mystical Texts* (D. S. Brewer).
Jantzen, G. (2000) *Julian of Norwich: Mystic and Theologian* (SPCK).
McAvoy, L. Herbert (2004) *Authority and the Female Body in the Writing of Julian of Norwich and Margery Kempe* (Studies in Medieval Mysticism, D. S. Brewer).

McAvoy, L. Herbert (2005) 'Virgin, mother, whore: the sexual spirituality of Margery Kempe', in Chewning, S. (ed.), *Intersections of Sexuality and the Divine in Medieval Culture: The Word Made Flesh* (Ashgate).

McAvoy, L. Herbert (ed.) (2008) *A Companion to Julian of Norwich* (Boydell and Brewer).

McInerney, M. (1996) 'In the Mayden's womb', in Parsons, J. and Wheeler, B. (eds), *Medieval Mothering* (Garland Publishing).

Nuth, J. M. (1991) *Wisdom's Daughter* (Crossroad).

Olson, L. and Kerby-Fulton, K. (eds) (2005) *Voices in Dialogue: Reading Women in the Middle Ages* (University of Notre Dame Press).

Parker, K. (2004) 'Lynn and the making of a mystic', in Arnold, J. H. and Lewis, K. J. (eds), *A Companion to the Book of Margery Kempe* (D. S. Brewer).

Robertson, E. (1993) 'Medieval medical views of women and female spirituality', in Lomperis, L. and Stanbury, S. (eds), *Feminist Approaches to the Body in Medieval Literature* (University of Pennsylvania Press).

Robertson, E. (2008) 'Julian of Norwich's "Modernist" style and the creation of audience', in McAvoy, L. Herbert (ed.), *A Companion to Julian of Norwich* (Boydell and Brewer).

Sikorska, L. (1996) *Voices against Silence: Julian of Norwich and Margery Kempe: A Feminist Approach to Language* (Motivex).

Watt, D. (2004) 'Political prophecy in the book of Margery Kempe', in Arnold, J. H. and Lewis, K. J. (eds), *A Companion to the Book of Margery Kempe* (D. S. Brewer).

Windeatt, B. (2004) 'Introduction: reading and re-reading The Book of Margery Kempe', in Arnold, J. H. and Lewis, K. J. (eds), *A Companion to the Book of Margery Kempe* (D. S. Brewer).

Chapter 6

Religious and Moral Stories

Religious and moral stories were the most popular kinds of vernacular texts. Like those discussed in Chapter 2, they are generally didactic, responding to the almost universal medieval expectation that what one read should do one good. That would certainly have been the expectation of the poor and illiterate, though they must have much preferred to have the Bible served to them as drama rather than in sermons, and their moral inspiration delivered as exemplary saints' lives or pious romances rather than as unadorned homilies. These are easily the most popular kinds of narrative in the period, and could also have been discussed in Chapter 2 were it not that they were read by all levels of society, from the lowest to the highest. I will look first at the largest group of 'literary' texts in Middle English: Saints' Lives. Although almost all the saints' plays in England were destroyed in the sixteenth century, over 350 manuscripts of Saints' Lives in English and Anglo-French survive. To judge by evidence in the Lives themselves, and from the later owners of manuscripts, this readership included many enclosed monks and nuns, secular clergy and many of the educated laity who lived in the towns, manor houses and castles of medieval England. The same wide audience, and probably an even wider and less educated one, would have enjoyed the Popular Romances I will discuss in the next section. I will introduce the whole genre (distinguishing it from the more literary and courtly Romances discussed in Chapters 7 and 8), and then look in more detail at Homiletic Romances, which are another kind of moral story. Though the vast majority of saints and romance heroes whose lives were recounted in Middle English were male (see collections edited by Whaley, 2004, and by Mills, 1979), I will focus the discussion by looking at two treatments of a female saint (Bokeman's and Chaucer's Lives of St Cecelia), and two romance heroines (Émaré and Chaucer's

Custance), in my Example Texts. I will try to see if these very popular but clearly unrealistic tales can be used to gauge positive images of women. Moral Exempla (Examples), my third genre, can also be found everywhere in sermons and texts read to or by all classes of society, and were taken from the Bible or from a variety of European Latin and French sources. I will use *Patience*, which is a retelling of the Book of Jonah taken from the *Pearl* manuscript, as my Example Text of a Biblical *exemplum*, and another story of patience, this time a woman's, namely Chaucer's *Clerk's Tale*, as my Example Text of a non-Biblical *exemplum*. The fourth genre I will include here is the Religious Dream Vision, which is often less didactic, more experimental, and so less conventional, than the other three genres discussed here. My Example Text here, *Pearl*, from the same manuscript as *Patience*, is at an opposite extreme of literary sophistication from some of the other texts discussed in this chapter.

Does the popularity of this group of genres mean we can use them to measure the tastes and moral preoccupations of the readers? Because these stories often describe the battle between good and evil through stereotypical heroes or heroines and villains, do they give clues about the common aspirations and ideals of their readers? Such questions are of particular importance when the readers appear to be women, who leave fewer records of their choices and wishes than men do. One could even say that the large group of texts introduced in this chapter holds a place similar to the novel in our modern readership, in their variety and breadth of appeal to both genders and all classes. Some are interesting because they are fine pieces of literature, but others are interesting simply because they were popular.

(a) Saints' Lives

(i) The Legends

Lives or 'Legends' of the Virgin Mary and of the Saints of the New Testament and early Church, as well as the Lives of more contemporary or local saints, were produced in England in large numbers in Latin, French and Middle English throughout the Middle Ages;

there survive the histories of nearly 290 saints, many in several versions. The essential 'hagiography' (the biography of each saint) was generally derived from the *Golden Legend* of Jacobus de Voragine (written in Latin in Italy, c. 1260, and surviving in Europe in more than a thousand manuscripts), but there were many other sources, such as the Biblical Apocrypha, the *Acta Sanctorum* attributed to St Ambrose, the *Meditations on the Life of Christ* attributed to St Bonaventura (see above, p. 126), and the many versions of stories and miracles credited to established, local and more recent saints. This was a kind of literature which reached everyone in every class of society, and is a genre which comprehends many kinds and levels of writing:

> Hagiography itself is a deeply syncretic genre, over the centuries incorporating oriental and western folktale, classical myth and legend, adventure story, political propaganda, biography, travel literature, and romance. (Delaney 1992, p. xxii)

Middle English Saints' Lives can be found from the period before this Guide begins, with the *Katherine Group* of Three Virgin Martyr Legends, dating from the early thirteenth century, and they continue to be written until the end of the Middle Ages, with Caxton's very popular translation of the *Golden Legend* published in 1483. There are two large collections of Saints' Legends in Middle English: the *South English Legendary*, which is nearly as old as the *Golden Legend* itself (using it and other sources) and which survives in over sixty manuscripts, and the *Gilte Legende* (1438), a prose translation of the French version of the *Golden Legend* surviving in eight manuscripts, and possibly written by Friar Osbern Bokenham. Myrc's very popular *Festial* (late fourteenth-century) used saints' lives as starting points for homilies for their feast days. New Middle English versions of individual *Legends* were commissioned throughout the period by Churches, Guilds or heads of households, giving them a kind of 'mission statement', and these can also provide evidence for the existence of more informal 'reading communities', such as the Yorkist noblewomen who commissioned Friar Bokenham to write individual lives of Saints Elizabeth and Mary Magdalene (see pp. 7 and 158; and Sanok 2007, ch. 3).

(ii) Modern and medieval readers

Forty years ago the study of hagiography was a relatively specialist field. Then critics like Bynum, Warner and Delaney began to use this vast repository of material to research such developing topics as gender studies and attitudes to the body, and social historians to use their reception to analyse class and community. The very popularity of the genre raises some key questions. For example, can these Legends be used to provide evidence of the qualities which were valued and actually practised in that society? On the one hand, the Legends, like the Romances to be discussed in the next section, tend to be conventional in their depiction of the Life, Passion and Miracles of individual saints, so that 'paradigmatic actions dominate the narrative structure', presenting 'models of behaviour' to inspire the reader or listener (Heffernan 1988, p. 6). On the other hand, these models are often quite inappropriate for medieval society, and as Sanok argues, were seen as safely locked into an unattainable past (2007, Preface; see also Heffernan 1988, p. 286). This dilemma has a particular pertinence when applied to the female saints' lives, which seem at considerable variance with the behaviour expected of most medieval women. St Cecelia and St Katherine refused to give their husbands their marital rights, and argued with male authority figures like judges and emperors, preaching the word of God with a feisty irrepressibility which would surely have been condemned by St Paul, who wrote in 1 Corinthians:

> Let the women keep silent in the churches. For they are not permitted to speak, but should be in submission, as the Law also says. If there is anything they desire to learn, let them ask their husbands at home. (14:34–5)

There is evidence that some medieval readers did not flinch from the implications of the Legends of female saints. Sanok points out that John Wycliffe used St Cecelia's *Life* to justify lay preaching, and at his trial in 1391 the Lollard Walter Brut used female saints as evidence that contemporary women should indeed be allowed to preach and minister:

> women, devout virgins, have steadfastly preached the word of God and have converted many men while priests dared not speak a word (quoted in Sanok 2007, p. 15)

Women tried in the Norwich heresy trials of 1428–31 used the same argument. Even Margery Kempe, always insistent that she was not a Lollard, claimed that her position as a wife and mother did not disqualify her from prominent Christian witness any more than it had disqualified the Virgin Mary herself. Could it be the case that the fifteenth-century hagiographer John Capgrave, who was living in Lynn at the Austin Friary when Margery was there, was implicitly supporting her by making his pagans condemn lay preaching (*Life of St Katherine* 4.431–5; see ed. Winstead 2011, p. 8)? Did Capgrave's contemporary Friar Bokenham accept commissions to write the Lives of 'liberated' female saints like Katherine of Alexandria or Elizabeth of Hungary, from educated and politically aspirant noblewomen, in order to encourage their independence? It is tempting to think so, although this was generally a period of anxious conventionality (see above, p. 55). Even the Knight of La Tour-Landry, in his book on good feminine behaviour (written about 1372), used the *Life of Mary Magdalene* to claim that women should learn to read (see Sanok 2007, 6–10). We can see from the cover of this Introduction that the Virgin herself provided another example.

Another question raised by modern critics is: how did contemporary readers of either gender respond to the verbal exposure of the female body in these Lives? Do the appalling tortures described as inflicted on both male and female martyrs reflect either sadism or salacious enjoyment in their very numerous readers? The deaths of three of the Virgin martyrs (Margaret, Anne and Christine) are analysed by Delaney in *Impolitic Bodies*:

> They do not die easily, these zealous adolescents (aged eleven, fifteen, and eighteen) who are flayed and burned and drowned and maimed and shaved and insulted and disembowelled and roasted and have their tongues and breasts torn off, their guts and bones exposed, and are then proposed to, whereupon they answer spiritedly: no. Their endurance is superhuman – indeed, surreal. They survive ordeals that would kill any of us ten times over. Yet there is a moment of truth that no saint survives, for the coup de grace is, most often, decapitation. (1998, p. 71)

Delaney argues that the physical details of literal bodies can reveal attitudes to metaphorical bodies; for example, the fact that the martyr only dies when she is decapitated indicates the crucial significance of the head to the body politic as well as the natural body. But modern readers are more squeamish than medieval ones, and tend to prefer the Legends where the battles with the persecutors are intellectual and verbal rather than physical (such as Bokenham's St Cecelia, St Katherine of Alexandria, St Mary Magdalene; see Delaney 1992, ch. 5).

(iii) Literary hagiographers

Hagiographies were written chiefly by clerics, but they were also written by most of the notable authors of the period, among them Chaucer and possibly the *Pearl* author from the fourteenth century, and Lydgate, Capgrave and Bokenham from the fifteenth. In the 1380s Chaucer wrote a book of 'secular' saints, the influential *Legend of Good Women*, and when he was writing the *Canterbury Tales* in the 1390s he gave his Physician the story of another Good Woman, the Roman virgin Virginia who chooses to die to preserve her chastity from a rapacious judge. He also gives the Legend of St Cecelia, which he had translated from the *Golden Legend* when he was younger, to the Second Nun (see the discussion in the Example Text below). He seems then to have written a Miracle of the Virgin for the Prioress, which has several analogues but apparently no direct source (see the Norton edition, Kolve 2005, pp. 418–27; Collette 1990). It is often discussed as throwing light on the assumptions and feelings of the Prioress herself. Was Chaucer the writer pointing to the divergence between the Prioress's sympathy for the child (or for her own pet dogs; see *Gen. Prol.* 148–9) and her satisfaction that the 'cursed jues' who were involved should be drawn by wild horses before being hanged (599, 629–31)? It is clear that the Tale is anti-Semitic, but far from clear whether this should distract the modern reader from its original focus on the Virgin (Collette cites different approaches to this issue by Frank, Hanning and Brody among others). So if we want to use the *Tale* to further the discussion of how one often-despised social group (women) were portrayed in Saints' Lives, we cannot disregard the way another such group (Jews) are also portrayed. However, it should be remembered that saints are often confronted by non-Christians, and that neither pagans nor Jews had much of a presence in Chaucer's England.

From the end of the fourteenth century there survives a single manuscript of an alliterative *Life of St Erkenwald*, which has in the past been attributed to the *Pearl*-poet, who used the same dialect. There was an established cult of St Erkenwald in St Paul's cathedral, where he had been bishop in the seventh century. However, the writer disregards these stories (including all the miracles associated with the horse-litter preserved in the Church), and instead gives him a miracle usually associated with Pope Gregory, who was supposed to have successfully prayed for the release of the just pagan judge Trajan, from Hell. The poem is dramatic and beautifully written, perhaps to contribute to a revival of the cult of this saint at St Paul's, or to the contemporary debate on the salvation of the righteous heathen (see Morse 1975, Introduction, and *Piers Plowman* B.11, for another example).

In the fifteenth century important hagiographies were written by John Lydgate, John Capgrave and Osbern Bokenham, all devout followers of Chaucer, and influenced by the structure of the *Legend of Good Women* and the rhyme royale of his two Saints' Lives. All three were clerics: Lydgate (1370–1461) was a Benedictine monk at Bury St Edmunds, though he was often in London and Europe as well. Capgrave and Bokenham were both born in 1393, Capgrave dying in 1464 and Bokenham probably at about the same time. Both were Austin (or Augustinian) Friars, Capgrave rising to be the Prior of his Convent at Lynn, 1441–53, and then for three years Prior-Provincial of all the Austin Friars in England. Bokenham, like the other two, lived in East Anglia, at the Augustinian Priory of Clare in Suffolk, though he too travelled abroad. All three moved in high social circles, Lydgate and Capgrave addressing work to Henry V and Henry VI, and taking commissions from Dukes like Humphrey of Gloucester. Bokenham openly supported the Yorkist side on the eve of the Wars of the Roses (see the *Prologue* to the *Mary Magdalene*) and wrote for Yorkist noblewomen like Isobel Bouchier, sister of the Duke of York, and Elizabeth Vere, Countess of Oxford, as well as for the local gentry.

Lydgate (see text-box on p. 216) was the most celebrated literary figure of his age and seen as the worthy successor to Chaucer, particularly for his long poems dealing with the classical past, such as the *Troy Book* and *Siege of Thebes*, which I will discuss in Chapter 7. In his earlier years he produced several short Saints' Lives for various patrons, and in 1433 wrote the long *Life of St Edmund and Fremund* for the twelve-year-old Henry VI while he was staying at Bury, and an even longer *Life of St Alban and Anphabell*, both produced in lavish manuscripts. But he was most personally involved in a Life which he wrote without a commission: the *Life of Our Lady*. Pearsall calls this 'one of the finest pieces of religious poetry in English' (1970, p. 285), and it was very popular in its own day with 42 manuscripts surviving. It is based on the *Meditations on the Life of Christ* ascribed to Bonaventura and translated into English by Love (see p. 126, above), together with other Marian texts, and so is more a 'rhapsodic meditation' on the principal Feasts of Mary than a Saints' Legend (Pearsall 1977, p. 236). It is written in rhyme royale.

Capgrave was a less sophisticated writer than Lydgate, though he too wrote in a variety of genres in both Latin and English. His long *Life of St Katherine* (again in rhyme royale, and surviving in four manuscripts) has much in common with Homiletic Romance in its movement and use of dramatic incident and colloquial dialogue (see below, and Pearsall 1975). Indeed, he ignored most of the detail in the Lives already written about Katherine, including the *Golden Legend* version, saying instead that he had found a more authentic contemporary source. This claim allowed him to fill the *Life* with encyclopaedic knowledge and to discuss contemporary issues, clearly envisaging a lay and often female readership. It too is written in rhyme royale, in imitation of Chaucer.

Capgrave's contemporary and friend the Austin Friar Osbern Bokenham, seems to have written hagiography throughout his life, and may be responsible for the *Gilte Legende* (see p. 156, above), so his *Legendys of Hooly Wimmen* (completed in 1447 and surviving in a single manuscript) was a collection of earlier *Lives* commissioned by individual local gentry and aristocracy, and it is the first collection devoted entirely to female saints. It is compiled from many different sources, and written in untidy rhymed couplets or French stanza forms (see text-box on English Rhymed Forms, p. 206). He imitates

Chaucer's structure, particularly in the *Legend of Good Women*, and includes many verbal echoes of Chaucer's works. Like Chaucer too, he included several details about himself in his *Legends*, which have what Delaney calls 'a substantial earthiness about them', and even 'personalises his pen as a snouted animal' (1992, p. xvi, referring to 898–908, and see pp. xxii–vi on Chaucerian influence).

I will now look at the *Golden Legend* version of the *Life of St Cecelia* as translated by Chaucer and later used as his *Second Nun's Tale*, and compare it with Bokenham's *Lyf of S. Cycyle*, which is a much freer version than the *Golden Legend* version.

Example texts: Chaucer's *Second Nun's Tale* and Bokenham's *Life of St Cecelia*

Chaucer never stopped bringing Latin, French and Italian literature to an English-speaking audience; indeed, Simpson argues that 'translation is the very life-blood of Chaucerian writing' (2006, p. 61). It was therefore easy for him to add to his *Canterbury Tales* a translation he had already made into rhyme royale of the *Golden Legend* version of the *Life of St Cecelia*, as the *Second Nun's Tale*, and it became one of the most popular Tales, to judge from the manuscript selections. He introduced it with an invocation to the Virgin taken from St Ambrose which goes some way to characterising the speaker, whom we scarcely met in the *General Prologue*. Although Pearsall finds the result static and lacking human feeling (1985, pp. 252–5), the reader my well be favourably struck by Cecile's personality, so different from that of the ideal medieval woman. This is particularly clear in her address to her husband Valerian, his brother Tibernius, and other new converts, with this uplifting imperative entirely appropriate to a saint whose name was interpreted as 'light' (Fr.8, 85–119):

> Now, christes owene knyghtes leeve and deere,
> Cast alle awey the werkes of derknesse,
> And armeth yow in armure of brightnesse....
> The rightful juge, which that ye han served,
> Shal yeve it yow, as ye han it deserved. (Fr.8, 383–90)
>
> *leve an deere*: beloved and dear; *yeve it yow*: give it to you (see Romans 13:12)

When Valerian, Tibernius and all the new converts have been slaughtered, she alone is left to debate with the pagan judge Almachius, whom she loudly condemns for his ignorance, his stupidity, and his impotence, goading him into ordering her death. Here, for example, she is discrediting his belief in the stone statue of Jupiter, to whom he demands she make sacrifice:

> I rede thee, lat thyn hand upon it falle,
> And taste it wel, and stoon thou shalt it fynde,
> Syn that thou seest nat with thyne eyen blynde.
> It is a shame that the peple shal
> So scorne thee, and laughe at thy folye;
> For communly men woot it wel
> That myghty God is in his hevenes hye (Fr.8, 501–8)
>
> *rede*: advise

Cecile calmly assumes that she, like the common people, can see the truth that the pagan authorities hide from themselves. Is the point that pagans are so weak that even a woman can best them? Or that God can give words and authority to whom he pleases at their time of trial? One cannot help feeling, as Hirsch does, that this is in some sense a feminist text in which it is the woman who exercises authority (1990, pp. 1161–71).

In Bokenham's fifteenth-century version, Cycyle has, if anything, even more wisdom and assertiveness than in the Chaucer translation. The Prologue emphasises her wisdom, and the passage where Cycyle explains the Holy Trinity to Tibernius (and so converts him) has been expanded to include more parallels to explain the paradox of Three in One:

> Anothir exauwnple by feer I may eek brywg,
> Wych threfold in propyrtees hath varyaimce
> Formally dystynct, & yet in substaunce
> Thei ben o feyr; so snow, hayl & yhs
> Dystynct ben, as seyn phylosophyrs wyhs,
> In name & formed, but substancyally
> They be but watyr. (7830–6)

> Another example of a single substance with three forms (snow, hail and ice) is water, as wise (natural) philosophers see.

This is much more philosophical than anything Chaucer's Cecile says. The *Lyf* moves quickly to focus on Valerian's and Tibernius's obedience to Cycyle, to Pope Urban (who baptises them in the catacombs) and to God. As in the *Golden Legend*, Valerian and Cycle convert the people sent to arrest them, and Cycyle encourages their immediate martyrdom by using the imagery of darkness and light (see Chaucer's translation, 384–5, quoted above), so that the final confrontation must be between Cycyle and Almachius, the pagan judge. Here as in the *Golden Legend*, Cycyle uses humour to deflate her opponent in language which is even more graphic (and sexually suggestive) than in Chaucer's more polished lines (I give the Chaucer below Bokenham's text):

> 'Alle youre power, as yt semyth to me,
> May wele to a bleddyr lyknyd be
> Bio we ful of wynd tyl yt hath starknesse,
> Wych who-so lyst may gone depresse;
> For wyth a nedlys poynt he may make
> The wynd oute to goon & the sterknesse slake.
> Euene thus it faryth by thi puyssaimce.' (Bokenham, *Legendys* 8127–33)
>
> *starkness*: tightness; *slake*: slacken; *puyssaimce*: power

> 'Youre myght,' quod she, 'ful litel is to dreede.
> For every mortal mannes power nys
> But lyk a bladdre ful of wynd ywys.
> For with nedles poynt, whan it is blowe,
> May al the boost of it be leyd ful lowe.' (Chaucer, *Canterbury Tales*, Fr.8, 437–41)

Bokenham's *Lyf* as a whole seems, therefore, to leave the reader with a stronger impression of this Virgin Martyr's intellectual victory rather than of her suffering and death.

Questions on two Lives of St Cecelia

- What evidence can you find for and against the claim that Bokenham's changes to the *Life of St Cecelia* exemplify the new 'decorous' heroines of fifteenth-century hagiography (Sanok 2007, pp. 2–3)?
- Compare Chaucer's or Bokenham's Cecelia with the heroines of the Homiletic Romances discussed in the next Example Texts. To what extent can any of them be used to provide a model example for contemporary women?

(b) Popular Romances

'Romances' are tales centring on the deeds of a secular hero or heroine, characteristically written in the 'romance' languages of French, Anglo-Norman or Latin. As this Guide is organised by both genre and readership, I deal with Romances in three different places. In the next chapter I will look at those courtly Romances in which the literary code of *fin amour* is the centre of attention, and where new ways of developing narrative are explored by the most experienced writers. These must have been enjoyed by the most educated of readers, including members of the clergy, the nobility and the court. The final chapter is devoted mainly to Romances of Arthur, which centre on chivalry as much as love, and which carried the prestige of a national myth. These seem to have held the interest well into the fifteenth century of a rather less sophisticated audience, including many of the better-off townspeople and gentry, whom we might describe as 'upper middle class'. The Popular Romances I discuss in this chapter attracted a less sophisticated and less wealthy, though much larger, group of readers, probably including both the provincial gentry and skilled working men of the lower middle class, members of the lower clergy, and women and illiterate listeners. Within the fifty-odd Middle English Romances which survive from the period between 1280 and 1400, when they were almost all written, there is a loose group of 'Homiletic Romances', tales where the morality and Christianity of the hero or heroine is the main focus of attention. These are much closer to the Saints' Lives, in their celebration of fortitude in suffering, than to the Chivalric Romances which are the subject of Chapter 8. As Cooper puts it, such tales occupy

> the point where romance shades into saint's life, as a kind of secular hagiography. Saints' lives are exemplary, providing a pattern of behaviour and belief for sinful mankind to strive to emulate; and the heroines of these tales offer similar patterns of perfection. (Cooper 1989, p. 122)

These Homiletic Romances are the main focus of this section. However, before I describe and exemplify them in more detail, I would like to give a brief account of Popular Romances in general, although many can scarcely be described as edifying (for evidence of their popularity, see Reiss 1985, pp. 112–13). There will be a corresponding account of Chivalric Romances in Chapter 8, focusing on the Arthurian tradition.

These Popular Romances were 'overwhelmingly popular and non-courtly' (Pearsall 1988, p. 11), versions probably made for a lower middle-class audience of the kind of material that their betters would read in French. About half of them survive in only one manuscript, and all are in verse, using simple four-stress rhymed couplets or the English 'tail-rhyme stanza' (see the text-box on English Rhymed Forms, p. 206). The writers almost always had a French or Anglo-Norman source, which they translated and adapted for English tastes, leaving out the discussion of the most courtly themes (as they did with Courtly Romance as well; see below, p. 247), and often giving the story a clearer sense of moral principle.Though using common motifs and plot elements, they can be described as either predominantly adventurous, or as more sentimental, or as more homiletic.

(i) Romances of adventure

Some romances are essentially tales of adventure, with descriptions of battles, and of long sea journeys to pagan lands, some (like *Havelock*) quite realistic, others more marvellous, including encounters with dragons and giants. Like other kinds of romance they are often structured on the exile and return of the hero, who is finally restored to his inheritance. Popular stories of this kind include *King Horn* (one of the earliest and most lyrical), *Havelock the Dane* (like *Horn*, recounting battles with the Vikings), and *Bevis of Hampton*; all three, part of what is known as 'The Matter of England'. In spite of their French origins, some of these tales are supposedly local and historical, such as *Guy of Warwick* (describing a humble steward who becomes a knight and saves England from the Danes), or *Gamelyn*, a story of the Robin-Hood type, which survives in a large number of manuscripts because it was thought to be Chaucer's *Cook's Tale* (for discussion of all these, see Pearsall 1977, p. 140; 1988, pp. 11–20). Chaucer the pilgrim parodies the popular romance in his 'own' tale of *Sir Thopas*, with its abundance of incident, its use of cliché, and the *drasty rymyng* (Fr.7, 930) of the 'tail-rhyme stanza'.

(ii) Sentimental Romances and 'Breton Lays'

The more sentimental romances are also full of adventures, but they generally involve separated lovers who undergo supernatural or other trials. One of the oldest surviving romances, the Tale of *Floris and Blanchefleur*, dating from the 1240s and extant in several other European languages, does have a religious motif, for the Christian Blanchefleur eventually converts her pagan lover. But the story is much more about young love than about young virtue, and indeed, Blanchefleur's love is finally revealed because she twice oversleeps after an illicit night with Floris. Many other romances, such as the Arthurian tale of *Yvain* discussed in Chapter 8 (p. 249), and the tales of the Custance group described below, similarly show the trials of separated lovers.

Also appealing to sentiment was the 'Breton Lay' (see Bennett 1986, pp. 137–41). It had the oldest pedigree of these Popular Romances, for there is good evidence of the existence of an oral tradition in Brittany of stories or recited songs, using material from Classical as well as Celtic folk tales. From these the early twelfth-century French authoress Marie de France said she had composed her *Lais*, narrative poems designed to be chanted to a simple (harp?) accompaniment, to convey the 'grands biens' of the noble love then being developed in France (see pp. 202ff.). Although some of the later

English upper class would undoubtedly have read Marie de France's *Lais* in French, there are surviving English versions of two of them in rhyming couplets, dating from the early fourteenth century: the *Lai de Fresne* and *Launfal*. The gentle story of the *Lai de Fresne* can serve as an example of the genre. It tells of a foundling who is treated as a live-in bedfellow by a local knight until he has married her legitimately-raised twin sister. But when she decorates their bedchamber for the nuptial night with the costly robe she was found in, her mother recognises it and reveals the truth of her parentage. The new marriage is dissolved and she is able to marry her lover. Her patience and generosity are mirrored nearly two hundred years later in Chaucer's Griselde (indeed Petrarch, Chaucer's source, may have known the story). The term *Lai* was used in the fourteenth century for stories of this kind, including *Sir Dégaré* and *Émaré* (to be considered below), which had no connection with Marie de France or Brittany.

The virtue which most clearly links the chivalric (such as it is) and the love elements in these popular genres of Romance and Lay is, however, faithfulness, either to one's fellow-heroes or to the beloved (see the discussion of *Yvain*, p. 249). Faithfulness or 'truth' is at the centre of another Lay, not narrated by Marie, a version of the story of Orpheus referred to in two thirteenth-century French romances. It survives as the haunting Middle English version known as *Sir Orfeo*, which still includes some of the Celtic elements (the fairyland with its dances and hunts, which replaces the Classical Underworld; see the quotation within the text-box on English Rhymed Forms on p. 216). Orfeo's faithful love or 'truth' is compared to his steward's faithful watch over his kingdom, showing the close link between 'courtly love' and the older feudal bond between a lord and his man.

'Trouthe' is also the virtue which lies at the centre of anther supposed Breton *Lai*, Chaucer's *Franklyn's Tale*, in which there are not two but three parallel stories of faithfulness (this is not true of its Italian source, the *Filocolo* of Boccaccio). The denouement is, however, much more problematic than that of *Sir Orfeo*; the knight Averagus demands that his wife Dorigen be true to her promise to her would-be lover Aurelius even though it will involve her in breaking her truth to him, her husband, because

Trouthe is the hyeste thyng that man may kepe (Fr.5, 1479)

As a result of his generosity, both Aurelius and the magician who helped him, decide to break their own agreements with Dorigen and each other. Is falseness to truth a greater truth? As in *Sir Orfeo*, the word 'trouthe' recurs like a motto, and points to the exemplary nature of these Tales.

(iii) Homiletic Romances

Some of these Popular Romances can also be described as 'homiletic', because they focus on the moral standing of the hero or heroine, and offer a model of repentance and reform, or of patience rewarded. *King Horn* itself has many homiletic elements, though the two versions of *Isumbras*, whose hero purges his pride by becoming a pilgrim, provide clearer examples; indeed, this story ends in the triumphant slaughter of more than thirty thousand pagans. The *King of Tars* is the tale of a miraculous baptism and conversion. A series of mid-fourteenth-century Romances, including *Octavian, Athelstan, Sir Eglamour* and one or two others, all show constancy in exile; *Octavian* in particular is 'full of piety and pathos' (Pearsall 1988, p. 29). This kind of tale need not celebrate the 'masculine' attributes of prowess and 'truth' to one's brother-knights, but rather, truth to God, chastity, patience in suffering and enduring faith. As Reiss puts it, 'the didactic and the religious are the warp and woof of Romance, and in fact had been from the beginnings of the genre in late antiquity' (1985, p. 115). *Sir Amadas* and *Sir Cleges* are particularly close to Saints' Lives; and see Pearsall (1975) on the romance elements in Capgrave's *Life of Saint Katherine*. As Reiss demonstrates (1985, p. 116), popular romances, lays and saints' lives are collected in the same manuscripts, often with other didactic pieces, and clearly appeal to similar tastes.

A comparison with the stories of female saints we have been considering in the last section can be made if we look in more detail at romances in a story group with a female protagonist, known as the 'Custance Group' (see Black 2003). Custance is an 'accused queen', sent away on an empty ship to suffer a series of adventures, often ending in marriage to, and conversion of, a pagan king. Early examples of the story can be found in the Latin *Gesta Romanorum* (see below, p. 174), and in the Anglo-Norman *Chronicles* of Nicholas Trevet or Trivet (c. 1335), both widely read throughout England. One of the surviving Middle English examples, John Gower's *Tale of Constance* in *Confessio Amantis* Book II, 587–1612, is a fairly close translation of Trevet, and offers the story as a piece of genuine history. Another and more original version is Chaucer's *Man of Law's Tale*, which also acknowledges a debt to Gower in the Prologue. I will now look at a fourteenth-century Homiletic Romance or Lay which tells this story, *Émaré*, as my Example Text, making some comparisons with Chaucer's more sophisticated but also more accessible version.

Example Texts: *Émaré* and Chaucer's *Man of Law's Tale*

The late fourteenth-century tail-rhyme romance *Émaré*, and Chaucer's rhyme-royal *Man of Law's Tale*, are taken from different versions of the story. *Émaré* (available to read on the TEAMS website) is an older version of the Constance-group of stories, and is full of folk-tale elements, such as the threat of incest from Émaré's father, the glittering robe she sometimes wears as a sign of her identity (or as a love charm?), and the reunion of Émaré with her husband through the agency of their child. Chaucer, on the other hand, takes Trivet's Christianised version from Gower, presenting Custance as ideal both in her faith and in her fortitude, and making her Tale a moral as well as a religious *exemplum*. Chaucer's Custance is a Christian princess who is married to a Saracen king in Syria but whose husband and household are murdered by her mother-in-law in (devilish) defence of her own Islamic faith. It is because of this murder that Custance is sent out in a rudderless boat. This punishment is repeated by her second mother-in-law. Thus the more masculine qualities of strength and cunning are displayed in two 'viragoes', the mannish women who cause all Custance's suffering, while Custance herself can only be patient and faithful. Chaucer takes pains to make his story one of faith triumphant by such additions as threatening astrological predictions, which are eventually defeated by God's Providence, and by giving his heroine several moving prayers to God, such as here, where she compares her plight to that of the Virgin Mary:

> Thanne is ther no comparison bitwene
> Thy wo and any wo man may sustene ...
> Rewe on my child, that of thy gentillesse,
> Rewest on every reweful in distresse. (Fr.2, 846–53)
>
> *rewe ... rewest ... reweful*: have pity ... pitied ... pitiable

Whereas Custance is a champion for the Christian Church, Émaré seems to stand alone in her moral refusal of her father's love – even against the Pope's written permission for the marriage (233–40):

> 'Nay syr, God of heven hyt forbede,
> Tha ever do so we shulde!' (251–2)

Hopkins explains that this 'threat of harm' is characteristic of the beginning of a Middle English Lay, particularly where the protagonist is a woman, and explores why 'rape, incest ... torture and abandonment flourish in the imaginary worlds of hagiography and romance'.

Her father, the emperor, puts her alone into a boat – an action he immediately regrets – and she drifts for a mere six days (as distinct from the three years of Chaucer's Tale). When she is washed up on the shores of Galicia, it is her glittering robe as much as herself which encourages the steward Kadore to send for the king.

> A boot he fond by the brym,
> And a glysteryng thyng theryn ...
> They askede her what was her name:
> She ... sayde she hette Émaré. (349–60)
>
> *brym*: edge; *glysteryng thyng*: flittering thing (the robe); *hette*: was called

This renaming of herself as 'outcast' can be seen as her taking control of her identity, keeping it until she eventually reveals her true name at the end – a pattern found in other Romances of this type (see Bliss 2008, pp. 141–4). The shining robe and her unearthly beauty win the king's love, and we might even sympathise with the fear shown by the king's mother:

> The olde qwene spakke wordus unhende
> And sayde, 'Sone, thys ys a fende'. (335–6)
>
> *unhende*: discourteous, unkind

This is the slander, which she then reinforces by pretending to her son that 'Émaré' has borne a child with three heads. Though her husband does not command her exile, her mother-in-law arranges that Émaré is once again put aboard an empty ship, where she lies with her baby in the depths of despair:

> She was aferde of the see,
> And layde her gruf uponn a tre,
> The chylde to her pappes. (655–7)
>
> *gruf uponn a tre*: face down on a plank; *pappes*: breast

She does, however, survive, earns herself and her son a life in Rome, and engineers a meeting with her husband, and another between him and the Emperor her father, so resolving the initial crisis of the story. In all this she shows strength as well as faithfulness.

In Chaucer's Tale, Custance is less alone as she feels herself to be under God's protection. Nor is she alone in her Christian endurance, for her second husband, a Viking king confusingly called Alla, goes even further than his predecessor in *Émaré* in his acceptance of a supposedly fiend-like son, patiently welcoming *Cristes' sonde*:

> Welcome the sonde of crist for everemoore
> To me that am now lerned in his loore! ...
> Kepeth this child, al be it foul or feir,
> And eek my wyf, unto myn hoom-comynge. (Fr.2, 760–8)
>
> *sonde of gd*: whatever God sends, destiny

Custance echoes these words when she is put back into the boat:

> But nathelees she taketh in good entente
> The wyl of crist, and knelynge on the stronde,
> She seyde, lord, ay welcome be thy sonde! (Fr.2, 824–6)

These words of acceptance clearly make both Alla and Custance types of patience, which in this Tale is ungendered. Both Custance and Émaré can therefore be seen as female saints, strong women who accept their suffering as a choice and – particularly in *Émaré* – have a role in resolving their destiny. Their stories are not believable, but this does not seem to imply that the God who supposedly sustained them is also unbelievable, or that their faith and patience should not be an example for the reader.

Questions on *Émaré* and Chaucer's *Man of Law's Tale*

- We are given different images of womanhood in these tales, through the heroine and her mothers-in-law. Can you find a reading of these which does not polarise them into the 'good' and the 'bad'? Are the men in each tale also polarised in this way?
- *Émaré* is unsophisticated but consistent in its tone and apparent purpose, unlike the *Man of Law's Tale*, which critics find uneven in tone, suggesting Chaucer's disillusion with the genre (as Edwards 1990). How does Chaucer deal with the problems of structure and characterisation raised by using a Homiletic Romance as his source?

(c) Moral Examples

Although Homiletic Romances, like Saints' Lives, do of course describe exemplary behaviour and faith, they are hardly examples that the reader can literally follow. In both cases the situations encountered are remote and extreme, and the supernatural – whether God or magical events – all too present. I am turning now to stories in which the hero or heroine exemplifies a moral quality that the reader can certainly emulate, even though the context may still be unrealistic. Clearly religious are the texts which retell a Bible story and then explain and discuss it to bring out its exemplary nature for the reader or listener. Very sophisticated examples of this type are the two other religious poems in the Cotton Nero Manuscript, which contains *Pearl*, *Cleanness* and *Patience* (see the text-box on p. 175).

Cleanness uses several Biblical stories (including the Parable of the Wedding Feast, Noah's Flood, and the destruction of Sodom) to illustrate the importance of cleansing away sin, a process which restores the innate innocence discussed in *Pearl*. *Patience* gives the story of Jonah in full as a negative example of the virtue of patience; I will be discussing it in more detail as the second Example Text in this section. This kind of writing is on the borders of Biblical Paraphrase, another kind of religious narrative I shall not cover as it does not really count as 'literature'. One example which does influence other literature is Grosseteste's *Cursor Mundi* ('Runner' or course of the World), written in Anglo-French, and used by Langland in Passus 18 of *Piers Plowman*. The Middle-English *Metrical Paraphrase of the Old Testament*, written at the beginning of the fifteenth century (see Peck 1991), is another example. These Biblical retellings were somewhat tainted by the Wycliffite Bible; in the fifteenth century, Bible retellings might have led to a suspicion of Lollardy.

Authors also liked to use non-biblical stories derived from popular history and European tradition to exemplify a moral quality. These were readily available in collections on Vices and Virtues, or in Latin 'Exemplum Books' (see Hanna 1978, p. 66). One secular source was the popular Latin story collection known as the *Gesta Romanorum*, compiled in the early fourteenth century from a mixture of Classical and Christian moral stories. It and similar sources were used in preachers' homilies (see Chapter 2 above, pp. 47–8), which offer a Bible text which is then illuminated by an *exemplum* or several *exempla*, stories taken from a non-biblical context. But this method was also used by notable writers like Chaucer and Gower. Chaucer's *Pardoner's Tale*, an old story of how three uncaring and greedy young man met with Death, illustrates St Paul's warning that 'The love of money is the root of all evil' (I Timothy 6:10). The story itself is not religious, having more of the sense of 'the biter bit' characteristic of the *fabliau*. However, Chaucer's ability to make a plot seem natural and inevitable, to flesh out characters, to combine black humour with the haunting sadness of the old man, make this one of the greatest of his *Canterbury Tales*. As explained in Chapter 4 above, Gower used an exemplary structure in his collection of stories the *Confessio Amantis*; each of seven Books exemplifies a particular sin or its opposite virtue, although some of the connections seem rather forced. Some critics of the *Canterbury Tales* have attempted to demonstrate that Chaucer uses individual Tales to exemplify the structure of Vices and Virtues presented in *The Parson's Tale* (see, e.g., Huppé 1964, discussed in Pearsall 1985, p. 291).

In the previous two sections I used stories with heroines who – particularly in the examples of Homiletic Romance – exemplified the characteristically female virtue of patience or long-suffering, particularly regarding what Chaucer called the *sonde of God*. My two Example Texts in this section, *Patience* and *The Clerk's Tale*, also exemplify this virtue, the first (eventually) exercised by a man, and the second by a woman. What does the need for this virtue say about the relationship between God and mankind, or between man and woman? Does a genre which is essentially didactic allow the difficult 'problem' of pain to be examined as well as the virtue which confronts it? Does the *exemplum* structure have to be broken for the story itself to define its own values?

The Pearl-*poet*

The *Pearl*-poet (or *Gawain*-poet) is generally thought to have written the four poems found in a unique manuscript in the British Library, Cotton Nero A.10: *Pearl, Cleanness, Patience* and *Sir Gawain and the Green Knight*, in that order, without titles, but with twelve simple illustrations. This modest manuscript was acquired from a Yorkshire collector by Robert Cotton in 1521, and was left to the nation in 1702. The poet is sometimes also credited with *St Erkenwald* (see above, p. 160), found in Harley 2250, as it shares many of the characteristic features of the poet. Both manuscripts date from the end of the fourteenth century. The poems are all written in Cheshire dialect, and *Sir Gawain* uses names for geographical features peculiar to the Wirral (see Elliott 1997, p. 109), though the poetry suggests a sophisticated London audience and *St Erkenwald* celebrates St Paul's Cathedral. It may be that the poet was a Cheshire knight living in London, perhaps at the court of Richard II (who employed Cheshiremen as his personal bodyguard). If we make the very dangerous assumption that the 'I' in *Pearl* and in the *Patience* prologue is an autobiographical I, then we can also deduce that the poet, despite his thorough clerical training, had taken only minor orders, was married and had a child who died when she was two, and was employed as a high-ranking retainer of a lord, or even the king (*Patience* 51–2). If he was at the royal court, his subsequent obscurity might be due to the change of government after the deposition of Richard II, though that fact did not seem to affect Chaucer's popularity. (It should be noted that alliterative poems are often found, and presumably were read, outside the area of their written dialect.)

The characteristics which link these poems are discussed by numerous critics; they include the dialect and vocabulary of the Cotton Nero poems, an extraordinary craftsmanship in the alliterative tradition, vivid characterisation, an unusually realistic and visual depiction of landscape, interiors and objects, a deep knowledge of both secular noble pursuits and religious learning and observance, and a concern for the many aspects of perfection which his own masterly skill makes particularly appropriate. He also has a sense of humour.

(For a summary of scholarship and criticism, see Bowers 2012; Andrew 1997; Elliott 1997; Putter 1996.)

Example Text: (i) *Patience*

Patience represents the first kind of *exemplum* mentioned above, for it retells the biblical *Book of Jonah*, used to exemplify the value of patience. It is a fine piece of writing which displays many characteristics of the *Pearl*-poet (see the text-box above). For example, it is extremely well constructed, both in its thematic unity and in its use of poetic form, and it shows an underlying interest in guilt and innocence, expressed in terms of dirt and cleansing. The character of Jonah, like that of Gawain, or of the dreamer in *Pearl*, is thoroughly believable, and presented with the poet's typically ironic detachment. Jonah is the least admirable and the funniest of these three characters, thin-skinned and irascible, and with a sense of his own rights which constantly puts him at odds with God. As Bowers puts it, the poet has 'a gift for broad humour shaded by seriousness' (2012, p. 82). For Jonah is an *exemplum* of impatience rather than patience; in the poem it is God who is patient, much to Jonah's annoyance. Through the poem he learns three meanings of 'patience', a word which came from the Latin *patio* meaning *to suffer, to accept,* and which is also the root of the word *passion*, as in the 'Passion of Christ'. We have already seen the meaning *endurance* exemplified in Chaucer's Custance, and both she and Émaré also exemplified suffering. The word can also suggest an active *obedience* to God's will which was not available to those somewhat passive maidens. Jonah however, as a man, is an active agent, who fails to obey God's will patiently, and is punished not by enduring suffering, but by learning of the patience of God himself.

The poet begins his presentation of patience by paraphrasing the Beatitudes of Matthew 5:11, which was in fact recommended in the *Ars Predicandi* (a preachers' handbook; see Newhauser 1997) as appropriate for a sermon on this virtue. It is the last of these (in the Vulgate *beati qui persecutionem patiuntur propter justitium*: Blessed are they who suffer persecution for the sake of justice) that the poet defines as patience; for him this represents the key virtue of self-control, the governing of one's own heart:

> Thay ar happen also that con her hert stere,
> For hores is the heuen-ryche, as I er sayde (27–9)
>
> *happen*: blest; *stere*: govern; *heuen-ryche*: kingdom of Heaven; *er*: before

The first situation in which Jonah is required to govern his heart is when he is obeying God's command to go to Nineveh and warn the inhabitants there of God's planned vengeance for their sins. He immediately blames God for putting him in danger of enduring a cruel punishment at the Ninevites' hands if he delivers this message, unwittingly contrasting himself with Christ's obedient acceptance of his Passion:

> 'Oure Syre syttes,' he says, 'on segge so hyghe
> In His glowande glorye, & gloumbes ful lyttel
> Thagh I be nummen in Nunniue & naked dispoyled,
> On rode rwly torent with rybaudes mony.' (93–6)
>
> *segge*: throne; *gloumbes ful lyttel*: worries but little; *nummen*: seized; 96: on a cross pitifully torn to pieces by many cruel men

Jonah decides to take a ship to Thrace instead, but when the ship he is in is caught in a terrifying storm, he is found in *sloumbe-selepe, & sloberande he routes* (in a deep sleep, and slobbering as he snores: 186), a situation of gross inactivity which is at the opposite extreme from active obedience. However, he somewhat redeems his credibility as a prophet here by readily acknowledging his sin and encouraging the sailors to throw him overboard, this time really typifying the sacrifice of Christ before Pontius Pilate as they pray that *thay in balelez blod ther blenden her handez* (innocent blood: 227; compare Matthew 27:24). These echoes of the Passion narrative are appropriate in a story that Jesus himself said was an anticipation of his own death and descent to Hell (Matthew 12:40); even if God's will seems careless of the pain obedience might involve, at least he was prepared to suffer it himself.

Once inside the whale, Jonah illustrates the first meaning of patience: the 'souffrance' or suffering (generally unavoidable) pain without 'gruching' or complaint, and without anger. Indeed, Jonah accepts the discomforts of the whale's belly as a penance:

> Thagh I be gulty of gyle, as gaule of prophetes,
> thou art God, & alle gowdez ar graythely thyn owen.
> Haf now mercy of thy man & his mysdedes. (285–7)
>
> *gaule*: scum; *graythely*: truly

That the pain encountered in one's daily life can be seen as penance for sin was a commonplace of penitential manuals. Jonah's penance in the whale seems to work, for he finds a clean nook in which to await deliverance (389–90), and soon has an opportunity to wash (342), the fastidious poet clearly empathising with this desire for cleanness. Later the Ninevites will impose fasting and prayer on themselves to show their repentance (371–404), and again God will show mercy (408). The poet applies this ideal of uncomplaining acceptance or 'souffraunce' of pain to himself, when he is called on to endure poverty:

> Forthy when pouerte me enprecez & paynez innoghe
> Ful softly with suffraunce saghttel me bihouez;
> Forthy penaunce & payne to preue hit in syght
> That pacience is a nobel poynt, thagh hit displese ofte. (628–31)
>
> *Forthy*: therefore; *enprecez & paynez*: presses and hurts; *suffraunce saghttel me bihouez*: I need to settle myself with patience; *poynt*: virtue

These are the last lines of the poem, and they indicate how patience can offer a meaning to inevitable suffering and hardship, paradoxically giving the sufferer an active role.

The final episodes of the poem – Jonah's preaching, the Ninevites' repentance, and Jonah's anger that retribution has not come as he had prophesied – illustrate another meaning of Patience: the endurance and even forgiveness of wrongs done to oneself. It is God who shows this patience towards the penitent Ninevites, which Jonah (with his usual self-importance) views with contempt:

> Wel knew I thi cortaysye, thy quoynt soffraunce,
> Thy bounte of debonerte & thy bene grace,
> Thy longe abydyng wyth lur, thy late vengaunce. (417–19)
>
> *quoynt soffraunce*: wise patience; *debonerte*: kindness; *bene*: good; *longe abydyng wyth lur*: long-suffering of injury; *late*: tardy

Jonah has conveniently forgotten that he implored God to be equally forbearing with him while he was in the whale (285–7, quoted above), and his anger here contrasts dramatically with God's withholding of anger. God patiently explains his reasons for not destroying the Ninevites through the rather curious episode of the withering woodbine (437–523), which gives the poet plenty of opportunity for comedy, especially when Jonah insists that God's destruction of the woodbine is

> '... not lyttel,' quoth the lede, 'bot lykker to ryght;
> I wolde I were of this worlde wrapped in moldez' (493–4)
>
> *lykker to ryght*: more a matter of justice; *wrapped in moldez*: buried in earth

So while at first Jonah accepted suffering for sin like a second Jesus, he now requires the punishment of sin like a second Jehovah. Is this man's inconsistency or God's? It is the task of the poet to present the case for a patient and caring God without discounting the human need for justice or his experience of injustice. The inbuilt ambiguity in this apparently didactic *exemplum* gives the reader all the literary independence needed to interpret it for himself in the light of his own experience.

Questions on *Patience*

- Medieval accounts of patience often show it to be triumphant over wrath (as in Prudentius' *Psychomachia* or in *Piers Plowman*, Passus 14). Does the poet seem to be demonstrating this idea in the themes and language of the poem?
- Compare the poem with the Book of Jonah, looking in particular at the portrayal of the landscape and the characters.

Example Text: (ii) Chaucer's *Clerk's Tale*

The *Clerk's Tale* is another example of Chaucer's translation project. It closely translates a very popular Latin story expanded in 1373 by the Italian poet Petrarch from one of the stories in Boccaccio's *Decameron* (see Norton ed. Kolve 2005). Chaucer makes the text so much his own that is hard to believe he did not write the whole story himself, though only a few– if significant – lines are wholly original. It tells the story of the exemplary patience of a wife called Griselde, but Chaucer, following Petrarch, specifically says that this is an example not for wives so much as for all mankind when smitten by adversity (Fr. 4, 1143-4):

> But for that every wight, in his degree,
> Sholde be constant in adversitee
> As was Grisilde; (Fr. 4, 1145-7)
> *wight, in his degree:* man, whatever his class

So, as in the poem *Patience*, or in *The Man of Law's Tale*, the virtue exemplified is constancy in the endurance of suffering, which is the primary medieval meaning of 'patience' (St Augustine says it is *to endure evils with an even mind*: Hanna 1978, p. 68). Here, however, the focus is much more clearly on the suffering, the 'Passion', and the cruelty of inflicting it, whether by a husband or God himself, than in *Patience*, where Jonah learned to 'steer his heart'. It was this refusal to deny human feeling which distinguishes Christian patience from the Stoic *apatheia* (see Hanna 1978, pp. 77–8). Griselde is a poor and powerless tenant of the Marquis, Walter, and when he offers to marry her, is prepared to agree to his condition of complete obedience in everything (which suggests that the origin of the *Clerk's Tale* is one of the 'rash promise' group of folk tales; see Sledd 1953). When this obedience involves giving up her little children to apparently certain death she does not flinch, or complain (*grucche* 354), or even cease to love her husband. Even when he apparently secures a divorce, from the Pope, and sends her back to her father so that he can marry again, she remains steadfast in her vow of unstinting compliance to his will. Chaucer not only adds his own comments to his source to lament Walter's obsessive cruelty, but also his own words of praise for all women:

> Though clerkes preise wommen but a lite,
> Ther kan no man in humbless hym acquite
> As womman kan, ne kan been half so trewe
> As wommen been, but it be falle of newe. (Fr.4, 935–8)
>
> *lite*: little; *acquite*: acquit himself; *falle of newe*: happened very recently

(This is in striking contrast to St Jerome, who says that a woman who is a true servant of Christ ceases to be a woman and becomes a man! See Oppel 1993, pp. 21–2.) The modern reader is, however, unlikely to admire her failure to protect her children from their clearly psychopathic father, or to share her unqualified joy when he then learns that his supposed new bride is in fact her daughter, who together with her son has been brought up secretly by his sister. It is hardly surprising that the *Clerk's Tale* has attracted the opprobrium of feminist critics, or that it seems to epitomise everything that was wrong with patience, legitimising as it does women's social and marital powerlessness and subservience (see, e.g. Hansen 1988, pp. 230–49, and further references in Morse 1990). Even the Clerk seems to disown its moral, for he adds an 'Envoy' at the end, 35 lines in a different rhyme scheme, in which he directly addresses (*envoy*) the Wife of Bath to insist that she should *not* follow this example, but that she should make her husbands suffer. Though such advice is clearly ironic, it suggests that the *Tale* is no more than the strait-laced Clerk's contribution to the 'Marriage Group' of Tales discussed above in Chapter 4.

But such thoughts, however insistent, are almost irrelevant to the story as an *exemplum* of patience. The *Tale* changes its effect completely if we follow Petrarch's direction and read it not as a realistic account of a marriage, where Griselde's patience is directed to her husband, but as an example of the way every man should meet the violent changes of fortune for which Walter's moodswings are only a paradigm. Discussions of patience (for example, in lists of sins and virtues) do not focus on exercising patience towards other people so much as towards God and the evil fortune He apparently fails to prevent, and they exhort obedience and lack of *grucching* or complaining, which Jonah so comically failed to display (St Gregory insisted that such *murmuratio* was a sign of impatience; see Hanna 1978, p. 73). Griselde conforms precisely to this pattern of patience, both in her obedience and in her uncomplaining fortitude. When Jankin, Griselde's father, agrees to the Marquis's will in words which echo the Virgin Mary's response to Gabriel (319–20), Griselde reinforces the promise to obey Walter in everything:

> And heere I swere that nevere willyngly,
> In werk ne thoght, I nyl yow disobeye
> For to be deed. (Fr.4, 362–4)

From that point onwards she accepts his will uncomplainingly, never expressing to him her agony at the loss of her children, and only hinting that he has changed towards her when he pretends to divorce her.

> O goode god! how gentil and how kynde
> Ye semed by youre speche and youre visage
> The day that maked was oure marriage! (Fr.4, 851–3)
>
> *visage*: face

It is her refusal to *grucche* or complain, even more than her obedience, which eventually conquers this cruelty of a husband who signally failed to govern his own desire to 'tempt' his wife:

> And whan this Walter saugh hire pacience,
> Hir glade chiere, and no malice at al,

> And he so ofte had doon to hire offence,
> And she ay sad and constant as a wal,
> Continuynge evere hire innocence overal,
> This sturdy markys gan his herte dresse
> To rewen upon hire wyfly stedfastnesse. (Fr.4, 1044–50)
>
> *chiere*: face, expression; *sad and constant*: stable and consistent; *dresse*: turn; *rewen*: have pity

That patience can conquer was a commonplace of Christian teaching (see Kirk 1978), but to a modern reader this does not appear to the best way to respond to a husband as unhinged as Walter, and Chaucer again adds some original lines to stress how unhinged he is (697–707). But perhaps it is the only way in which one should respond to God, who has complete power over mankind and can inflict what blows he wishes. To many mothers in the Middle Ages, when possibly half of all childen died in infancy, He must have seemed to wear the face of Walter, as He took one child after another. The bereaved parents could hope for the children to be restored at the final feasting in heaven, as Griselde's children are restored at the marriage-feast, but lamenting their loss and raging against the power which had inflicted it would not bring them back. Indeed, patient acceptance of God's will, so much resisted by Jonah in *Patience*, and so wholly exemplified by Griselde's acceptance of Walter's will, is probably the only way to deal with unavoidable adversity, at least for those who have faith in God and wish not to lose their faith as well as their loved ones. Thus the *Clerk's Tale*, like *Pearl*, can be read as a consolation text for those who have suffered the death of their children. This way of reading the *Tale* is taken even further by Mann when she argues that Griselde typifies not only the obedient sacrifice by Christ of his life, but also the willing sacrifice by God himself of his son. Chaucer, like Julian of Norwich, suggests that such acts of loving sacrifice are more typical of a woman than a man. 'In Griselde human suffering and divine patience are united in one person, as Christ united manhood and Godhead. And it is her 'womanhede' that is the ground of the union. Patience, like pity, is a *womanly* quality' (Mann 1991, p. 160).

Questions on the *Clerk's Tale*

- Do you agree with the 'Petrarchan' interpretation of the *Tale* offered above, or do you think that Chaucer's own *Envoy* shows that the *Clerk's Tale* should be read primarily as a critique of *maistrie* (mastery) in marriage, whether apparently legitimised by traditional gender-roles or not?
- To what extent does the success – or failure – of the story depend upon realistic characterisation? In many ways Griselde and Walter function as types, opposing her truth to his lies, her love to his cruelty, her steadfastness to his inconsistency, even her inner value to his sense of aristocratic worth. Is the problem with the *Clerk's Tale* that Chaucer makes them individuals rather than types, disrupting the allegorical patterning?
- In the two *exempla* of Patience that I have been discussing, one protagonist (Jonah) is a man and the other (Griselde) a woman. Does this affect the point of the stories significantly?

(d) Religious Dream Visions

A medieval author who wished to write a religious narrative which was more personal and self-expressive than a Biblical paraphrase, a Saint's Life, or even a moral *examplum* could be, would probably present it as a Dream, since this freed him to be as inventive as he wished. This genre had two other differences from those we have been discussing so far in this chapter: the 'dreamer' narrates in the first person and so seems to represent the author's – or his *persona*'s – own consciousness, and secondly, since this *persona* need not understand or even finish his own dream, the poem he writes need not be didactic, but could simply recount a puzzling experience. We have already seen it used by writers of Debate Poetry (see above, p. 75), where its open-endedness was a clear advantage. In the next chapter we will see it used again and again by writers on love, where the autobiographical truth of the dreamer's experience is nearly always asserted (though we don't need to believe in it).

Though the form was thus very flexible, the writers using it were still working within a tradition. Love-dreams, as we shall see, generally imitate at some level the *Romance of the Rose*, written in thirteenth-century France and read widely throughout Europe (see pp. 202–5 below, for a fuller discussion). Although this tradition certainly influenced religious visions as well, religious dreams came from an older tradition (see the text-box on Religious Dream Visions, below). They are less playful, more rooted in the authority of Christian revelation, but they could still share the effect of personal disclosure and ambiguous meaning of the secular dream visions. In this section I will introduce some examples of the form, including *Piers Plowman*, and look in some detail at *Pearl*, as my Example Text. This is another poem from the manuscript which includes *Patience*, and is a very personal debate between a father and his dead child, which concludes with a Biblical vision of Heaven. Like *Piers Plowman* and *Wynnere and Wastoure* discussed in Chapter 3, it is a combination of debate and vision, and written in an updated form of the native alliterative tradition. The use of such traditions does not prevent such a poem from being strikingly original, or from being apparently self-expressive to a degree that we have so far only encountered in the mystics.

Religious Dream Visions

Religious and philosophical Dream Visions go back to Biblical and Classical times. Important Biblical models include the Vision of the Valley of Dry Bones (Ezekiel 37), of God enthroned in Heaven (Isaiah 6) from the Old Testament, and St Paul's Vision of Heaven (2 Corinthians 12) and St John's Apocalypse or showing of the end of the world and the New Jerusalem (Book of Revelation) from the New. The most important Classical Vision was Cicero's Dream of Scipio, which is all that survived in the Middle Ages of his *De Re Publica* (first century AD). It was a commentary on this Dream, by the fifth-century Roman author Macrobius, which in Chapter 3 was shown to have provided the Middle Ages with a theory of dreams. Macrobius discounts nightmares and waking dreams as insignificant, and divides significant dreams into three principal kinds:

- the *somnium* or enigmatic dream, which 'conceals with strange shapes and veils with ambiguity the true meaning of the information given'
- the *oraculum*, in which the dreamer is present and is addressed by authority figures who tell him 'what action to take or to avoid'
- the *visio* or prophetic vision.

Chaucer describes the *Somnium Scipionis* or *Cicero's Dream* in his *Parliament of Fowls*, part of which is an Oraculum where the authority-figure is Scipio himself.

These categories can be applied to dreams widely read in the later Middle Ages. For example:

> The Book of Revelation in the New Testament is a prophetic *Visio* but also a *Somnium* because the strange events can be interpreted allegorically (for example, the dragon with seven heads as the seven deadly sins). This is also true of the many visions found in the Old Testament, such as Pharaoh's dream of thin and fat cows which is explained by Joseph (Genesis 37 and 40).
>
> The immensely popular *Consolations of Philosophy* by the fourth-century writer Boethius is an *Oraculum* where the author is consoled for being in prison by Lady Philosophy.

The tradition of courtly Love Visions which expanded the genre from the thirteenth century is discussed in Chapter 7 (pp. 203–6). Some of their characteristic features, such as the poet's sleep beside a stream and his dream-entry into a beautiful garden full of birdsong and flowers, are used in late medieval religious Dream Visions.

Sources: Stahl (1952, ch. 3); Nolan (1977); Lynch (1988); Piehler (1971); Spearing (1976).

The most influential religious Dream Vision in the period is *Piers Plowman*, which survives in some 56 manuscripts, and was written between about 1378 and 1390 in three versions (see the text-box on Langland, above, p. 19). Following its publication several political and religious Dream Visions were written, including *Mum and the Sothsegger* and *Death and Liffe*, in the early fifteenth century (see Turville-Petre 1977). This may be partly due to the plain style of verse that Langland adopted, avoiding the specialist vocabulary and formulae of the more traditional alliterative style (see text-box below, p. 25), and so allowing for a wide audience with a taste for pious rather than Romance writing. The first part of the poem (B. Passus 1–7) is known as the *Visio*, and is the most accessible section, containing some of Langland's liveliest poetry; we have already looked at the Prologue and the Trial of Lady Meed in Chapter 3, and the Ploughing of the Half-acre in Chapter 1. These events took place while the narrator or Dreamer was supposedly asleep in the Malvern Hills, and are structured as two Visions in which the Dreamer plays little part. I now want to give a brief sense of the structure of the rest of the poem, the part known as the *Vita* (B. Passus 8–20). Here the Dreamer has six more Visions, in which he now plays an active role, pursuing a personal and life-long search for Do-well (moral and religious rectitude), in the kind of allegorical pilgrimage that the French author Deguileville had made popular with his *Pilgrimage of the Human Life* (1330). These dreams are constructed as a series of debates with authoritative and more ambiguous allegorical figures, in the manner of an *Oraculum*, interrupted by the more active and often allegorical scenes characteristic of a *Somnium*. We move towards a Sixth Vision of the Life and Death of Christ, including a scene in Hell where the Four Daughters of God debate the justice of Christ's atonement, before he appears himself and frees the souls trapped by Original Sin (B.18; C.20). This dramatic scene is inspired by Grosseteste's depiction of the Four Daughters of God in the *Cursor Mundi* (see above, p. 174; compare the debate between Christ and Lucifer in the York Mystery Cycle *Harrowing of Hell*). The last two Passus of the poem, however, show two apocalyptic visions of the establishment and disintegration of the contemporary Church, and end with the Dreamer once again taking to the road to seek for Truth:

> 'By Crist!' quod Conscience tho, 'I wole bicome a pilrym,
> And walken as wide as the world lasteth,
> To seke Piers the Plowman, that Pryde myghte destruye,' ...
> And sithe he gradde after Grace, til I gan awake. (B.20.281–7)
>
> *sitthe*: the; *gradde*: cried

Through all the visions the mysterious figure of Piers Plowman comes and goes, appearing sometimes as the common man, sometimes as Jesus, sometimes as the Pope; is he an embodiment of the *Dowel* that the poet seeks? Or the spirit of God working within every man? This figure, as well as the shifting movement and ambiguities of the poem, give it some characteristics of a real dream.

I shall now look in more detail at a poem which was written at about the same time as *Piers Plowman* but in a different alliterative tradition by a poet who uses the Dream Vision in a less didactic way. This, the last of my religious stories, will then bring us back to the kind of expressive and visionary language we considered in the last chapter.

Example Text: *Pearl*

The *Pearl*-poet, who was introduced in the previous section (p. 175), uses all the three kinds of dream in a progression through the extraordinarily complex and decorative stanzaic alliterative poem which is the first in the Cotton Nero A.X (see text-box below, p. 206). It opens like a love-dream, in which the narrator, suffering *luf-daungere* from the maiden's loss, falls asleep beside a stream, and sees a vision of a beautiful woman in a fantastic landscape. He recognises her at once as the two-year-old child (483) whose death has so filled him with grief, and addresses her familiarly in the second person. She, however, acts as his mentor, making this an *oracular* in Macrobius' categories (see text-box above). Always literal-minded, he is at first delighted that he seems to have recovered her, but he quickly learns that she is in a better world, and that it would be selfish as well as futile to wish her back in this one. At this point the poem is a consolation-dream like Boethius' *Consolation of Philosophy*, but after the poet has been further enlightened about the child's situation, it becomes a *visio* or prophetic revelation. With all the authority of St John's Apocalypse, parts of which are translated and paraphrased, the poet conveys a sense of the glory of Heaven, and when the dreamer tries to cross the stream to it and to reach his Pearl, he awakens.

Like the *Vita* of *Piers Plowman*, the poem is constructed as a journey, in which each stage has an appropriate setting. The dreamer falls asleep in a literal 'spot' or place (on the burial mound of the little girl), its secondary meaning of 'flaw' or 'strain' also present to suggest the mortal limits of human life. The maiden, by contrast, inhabits a beautiful dream landscape, first seen adorned like an art object, which has more permanence (Section 2), and then as a city of jewels and light, which suggests an eternal perfection beyond nature. We witness these three locations through the eyes of the dreamer, sharing, as Stanbury argues, his moving gaze with a realistic perspective rarely found in medieval literature (1991, ch. 2).

The journey proceeds in a series of contrasts. When the dreamer falls asleep in the graveyard, the contrast is one between the real and the imagined worlds, and between the dreamer's grief and the maiden's calm joy (*Pensyf, payred, I am forpayned / And thou in a lyf of lykyng lyghte*: I was pensive, enclosed and very unhappy while you lived a life of joy: 246–7). As the poem develops into the consolation dialogue, the contrast is seen to be between the dreamer's human expectations and the looking-glass world inhabited by the maiden. He expects God only to reward the virtuous, and only according to the amount of the virtue, and that his daughter, if she is in heaven, will be at the bottom of the hierarchy. She explains that *The innosent is ay saf by ryght* (694), and that there is no distinction made between the rewards earned by the virtuous, the penitent, and the innocent, and that she is one of the 144,000 virgin brides of the Lamb of God. In the third and most visionary part of the dream, the contrast is between the innocence of the maidens, who have acquired no fault or blemish, and the perfection of the Lamb, who is blemished by the wound in his side (1135–6). Whereas the maidens are white and covered with pearls, the Lamb is a source of light, and his red blood (as the maiden explains at 649–55) washes sinful mankind and fits them for heaven. The maidens, the children who die in babyhood, have had the image of God restored by baptism; the dreamer and his fellow-Christians have had it restored by the sacraments, but the Lamb of God is the paradigm from which such images are made; where they represent an absence of fault, he represents the source of goodness.

The contrasts in each part of the poem are conveyed visually by the contrast between the three settings. The graveyard is filled with living flowers (*Gilofre, gyngure and gromylyoun*: wallflowers, ginger and gromwell, 143); the dream landscape is more like an adorned art object, with crystal cliffs, blue woods and silver leaves (74–84). The final landscape is even less natural, taken as it is from a Biblical book, like a visualisation of an illuminated manuscript (985ff.). We may admire this progression without wishing to share in it, and will probably empathise with the dreamer's resistance to losing his particular affection for his daughter. The dream is broken when he demonstrates his inability to resign his Pearl to this strange country and its stranger inhabitants. The poet's apparent recognition that the reader may prefer a living girl in a living landscape to a dead girl in a visionary landscape, however truly splendid, makes the poem a true depiction of grief as much as it is a consolation for that grief.

Questions on *Pearl*

- How do the link-words [linking sections] and refrain lines [at the end of each stanza] carry the themes forward, and help to delineate the differences between earth and heaven (e.g., see if 'the refrain-words apply differently to the Dreamer and to the Maiden', as suggested by Davenport 1978, p. 43)?
- Look in detail at how the dreamer's eye moves over the landscapes he moves through, and discuss the interrelation of the real and the imagined. His focalisation of landscape is discussed in detail in Stanbury (1991).
- Analyse the relationship between the dreamer and the maiden as it changes through the poem, and see how this externalises the changing stages of grief and consolation. Perhaps comparing the poem to Chaucer's *Book of the Duchess* (but see Spearing's suggestion that he is an 'unreliable narrator', 1997)?
- Compare *Pearl* with some of the other religious visions you have read. How does the *Cloud*-author's refusal to visualise God, and his resistance to figurative language, compare with the *Pearl*-author's surreal landscapes and the *Pearl*-maiden's defiance of logic? How does the discussion of salvation by works or by grace

compare with Julian's conviction that 'all shall be well' in spite of human sin?
- Is this story another *exemplum* of impatience, like Jonah's story in *Patience*? Is it significant that both these characters are male?

Texts, Sources and Further Reading

Texts

(For Chaucer texts, see Chapter 4.)

Delaney, S. (1992) *A Legend of Holy Women: A Translation of Osbern Bokenham's Legends of Holy Women* (University of Notre Dame Press).

Kolve, V. A. (ed.) (2005) *Geoffrey Chaucer: The Canterbury Tales: Nine Tales and the General Prologue* (Norton Critical Editions, Norton).

Laskaya, A. and Salisbury, E. (eds) (1995) Émaré (from *The Middle English Breton Lay*), (TEAMS Middle English Texts, http://d.lib.rochester.edu/teams/text/laskaya-and-salisbury-middle-english-breton-lays-emare). This is the text used for quotation.

Mills, M. (ed.) (1973) *Six Middle English Romances* (Everyman).

Morse, R. (ed.) (1975) *St Erkenwald* (D. S. Brewer).

Peck, R. (1991) *The Middle English Metrical Paraphrase of the Old Testament* (http://d.lib.rochester.edu/teams/text/peck-heroic-women-middle-english-metrical-paraphrase-of-the-old-testament-introduction).

Serjeantson, M. (ed.) (1938) *Legendys of Hooly Wummen by Osbern Bokenham* (Early English Text Society, EETS o.s. 206).

Stahl, W. (1952) *Commentary on the Dream of Scipio by Macrobius* (Columbia University Press).

Whaley, G. et al. (eds) (2004) *Saints' Lives in Middle English Collections* (TEAMS Middle English Texts).

Winstead, K. (ed. and transl.) (2011) *John Capgrave: The Life of St Katherine of Alexandria* (University of Notre Dame Press).

Saints' Lives

(See also, the Chaucer texts below.)

Brenau, A. (2006) 'Gender and sexuality', in Salih, S. (ed.), *The Companion to Middle English Hagiography* (D. S. Brewer).

Delaney, S. (1992) 'Introduction', in *A Legend of Holy Women: A Translation of Osbern Bokenham's Legends of Holy Women* (University of Notre Dame Press).

Delaney, S. (1998) *Impolitic Bodies: Poetry, Saints, and Society in Fifteenth-century England* (Oxford University Press).

Heffernan, T. (1988) *Sacred Biography: Saints and Their Biographers* (Oxford University Press).

Pearsall, D. (1970) *John Lydgate* (Routledge).

Pearsall, D. (1975) 'John Capgrave's *Life of St Katharine* and popular Romance style', *Medievalia et Humanistica*, 6, pp. 121–37.

Salih, S. (2001) *Versions of Virginity in Late Medieval England* (D. S. Brewer).

Salih, S. (ed.) (2006) *A Companion to Middle English Hagiography* (D. S. Brewer).

Sanok, C. (2002) 'Performing feminine sanctity in late medieval England: Parish Guilds, Saints' Plays, and *The Second Nun's Tale*', *Journal of Medieval and Early Modern Studies*, 32(2), pp. 269–304.

Sanok, C. (2007) *Her Life Historical: Exemplarity and Female Saints' Lives in Late Medieval England* (University of Pennsylvania Press).

Scanlon, L. and Simpson, J. (eds) (2006) *John Lydgate: Poetry, Culture and Lancastrian England* (University of Notre Dame Press).

Simpson, J. (2009) 'John Lydgate', in Scanlon L. (ed.), *Cambridge Companion to Medieval English Literature 1100–1500* (Cambridge University Press; also available as Cambridge Companions Online).

Popular Romances

Bennett, J. (1986) *The Oxford History of English Literature: Middle English Literature* (Oxford University Press).

Black, N. (2003) *Medieval Narratives of Accused Queens* (University of Florida Press).

Bliss, J. (ed.) (2008) *Naming and Namelessness in Medieval Romance* (D. S. Brewer).

Brewer, D. (1988) *Studies in Medieval English Romances: Some New Approaches* (D. S. Brewer).

Heffernan, T. J. (ed.) (1985) *The Popular Literature of Medieval England* (Tennessee Studies in Literature, University of Tennessee Press).

Hopkins, A. (2002) 'Female vulnerability as catalyst in Middle English Breton lays', in Hardman, P. (ed.), *The Matter of Identity in Medieval Romance* (D. S. Brewer).

Orme, N. (1973) *English Schools in the Middle Ages* (Methuen).

Pearsall, D. (1974) 'John Capgrave's *Life of St Katharine* and popular Romance style', *Medievalia et Humanistica*, 6, pp. 121–37.

Pearsall, D. (1977) *Old English and Middle English Poetry* (Routledge).

Pearsall, D. (1988) 'The development of Middle English Romance', in Brewer, D. (ed.), *Studies in Medieval English Romance: Some New Approaches* (D. S. Brewer).

Pearsall, D. (1990) 'Chaucer's religious tales: a question of genre', in Benson, C. D. and Robertson, E. (eds), *Chaucer's Religious Tales* (D. S. Brewer).

Reiss, E. (1985) 'Romance', in Heffernan, T. J. (ed.), *The Popular Literature of Medieval England* (Tennessee Studies in Literature, University of Tennessee Press).

Robson, M. (1996) 'Cloaking desire: re-reading "Émaré"', in Fellows, J. et al. (eds), *Romance Reading on the Book: Essays on Medieval Narrative presented to Maldwyn Mills* (University of Wales Press).

Dream Vision and *Pearl*-poet

Andrew, M. (1997) 'Theories of authorship', in Brewer, D. and Gibson, J. (eds), *A Companion to the Gawain-poet* (D. S. Brewer).

Barr, H. (2000) 'Pearl or "The Jeweller's Tale"', *Medium Aevum*, 69(1), pp. 59–79.

Beal, Jane (2003) 'The Pearl-Maiden's two lovers', *Studies in Philology*, 100(1), pp. 1–21.

Bennett, J. M. (2012) 'Death and the Maiden', *Journal of Medieval and Early Modern Studies*, 42(2), pp. 269–305.

Bloomfield, J. (2011) 'Stumbling toward God's Light: The *Pearl* Dreamer and the impediments of hierarchy', *Chaucer Review*, 45, pp. 390–410.

Bowers, J. (2001) *The Politics of Pearl: Court Poetry in the Age of Richard II* (D. S. Brewer).
Bowers, J. (2012) *An Introduction to the Gawain Poet* (University of Florida Press).
Brewer, D. and Gibson, J. (eds) (1997) *A Companion to the Gawain-poet* (D. S. Brewer).
Burrow, J. (2012) 'Thinking in poetry: three medieval examples. 1: Pearl and Piers Plowman; 2: St Erkenwald' in *English Poets in the Late Middle Ages: Chaucer, Langland and Others* (Ashgate Variorum).
Coley, D. (2013) 'Pearl and the narrative of Pestilence', *Studies in the Age of Chaucer*, 35, pp. 209–62.
Cox, C. (1998) 'Pearl's 'precios pere': gender, language, and difference', *Chaucer Review*, 32(4), pp. 377–90.
Davenport, W. A. (1978) *The Art of the Gawain-poet* (Athlone).
Elliott, R. (1997) 'Landscape and geography', in Brewer, D. and Gibson, J. (eds), *A Companion to the Gawain-poet* (D. S. Brewer).
Hanna, R. (1978) 'Some commonplaces of late medieval Patience discussions: an introduction', in Schiffhorst (ed.), *The Triumph of Patience: Medieval and Renaissance Studies* (University of Florida Press).
Kirk, E. (1978) 'Patience in *Piers Plowman*', in Schiffhorst (ed.), *The Triumph of Patience: Medieval and Renaissance Studies* (University of Florida Press).
Kleine, D. (2003) 'Female childhoods', in Dinshaw, C. and Wallace, D. (eds), *The Cambridge Companion to Medieval Women's Writing* (Cambridge University Press).
Lynch, A.(1988) *The High Medieval Dream Vision* (Oxford University Press).
Newhauser, (1997) 'Scriptural and devotional sources', in Brewer, D. and Gibson, J. (eds), *A Companion to the Gawain-poet* (D. S. Brewer).
Nolan, B. (1977) *The Gothic Visionary Perspective* (Princeton University Press).
Piehler, P. (1971) *The Visionary Landscape: A Study in Medieval Allegory* (Edward Arnold).
Putter, A. (1996) *An Introduction to the Gawain-poet* (Longman).

Riddy, F. (1997) 'Jewels in *Pearl*', in Brewer, D. and Gibson, J., *A Companion to the Gawain-poet* (D. S. Brewer).
Scanlon, L. (1994) *Narrative, Authority, and Power: The Medieval Exemplum and Chaucerian Tradition* (Cambridge University Press).
Spearing, A. (1976) *Medieval Dream Poetry* (Cambridge University Press).
Spearing, A. (1997) Poetic identity', in Brewer, D. and Gibson, J. (eds), *A Companion to the Gawain-poet* (D. S. Brewer).
Terrell, K. (2008) 'Rethinking the "Corse in clot": cleanness, filth, and bodily decay in *Pearl*', *Studies in Philology*, 105(4), pp. 429–47.
Turville-Petre, T. (1977) *The Alliterative Revival* (D. S. Brewer).

Chaucer's *Second Nun's Tale, Prioress' Tale, Man of Law's Tale* and *Clerk's Tale*

Ashton, G. (2000) 'Her father's daughter: the re-alignment of father–daughter kinship in three Romance tales', *Chaucer Review*, 34, pp. 416–27.
Barlow, G. (2010) 'A thrifty tale: narrative authority and the competing values of the *Man of Law's Tale*',*Chaucer Review*, 44, pp. 397–420.
Benson, D. and Robertson, E. (1990) *Chaucer's Religious Tales* (D. S. Brewer).
Boitani, P. and Mann, J. (2003) *The Cambridge Companion to Chaucer*, 2nd edn (Cambridge University Press).
Brown, P. (2000) *A Companion to Chaucer* (Blackwell).
Collette, C. (1990) 'Approaches to the *Prioress' Tale* and the *Second Nun's Tale*', in Benson, D. and Robertson, E. (eds), *Chaucer's Religious Tales* (D. S. Brewer).
Cooper, H. (1989) *The Canterbury Tales* (Oxford Guides to Chaucer, Oxford University Press).
Ellis, R. (1986) *Patterns of Religious Narrative in the Canterbury Tales* (Croom Helm).
Edwards, A. (1990) 'Critical approaches to the *Man of Law's Tale*', in Benson, D. and Robertson, E. (eds), *Chaucer's Religious Tales* (D. S. Brewer).
Erler, P. and Kowaleski, M. (eds) (1988) *Women and Power in the Middle Ages* (University of Georgia Press).

Evans, R. et al. (eds) (2003) *Medieval Virginities* (University of Toronto Press).
Goodwin, A. (2006) 'Chaucer's *Clerk's Tale*: sources, influences, and allusions', *Studies in the Age of Chaucer*, 28, pp. 231–5.
Gray, D. (2003) *The Oxford Companion to Chaucer* (Oxford University Press).
Grossi, J. (2002) 'The Unhidden Piety of Chaucer's "Seint Cecilie"', *Chaucer Review*, 36(3), pp. 298–309.
Hansen, E. (1988) 'The power of silence: the case of the Clerk's Griselda', in Erler, P. and Kowaleski, M. (eds), *Women and Power in the Middle Ages* (University of Georgia Press).
Hirsh, J. (1990) 'The Second Nun's Tale', in Benson, D. and Robertson, E. (1990) *Chaucer's Religious Tales* (D. S. Brewer).
Huppé, R. (1964) *A Reading of the Canterbury Tales* (State University of New York Press).
Krug, R. (2010) 'Natural feeling and unnatural mothers', in Toswell, M. and Tolmie, J. (eds) *Laments for the Lost in Medieval Literature* (Brepols).
Lavezzo, K. (2002) 'Beyond Rome: mapping gender and justice in the *Man of Law's Tale*', *Studies in the Age of Chaucer*, 24, pp. 149–80.
Mann, J. (1991) *Geoffrey Chaucer: Feminist Readings* (Harvester).
McKinley, K. (1998) '*The Clerk's Tale*: hagiography and the problematics of lay sanctity', *Chaucer Review*, 33, pp. 90–111.
Mitchell, J. A. (2005) 'Chaucer's *Clerk's Tale* and the question of ethical monstrosity', *Studies in Philology*, 102(1), pp. 1–26.
Morgan, G. (2010) 'Chaucer's Man of Law and the Argument for Providence', *Review of English Studies*, 61(248), pp. 1–33.
Morse, C. (1990) 'Critical approaches to the *Clerk's Tale*', in Benson, D. and Robertson, E. (eds), *Chaucer's Religious Tales* (D. S. Brewer).
Oppell, J. (1993) 'St Jerome and the history of sex', *Viator*, 24, pp. 11–22.
Pearsall, D. (1985) *The Canterbury Tales* (Unwin Critical Library, Allen and Unwin).
Phillips, H. (2010) *Chaucer and Religion* (D. S. Brewer).
Saunders, C. (2004) 'Chaucer's Romances', in Sanders, C. (ed.), *A Companion to Romance: From Classical to Contemporary* (Blackwell).
Saunders, C. (2006) *A Concise Companion to Chaucer* (Blackwell).

Scanlon, L. (2009) *The Cambridge Companion to Medieval English Literature, 1100–1500* (Cambridge University Press).

Simpson, J. (2006) 'Chaucer as European writer', in Lerer, S. (ed.), *Yale Companion to Chaucer* (Yale University Press).

Sledd, J. (1953) 'The *Clerk's Tale*: the monster and the critics', *Modern Philology*, 51, pp. 73–82.

Staley, Lynn. (2002) 'The man in foul clothes and a late fourteenth-century conversation about sin', *Studies in the Age of Chaucer*, 24, pp. 1–47.

Stanbury, D. (1991) *Seeing the Gawain-poet: Description and the Act of Perception* (University of Pennsylvania Press).

Stanbury, S. (2010) 'The *Man of Law's Tale* and Rome', *Exemplaria*, 22, pp. 119–37.

Watt, Diane (1997) *Medieval Women in their Communities* (University of Toronto Press).

Chapter 7

Aristocratic Love

The writing about love in the later Middle Ages which has survived is remarkably homogeneous and remarkably European. A few songs and folk tales which seem to be a part of an English oral tradition do survive (see pp. 37, 127). But it was in Europe that human love had been ennobled into art, and some of the most striking and sophisticated Middle English poetry is written within the European tradition of *fin amour* or 'courtly love', either in texts wholly concerned with love, or as part of the Chivalric Romances I will be discussing in the next chapter. What this tradition provided was an intellectually and imaginatively rich alternative to the strictly Christian valuing of passionate human love only when directed towards God or the family. Instead, philosophers, allegorists and poets had built on pagan and semi-pagan sources to build a proto-humanist tradition which honoured human passion for its own sake and as a mirror of a divine (but not specifically Christian) love. This was an approach which would develop into Renaissance humanism in the Italy of the later fifteenth century. I have called this chapter 'Aristocratic Love' partly with reference to the lovers within these texts, who are generally (if vaguely) 'noble', to distinguish their stories clearly from the sexual comedy associated with the 'low-life' characters discussed in chapter 4. But I also want to indicate that these final two chapters will discuss the reading of the highest classes, the wealthy gentry and the aristocrats, which included the men and women who commissioned and purchased lavish manuscripts of Saints' Lives and Romances and the works of Chaucer, Gower and their followers. This group, as I will be explaining (pp. 239–40 below), was itself diverse, and of course there was no reason why texts about love should not also be enjoyed by people of a lower social status; Absalom the Town Clerk in the *Miller's Tale* was clearly modelling his wooing on *fin amour*. And this sophisticated readership was destined to become vastly more diverse with the bringing of printing to England by Caxton in 1475.

I will leave my usual historical contextualisation of this readership until the beginning of the next chapter, where literature more nearly reflects a country at war, and will start this chapter by outlining this European tradition of writing about love (section a). I will go on (section b) to show how the new attitude to love permeated the lyrics and shorter poems of the fourteenth and fifteenth centuries. I will then demonstrate (section c) how English and Scottish Love Visions develop what is essentially a French form with puzzled narrators confronted by images and events gleaned from an eclectic mixture of sources. Chaucer's Love Visions will be exemplified in an analysis of the *Parliament of Fowls* (late 1370s?), and I will end this section by describing some of the Love Visions that this text inspired in the English and Scottish Chaucerians of the fifteenth century. Finally (section d) I will provide my first survey of courtly Romance, the Love Romances of Chaucer and Henryson. (The second survey, of non-Chaucerian Chivalric Romance, will be the subject of the next chapter; non-courtly or Homiletic Romances were discussed in Chapter 6.) I will focus on what could be considered the finest text in this period: Chaucer's *Troilus and Criseyde* (1380s), a text which often makes a direct use of the sources discussed in section a. I will end the chapter by contrasting Chaucer's account of Criseyde with that of another Scottish Chaucerian, Henryson. His 'sequel' to Chaucer's Romance, *The Testament of Cressid* (later fifteenth century), is my third Example Text. It takes the story into a new direction, and demonstrates how varied and inspiring was Chaucer's influence.

(a) The European Tradition of Writing about Love

The multiplicity of sources in this tradition helps to explain the multiplicity of genres we encounter, often in a single text, and the presence of ambiguities and even contradictions within it. In particular there is a problem about the divinity of Love in these extended poems. Is Love a cosmic force, described by philosophers and scientists, by which the

Lord of the Universe rules His creation? Or is it the pagan God of Love, Cupid, or his mother, Venus, as fickle as Fortune herself, who embody the physical desire vilified by such theologians as St Jerome and Gregory the Great? Or should Love be seen as only a social construct, the kind of human good promoted by the pagan Stoics? The different sources I will outline below promote different answers to the question of the nature and divinity of love, and its positive or negative effects on human beings. I will divide these into three groups: Classical and late Classical texts (1BC–6AD), medieval Latin and French allegories and 'handbooks' on the Art of Love (twelfth and thirteenth centuries), and European Love Visions and Romances from the fourteenth century (C. S. Lewis 1936 and 1964, still gives the most readable account of these texts, but see also Taylor 1996).

(i) Classical and post-Classical texts

(1) Ovid

Publius Ovidius Naso (43BC–18AD) wrote three light-hearted poetic treatises on love, the *Ars Amatoria*, the *Amores*, and the *Remedia Amoris* (the *Art of Love, Love Affairs,* and the *Remedy for Love*). He also told tragic stories of love, such as the *Heroides* (*Heroines*) and the love stories included in *Metamorphoses* (*Transformations*). These texts were extremely popular in the later Middle Ages, and their influence on such medieval texts as Andreas Capellanus' *Ars Amandi* and Guillaume's *The Romance of the Rose* is clear (see below). As Calabrese, one of a number of modern critics exploring Chaucer's debt to Ovid, puts it:

> Ovid takes his place in a spectrum of medieval texts in any number of guises: noble author of history, doctor of love, father of anti-feminist love, advocate of female power, prophet of mutability, and, at times, dreaded corruptor of youth and peer of Satan. (Calabrese 1994, p. 1)

It was, however, more likely to have been Ovid's style and wit, rather than his attitude to women, which attracted Chaucer (see Simpson 2006, for a detailed discussion).

(2) Cicero's *Dream of Scipio* and Macrobius' *Commentary*

The first-century BC Latin writer and politician Cicero described, in *De Re Publica*, a dream in which his adoptive grandfather, Scipio Africanus, showed him a Platonic cosmos and taught him the importance of serving the 'common profit' of all mankind. The fifth-century Latin writer Macrobius produced a *Commentary* on this dream which was immensely popular in the Christian Middle Ages, partly because of its vision of an earth-centred Universe moved by God, and partly because it includes a pseudo-science of dream-categories useful to the writers of all kinds of Dream Visions (see p. 185). It thus has a direct influence on many of the Love Visions described below, and Chaucer opens his *Parliament of Fowls* as if writing a sequel to it.

(3) Boethius' *Consolation of Philosophy*

This sixth-century Latin work survives in more European manuscripts than any other apart from the Bible. It is well worth reading both for its beauty and wisdom and for the light it throws on such important Chaucerian texts as the *Knight's Tale* and *Troilus and Criseyde*. It consists of a dialogue between Boethius, a statesman in post-Empire Rome, unjustly imprisoned by his pagan ruler, and Philosophy. He is tormented by the conviction that Fortune and not God rules the affairs of men, and discusses this with Philosophy, who argues that God's Love does indeed determine what is going to happen. She (Philosophy) describes God's Love as a cosmic force which holds all creation together, rather as we describe the (still mysterious) law of gravity. The text includes several hymns to love, which are used by Petrarch and Boccaccio and then by Chaucer, to assert that what binds lovers together is not just a natural or social attraction, but a divine power working through them: '*O weleful weere mankynde / yif thilke loue that gouerneth heuene gouerned[e] yowre corages*' (*weleful*, joyful; *corages*, hearts; Chaucer's *Boece* II, *metrum* 8). Boethius was a Christian, but here he is writing as a Platonic philosopher, and so was able to give the Christian West a non-theological account of divine love.

(ii) 12th- and 13th-century Love Allegories and Handbooks

(1) Alain of Lille, *The Complaint of Nature*

This allegory from the twelfth-century 'Chartrian Renaissance' must stand for all the others, one or two as influential as Alain's. Here we meet Nature, God's deputy on earth, as the director and regulator of three artisans, Venus, Hymen (God of Marriage) and Cupid, who carry out Love's work from the suburbs of the Universe. This 'Trinity' creates all living things, but Nature complains (as Philosophy did in Boethius' *Consolation*) that she is unable to bind mankind into the happy unions or just societies enjoyed by the rest of Creation:

> All things are, by the law of their being, held subject to my laws, and ought to pay to me a rightful and established tribute ... but from this general rule Man alone is excluded by an abnormal exception. He, stripped of the cloak of decency ... dares to stir tumult and strife ... (Halsall, 1996)

Jean de Meun included some 5000 lines from this text in his *Roman de la Rose* continuation, where Chaucer might have read it before including the character of Nature in his *Parliament of Fowls*.

(2) Andreas Capellanus, *Ars Amandi*

This widely read and translated thirteenth-century Latin treatise can be enjoyed as a handbook to courtly love. At its centre in the second half of Book II is a series of 'judgments' before the noble ladies of the Countess Marie de Champagne, of whose court Andreas was a part. (Although Marie did indeed rule for six years after the death of her husband in 1181, it is not known if she really held the kind of love courts he describes in his book.) Andreas precedes this account by a dialogue between himself and his pupil Walter about the right conduct to be pursued in affairs of love. In Book I the lover is taught how to choose his lady, respecting true goodness rather than mere nobility or riches, and how to woo her by a demonstration of his personal attractiveness, his fluency, his valour and his virtue. In the first half of Book II she seems to have been won, and the lover is advised how to keep and even to increase their love, and to keep it secret. This Book ends with 31 'Rules of honest love'. (These procedures and rules are satirised in such texts as the *Miller's Tale*.) But in Book III Andreas denounces the kind of love he has been describing as illicit and sensual – though in fact it has been both idealistic and often chaste. It is tempting to assume that he condemns *fin amour* because it is adulterous, for throughout he has insisted that lovers cannot be married as the lady's love must be freely given, whereas in marriage she is compelled to love. Indeed, Judgment 19 insists that a lady who marries her knight must then accept another admirer, because 'love cannot extend its domination to married couples' (*On Love*, p. 267 – presumably because the husband now dominates instead). But the chief reason why Andreas turns against human love of this kind is that it distracts a cleric such as himself from the true devotion which should be offered to God. Andreas has thus carved out the territory, avoiding both religious devotion and marriage, to be inhabited for the following centuries by this the noblest kind of love between human beings.

(3) The *Romance of the Rose*

After the Bible and Boethius' *Consolation*, the next most copied text appears to be the *Romance of the Rose*, surviving in more than 300 manuscripts, and translated or adapted from its original French into the important European languages. The poem is a composite of Guillaume de Lorris' original story (1–4068) written about 1230, plus Jean de Meun's 17,000-line continuation, made some fifty years later. The fourteenth-century English translation covers all of Guillaume's poem plus some selections from Jean de Meun's, and the first 1705 lines (Fragment A) are in Chaucer's dialect and style and may well be part of the translation that he claims to have made (in the *Legend of Good Women*, Prologue 255); their limpid couplets are a pleasure to read. The other two Fragments are probably parts of another complete translation (see Sutherland 1967, pp. xv–xviii). Chaucer's own work is, however, influenced by far more of the poem than this remaining Fragment might imply; not only does he borrow from Jean de Meun's satirical continuation in characters like the Wife of Bath and the Pardoner (see La Vieille and Faux-Semblaunt), but he uses Guillaume's allegorical method in his Love Visions, and images from the *Romance* in his own Romances.

The poem allegorises the progress of a love affair as the episodes in a dream. It first shows the Lover's social milieu by describing a garden which (like the court or the class or maybe merely the literature he inhabits) excludes the social ills of old age and poverty as well as the moral defects of hatred, avarice, hypocrisy ('Pope-holy') and the like. The garden belongs to 'Deduit' (Delight, but translated in the Middle English as Mirth), and the tiny wicket gate is guarded by Idleness, suggesting that only the leisured can afford the time to be in love. Having got inside, the Lover finds Mirth dancing with allegorisations of an ultra-polite social life (Courtesy, Sweet-looking, Candour etc.), but also with the more menacing figure of the God of Love (Cupid armed with arrows). Indeed, Cupid soon gives a personal, painful focus to the Lover's journey through the garden, for when he sees a rose-bed reflected in a crystal fountain (does this represent the Lady's eyes?) and 'chooses' a particular rose as the best, Cupid shoots him with the darts of Love. If the rose represents the Lady's love, the arrows represent the emotional development of a relationship from the first sight of beauty into companionship and love. The Lover swears fealty to the god of Love and his law, even if it means denying Reason (a representative of God) and accepting a life of unrequited longing. The Lover thereafter pursues the Lady, allegorically encountering her Fair-welcome (friendliness?), her Shame (timidity?), and her Daunger (her desire to remain in control? I am suggesting these interpretations tentatively, because the allegory is not explained, leaving the readers free to see their own experience in the story; see, for example, D. Kelly (1978, p. 89), for a different interpretation, suggesting Daunger represents 'aristocratic prerogatives'). It may have been this openness to interpretation which attracted Chaucer to this new genre of allegorical Love Vision. Guillaume's poem continues in this way until Jealousy discovers the Lover's pursuit of the Rose and claps her into a castle. The poem was left unfinished until Jean de Meun, a learned and anti-romantic cleric, continued it in a rather different spirit, making it a kind of encyclopaedia of secular satire which ends with the Lover achieving the Rose.

(iii) Some 14th-century European Love Visions and Romances

Following the extraordinary success of the *Romance of the Rose*, writers began to produce their own Love Visions. A group of such writers flourished in the decades before and during Chaucer's early career as a poet. Its leader, writing in the 1349s and 1350s, was Guillaume de Machaut (1300–77), followed in the next generation by Eustace Deschamps (1346–1406) and Jean Froissart (c. 1337–1405). The latter was a diplomat and historian as well as a poet, and he spent some years at the English court in the 1360s when Chaucer was beginning his career as a courtier and diplomat there. Froissart came from Hainault in Flanders, from where Chaucer's wife also came. The French Love Vision was generally set in a perfect spring garden full of flowers and birdsong, where running water could suggest tears or the separation of the dream from the real world. Here the Dreamer encounters various allegorical figures, including his own Lady, before whom he generally appears naive and timid. Both Machaut and Froissart wrote long narrative poems or *Dits* in which the Lover complains of the cruelty of Fortune, the intensity of his desire, the indifference of his Lady, and so forth, and is consoled by a Friend such as Esperance (Hope, see the *Remede de Fortune*) or the poet himself (see *La Fontaine Amoreuse*). The French Love Visions attracted Chaucer very much and, as we shall see, his first original significant works develop this genre. Their influence on European interpretation of dreams has been surprisingly long-lasting, as one can see from Freud's observation of some of the same symbols used to disguise suppressed desires (see his 'Symbolism in Dreams' and 'The Dream Work in Freud', in Strachey 1917).

In Italy it was shorter love poems and Romances which were developing, with Dante writing his great religious poem the *Comedia* as a tribute of personal love, Petrarch inventing the sonnet form, and Boccaccio the prose novella. Chaucer was introduced to the work of all three authors when he went to Italy in 1372–3 and 1378 on diplomatic missions, and he introduced much of what he had enjoyed to English readers through translations and adaptations. The encounter with Boccaccio's work in Italian was particularly fruitful, though Chaucer never acknowledged it, only referring to Boccaccio in *Troilus and Criseyde* as *myn auctor*, and even as *Lollius* (which might mean a liar; see p. 222). Boccaccio lived from 1313 to 1375, and his Italian (rather than Latin) works include the hundred tales of *The Decameron* (see above, p. 104) and the historical Romances *Teseida* and the *Filostrato*, which drew their stories from the Classical past rather than Arthurian legend. Lydgate, too, was to find Boccaccio an inspiration, though he never used him as a source. Boccaccio used love stories as a focus for his stories of Thebes and Troy, and was able to depict them in a realistic and contemporary way as well as using the traditions I have been outlining. For the Italians this direction of travel led towards humanism and the Renaissance. Although Chaucer, in his *retraction* at the end of the *Canterbury Tales*, asks for forgiveness for his secular works, which include *Troilus and Criseyde* and *Many a song and Many a lecherous lay* (Fr.10, 1088–9), he had made sure that English literature too should be part of this new European movement.

This survey of the European tradition of writing about love has inevitably taken us forward into the end of the Middle Ages. I will now return to the beginning of the fourteenth century in England, to see how English poetry was affected by it, and then move forward to Chaucer in the 1370s and 1380s, and to his imitators in the fifteenth century.

English Rhymed Forms

Lyrical Forms

French and Latin verse is easily rhymed, and developed several rhymed forms early. French *chansons* (courtly songs) of the fourteenth and fifteenth centuries were often written in three 'fixed forms' of increasing complexity: the *ballade* (three stanzas, each ending with a refrain), the *rondeau* (an 8-line stanza where the first two lines are repeated at the end), and the *virelai* (three stanzas beginning and ending with a refrain and using some of the refrain rhymes in the verse). Each of these forms had English equivalents and variations, and there were also other forms popular in England such as the *chanson d'aventure* (where the poet acts as an observer of a love situation), the *pastorelle* (a dialogue between a young man and a shepherdess), the *carol* (a round dance) and the *villanelle* (up to five 3-line stanzas with only two rhymes running throughout, and two alternating lines used as a refrain; Chaucer ends his *Parliament of Fowls* with one).

The rhythm of these forms was quite strict so that they could be set to music. Four-stressed lines with a 7- or 8-syllable count could be used in a variety of patterns. A line could begin with a stressed syllable (/ ' / ' / ' / ' – trochaic) as in **Len**ten is **com**e with **love** to **towne**, or begin with an unstressed syllable (' / ' / ' / ' / – iambic) as in An **hen**dy **hap** ich **habbe** i**hent** (see below for references). The trochaic lines (which begin with the stress) are the more musical ad rhythmic because in music the first beat of a bar tends to be the stressed.

Chaucer's poetic forms

Chaucer can be credited with introducing the ten-syllable *iambic pentameter*, probably in imitation of Italian poets, perhaps for the first time in the *Parliament of Fowls*: The **Lif** so **short**, the **craft** so **long** to **lere** (1). Unlike the four-stress line, the pentameter does not have a natural mid-line break, and so is more flexible and more like prose. Chaucer used it in a variety of ways. In the *General Prologue* he liked the *iambic couplet* with its possibilities of comic dialogue:

> He yaf nat of that text a pulled hen,
> That seith that hunters ben nat hooly men. (Fr.1, 177–9)

For more dignified narratives he preferred *rhyme royale*, an iambic five-stress line arranged in 7-line stanzas that rhyme ABABBCC (see the example above on p. 172). This was much imitated by his followers, particularly Lydgate.

Romance forms

Stress is probably a better indication of metre than syllable-count here, though the rhymed narratives are much tighter than the unrhymed alliterative verse discussed in the text-box on p. 25 above. Fourteenth-century English rhymed Romances at first used simple four-stress *couplets*, as in the Romance or 'Breton Lay' *Sir Orfeo*:

> He might se him bisides,
> Oft in hot undertides,
> The king o fairy with his rout
> Com to hunt him al about (*Sir Orfeo* 281–4)

In the middle of the century there also developed a native variant, the *tail-rhyme*, which used stanzas of 2 or 3 sections each, rhymed AAB,

CCB, DDB, the running B line having three stresses, while the other lines have four. An example is another supposed Breton Lay, the Romance *Émaré*:

> Jhesu, that ys kyng in trone,
> As Thou shoope bothe sonne and mone,
> And all that shalle dele and dyghte,
> Now lene us grace such dedus to done,
> In Thy blys that we may wone –
> Men calle hyt heven lyghte. (1–6)

(Both these Romances are discussed in Chapter 6.)

Sources: Duncan (2005); Dobbins, F. (2002) 'Chanson', in Latham, A. (ed.), *The Oxford Companion to Music* (Oxford Music Online); Moore (1951).

(b) English Love Lyrics of the 14th and 15th centuries

There is abundant evidence for an English tradition before Chaucer of love songs and dances, spread through Europe by the troubadours, minstrels and jongleurs who entertained the richer households from the thirteenth to the fifteenth centuries; retained minstrels even formed their own Guild in 1469 (see Moore 1951). Little of their material survives, apart from fragments jotted on flyleaves of more serious manuscripts (these fragmentary poems and the two collections I will mention are discussed in Scattergood 2005, pp. 47–65). The first is a small group of poems on a parchment strip (a minstrel's song sheet?) from about 1325 found in Bodleian MS Rawlinson D013. Burrow prints four of these in *English Verse* (1977), including the dance-song or 'carol' 'Maiden in the moor lay' (I.3) and this enigmatic symbolic poem:

> Alnighte by the rose
> Alnighte by the rose I lay
> Dorst ich noght the rose stele
> And yet I bar the flour away. (Burrow 1977, p. 5)
>
> *Dorst ich noght*: I dared not

The implication that the love is adulterous and that the rose represents the lady's free gift of her love, immediately reminds us of the *Romance of the Rose*. So it appears that English love lyrics give us very early evidence of the influence of the French tradition of *fin amour*. It may have been brought to England first by troubadours and minstrels, and consolidated by the contact between the English and Provençal courts in the thirteenth century.

The European nature of early love songs is further demonstrated by the second collection which is preserved, the fourteen secular *Harley Lyrics* included in British Library MS Harley 2253. This is virtually the only collection of love lyrics before Chaucer which survives, in a manuscript from about 1340 which includes the 'Song of the Husbandman' discussed in Chapter 1 and 'The Simonye' discussed in Chapter 3 (see pp. 83 and 74 above). The love lyrics use the French forms of *roundel* (with repeated refrain), *chanson d'aventure* (a narrative) and *pastorelle* (a seduction dialogue) among others, and they use French rhyming schemes often further decorated with thoroughly English alliteration (see the text-box on p. 25). The themes and methods clearly come from the European tradition of *fin amour* and include the spring opening which excludes the suffering lover from nature's happiness (e.g., No. 11, *Lenten ys com with loue to toune*); the lover's praise for each detail of his lady's body (e.g., No. 9, *A wayle whyt as whalles bone*: woman); comparing her to flowers and jewels (e.g., No. 3, *Ichot a burde in a bour*: woman); and entreating her to yield to his embraces, in a dialogue (e.g., No. 24, *My deth y loue, my lyf ich hate*). In spite of this conventionality of subjects, however, the lyrics are rarely stiff and often amusingly unexpected, giving glimpses of real feeling (see discussion in Pearsall 1977, pp. 125–9). No. 4, *Alysoun*, demonstrates some of these characteristics: the poem is an Anglicised *chanson*, written in a complex stanza-form with a refrain but also using alliteration as well as rhyme. It has a spring opening, compares the lady to flowers and birds, and complains of love sickness. It is, however, still fresh and lively:

> Bytuene Mersh ant Aueril,
> When spray biginneth to springe,
> The lutel fowl hath hire wyl
> On hyre lud to singe ...

> *An hendy hap ichabbe yhent,*
> *Ichot from heuene it is me sent;*
> *From alle wymmen mi loue is lent,*
> *Ant lyht on Alysoun ...*
>
> Nihtes when y wende ant wake,
> Forthi myn wonges waxeth won ...
> Hire swyre is whittore then the swon,
> Ant feyrest may in toune ...
>
> Geynest vnder gore,
> Herkne to my roun.
>
> *An hendy ...* etc. (Brook 1956, p. 33)

How convincing do you find the mixture of sorrow and joy here? Do the two lines before the final refrain suggest that she is already his anyway?

The higher prestige of the love lyric in the fifteenth century follows Chaucer's use of the form within his longer poems, for example the catalogue of the lady's beauty in the *Book of the Duchess*, or the songs and letters within *Troilus and Criseyde*. Shorter free-standing poems such as the *Complaint of Mars* read as intended for unwritten Dream Visions (see Quinn 1999, p. 384), or simply as experimental adaptations of the French 'complaint' genre. Some short poems, like *To Rosemounde*, seem to laugh at the lover:

> Nas never pyk walwed in galauntyne
> As I in love am walwed and iwounde (Fisher 1989, p. 695)
>
> *pyk walwed in galauntyne*: cooked pike wallowing in wine sauce

Cultural exchange between England and France during the Hundred Years War also helped the development of the English love poem (in France ten times the number of medieval lyrics – often with music – survive as in England; see Moore 1951). Charles Duke of Orleans, heir to the French throne, was a prisoner in England for twenty-five years (1415–49), during which time he wrote two hundred love poems in English, a number of which are included in the costly manuscript British Library Harley 682 (1440; see Gray 2005, pp. 134–9). Most of them have polished French equivalents; Charles seems to have translated them himself, not like the somewhat rougher and more lively English versions (see Davies 1964, pp. 181–4). The themes and methods of fifteenth-century love lyrics are not very different from those in the fourteenth-century *Harley Lyrics*, but it is interesting to compare the final effect of poems on similar subjects, and to see how the poet-lovers have changed. As the prestige of non-religious poetry rose, poets began to write on a wider variety of secular subjects apart from love and social or political satire (the poem *Swarte-smecked smithes* is one startling example (Davies 1964, No. 115; see p. 25 above), paving the way for the new individuality of Renaissance poetry.

(c) English and Scottish Love Visions

(i) Chaucer's Love Visions

Having travelled several times to France in the 1360s and 1370s, Chaucer could almost consider himself a member of the circle of French poets engaged in writing Love Visions (see above, p. 205, and Wimsatt 1968, ch. 6). His first important poem, the *Book of the Duchess,* written after the death of Blanche Duchess of Gaunt in 1368, was particularly influenced by Machaut and Froissart. Here he casts himself as a rather inept comforter, consoling the bereaved Duke of Gaunt, who is represented by a Man in Black. This is his most French Love Vision, but he returned to the Vision form again in the *House of Fame*, the *Parliament of Fowls*, and the rather later *Prologue to the Legend of Good Women* (all discussed in Williams 2006). These later Visions, though still showing French influence (see Wimsatt 1968, pp. 118–23), drew also on the learned traditions of writing that I described in Section a), some of which Chaucer had himself translated. Thus the *House of Fame* (mid-1370s?) is not a Love Vision, but an extraordinary pot-pourri of learning, centring on a moral vision of a Castle of Fame where statues of the great poets stand in glory. The *Parliament of Fowls*, discussed below as an Example Text, uses Cicero's *Dream of Scipio* and Macrobius' *Commentary* on it (see p. 201) to introduce a rather distasteful love garden ultimately derived from the *Romance of the Rose*, and then switches to Alain of Lille's vision of Nature, now presiding over an assembly of birds. This poem then becomes part of the tradition of Debate Poetry which had flourished in England before Chaucer introduced the European Love Vision into the literature (see Chapter 3, pp. 75). Chaucer's fourth and last Vision is the *Prologue to the Legend of Good Women*, which is at last like a Love Vision in that it centres on a dream of a beautiful girl, Queen Alceste, who instructs him to tell the stories of women who were faithful (though unhappy) lovers, to counteract the bad effect of his *Troilus and Criseyde*. However, this is much more like a religious vision of an authority figure like Lady Philosophy from Boethius' *Consolations* than a French dream of a desired woman, and like the other two later Visions, indicates the originality with which Chaucer developed the genre.

Example Text: The *Parliament of Fowls*

This amusing – if learned – poem is an excellent place to start one's reading of Chaucer beyond the *Canterbury Tales*. It is probably his first poem in his characteristic *rhyme royal* (the 7-line stanza rhymed ababbcc; see the text-box on English Rhymed Forms on p. 206). Its astrological references and subject suggest that it may have been written for the betrothal of Richard II to Anne of Bohemia in 1381/2, when Chaucer was living at court with his wife; though Benson (1999) and others place it in the early 1370s. It is intriguingly open-ended in its answer to the opening question of what love can be, and it culminates in a bird parliament so charming that (as we will see) it continued to be imitated by poets into the Renaissance.

The narrator is characterised as a bookworm who knows little about real-life love, and whose dream is confused rather than clarified by his eclectic knowledge of different 'authorities'. The first of these is the section of Cicero's *De Re Publica* used by Macrobius, in which Cicero dreamt of his adoptive grandfather, Scipio Africanus (see above, p. 201), a text which seems unlikely to provide an explanation of the paradoxical power of love:

> The dredful joye alway that slit so yerne,
> Al this mene I by Love. (*Parliament* 3–4)
>
> *The dredful joye alway that slit so yerne*: the fearful joy that always passes away so early

The narrator falls asleep after reading this book, and dreams that Africanus guides him through the planetary spheres towards heaven, which he warns him is only achieved by those who think of social duties rather than personal desire (see discussion in Olson 1980; St John 2000, pp. 127–8):

> what man, lered other lewed,
> That loved commune profit, wel ythewed,
> He sholde into a blisful place wende (46–8)
>
> *lered other lewed*: learned or ignorant; *commune profit, wel ythewed*: the good of the whole community, when endowed with virtue; *wende*: go

The narrator then dreams that Africanus leads him into a beautiful garden where the very trees seem to serve the common profit (176–82), and where the banks are full of flowers and the streams full of little lively fishes (182–9; compare 139). In the garden stands a temple, full of sighs and heat, where he sees both Venus and Priapus, and also some weeping lovers. Outside the temple can be found Bribery and Message-sending (*Meede and Messagerye* 228) and inside he hears agonised jealous groans – all of which might well suggest that any love to be had there must be adulterous and unhappy. Much of this section is adapted from the Temple of Venus section in Boccaccio's *Teseida* (the source of the *Knight's Tale*), which is itself derived from the *Romance of the Rose*, so this vision too is bookish; indeed, it is self-consciously literary. Should we condemn the literary tradition which celebrates an artificially-intensified and individualistic love? Are we more simply to see this scene as representing *likerous folk* (*Parliament of Fowls* 79)?

In the third and final part the narrator returns from the Temple to the beautiful garden and discovers another goddess, one who is far superior to Venus and indeed who controls both Venus and Cupid in yet another of Chaucer's bookish 'authorities' – the *Complaint of Nature* by Alain of Lille (see above, p. 202):

> And right as Alain in the 'Plainte of Kinde'
> Deviseth Nature in array and face,
> In swich array men mighte hire there finde.
> This noble emperesse (316–19)
>
> *'Plainte of Kinde'*: 'Complaint of Nature'; *Deviseth*: describes; *array*: clothes

However, Chaucer seems to leave his books at this point to describe a bird debate surely stemming from the early Middle English tradition which produced *The Owl and the Nightingale* (see the text-box on Debate Poetry, p. 75). He imagines that all the birds have come together under Nature's law to choose their mates on St Valentine's Day. They sit in a due order, which Chaucer has taken from the encyclopaedist Bartholomeus Anglicanus, and which categories them by their food or their habitat rather than putting them in a hierarchy of estates – a natural rather than a socially-imposed order. However, their society does include aristocrats, the birds of prey, and these seem determined to follow the rules of *fin amour* rather than the laws of nature. In the first place three eagles have each chosen the same *formel* or female eagle, and insist they will remain true even if they fail to win her. In the second place she herself chooses none of them, but asks to remain single for another year. What are we to make of this unnatural procedure? Do the eagles represent Mankind, who alone of all creatures refuses to follow Nature in Alain's poem, or to serve the 'common profit' of society valued by Cicero (see discussion in Aers 1981)? Or do they represent a higher kind of love, one more able to control physical needs than the procreative marriages that the lower orders of birds are eventually allowed to make:

> To every fowl Nature yaf his make
> By evene accord, and on hir way they wende.
> But Lord, the blisse and joye that they make,
> For eech gan other in his winges take,
> And with hir nekkes eech gan other winde,
> Thanking alway the noble queen of Kinde. (667–72)

Perhaps this *blisse and joye* is the real love which has eluded the narrator so long, and which he might have found in Alain's book, where Nature 'places lawful sexuality within the structure of marriage' (in contrast to Venus and her adulterers' Temple; see Edwards 1989, p. 138). The poem ends with a *villanelle* (see the text-box on p. 206) and presumably a dance.

Questions on the *Parliament of Fowls*

- Should this poem be related to the political debates discussed in Chapter 3? Can we relate the different contributions of the birds to political positions discussed at the time, for example on the right relation between the aristocracy and the commoners (see Olson 1980, p. 266)?
- How important is it that the female eagle is allowed to *choose* either one or none of her suitors? Is this a significant aspect of courtly love and does it relate at all to the choice that Chaucer also offers to the reader between different definitions of love?

(ii) Love Visions of English and Scottish Chaucerians

Chaucer's Love Visions, particularly the *Parliament of Fowls*, had an enormous influence on later poets, already familiar with some of the texts from the European tradition of love writing, and now struck by the original possibilities that Chaucer had opened up. The combination of French love lament with other forms, particularly the bird debate, and the much more learned writing on Divine Love found in Boethius or Alain of Lille, attracted the intellectuals of the late fourteenth and fifteenth centuries. These included three poets with close ties to the royal court at the turn of the century, John Clanvowe, John Lydgate and King James I of Scotland. James was imprisoned in London or Nottingham from 1409 until 1423, where he no doubt exchanged laments with the imprisoned heir to the French throne, Charles d'Orleans. Chaucer's influence, perhaps through James I, reached as far as the Scottish court, where he was imitated by later fifteenth-century poets like William Dunbar and Robert Henryson. Spearing argues (1976, pp. 169–70) that the best of these imitators also explored some of the new directions in which Chaucer was taking the form, such as increasing the distance between the narrator and the poet, or between periods of sleep and wakefulness, which allow for interpretative possibilities (see pp. 105–6 for Langland's development of such possibilities).

Among the English Chaucerians of the late fourteenth and fifteenth centuries, this distancing of author and narrator is exemplified in one of the earliest Love Visions to show Chaucer's influence: the *Book of Cupid* (or *The Cuckoo and the Nightingale*) was written by John Clanvowe (1341–91) towards the end of his life. Clanvowe was a personal friend of Chaucer at Richard II's court, and was one of the knights who are now thought to have had Lollard sympathies (see his religious treatise *The Two Ways*). The poem is a Love Vision which centres on a surprisingly balanced debate between two birds about the value of love. The humour and the ambiguities of Chaucer's bird debate are well caught, as the Dreamer and Nightingale enthuse about love while the Cuckoo is cynical, though more realistic. Although the Cuckoo is beaten physically at the end he does seem to express the feelings of his narrator more than do his romantic opponents.

John Lydgate

John Lydgate (1370–c. 1451), the most celebrated English poet of the fifteenth century, was a Benedictine monk, based at the great Abbey at Bury St Edmunds, which he had entered as a novice when he was only 15. He was far from being a cloistered monk, however, travelling extensively in Europe and living in London and at court until the late 1430s. His work was from the first much influenced by Chaucer in form and subject matter, though not in style as he was always considerably more ornate, rhetorical and verbose than his master (for discussion of his style, see essays in Scanlon 2006). His earlier works include courtly love poetry (such as the *Compleynt of a Loveres Lyfe*, and the *Temple of Glass* discussed below) and several Saints' Lives (see pp. 159–60, above). In 1412 he secured a commission from Henry V to write his *Troy Book*, a detailed translation, with additions, of Guido de Collonne's *Historia Destructionis Troiae*, which he completed in 1420. He then wrote (without commission) a companion piece, the *Siege of Thebes*, using the same French author as source (these are both discussed below, pp. 259–60). The success of these works meant that Lydgate acquired 'the de facto status of a public orator' (Pearsall 1970, p. 160), writing for a wide variety of occasions at the request of people, from the three Lancastrian kings and the Dukes of Warwick and Gloucester, down to wealthy London citizens. For example, he recorded in verse the important processions and pageants which welcomed Henry VI to London after his French coronation in 1432, and celebrated the opening of Parliament in 1417 with a 'London Mumming' (a mime with declaimed verse; see Benson 2006, pp. 152ff.) which recommended that the citizens use the Cardinal Virtues. Other Mummings, including those written for City Guilds, are discussed on p. 36 above. In his later years Lydgate somewhat withdrew from public life to Bury Abbey, where he continued to work on translations and amplifications (including Deguileville's three *Pilgrimage* poems, which Lydgate had started in 1426, and Boccaccio's *On the Falls of Illustrious Men*, which he called *The Fall of Princes*). It may have been then that he wrote the immensely popular *Life of Our Lady* (see below, p. 161).

Sources: Pearsall (1970); Simpson (2009); Benson (2006).

The more serious but less engaging John Lydgate (c. 1370–1451; see text-box above) was the most prolific of the Chaucerians, and also quick to imitate his master in Dream Visions. The ponderous *Temple of Glass* (c. 1401) was one of his earliest poems, and begins dramatically with a genuinely dream-like description of a blindingly-bright temple of Venus, which suggests to me that he had come across *Pearl* and is half-quoting *more and more*:

> And as I did approche
> Again the sonne that shone, me thought, so clere
> As eny cristal, and ever nere and nere
> As I gan neigh this grisli dredful place,
> I wex astonyed: the light so in my face
> Bigan to smyte, so persing ever in one
> On evere part, where that I gan gone,
> That I ne myght nothing [see], as I would,

> Abouten me considre and bihold
> The wondre hestres, for brightnes of the sonne;
>
> *Again*: against, away from; *in my face*: i.e. from the Temple; *so persing ever in one*: so continually piercing

However, after this opening the poem does little more than report the long laments of a pair of lovers before the statue of Venus, and allow them to be joined at the end of the poem.

The anonymous late fifteenth-century poem *The Floure and the Leafe*, once attributed to Chaucer, is in the Love Vision tradition, though not actually cast as a dream. Like the contemporary *Assembly of Ladies*, it claims to have been written by a woman, and describes an encounter in an idealised landscape between the Company of the Leaf and that of the Flower. The Leaf represents those who are strong, chaste and valorous, while the Flower suggests people who are pleasure-loving and weak. The Company of the Leaf protects the Company of the Flower from bad weather, before a nightingale explains the allegory. The refusal of the author to equate strength and weakness with gender here is interesting. *The Floure and the Leafe* leads us into the Renaissance development of courtly love.

Of the Scottish Chaucerians the most notable writer in the form was King James I, who did anything but distance himself from the narrator of his Love Vision, for *The Kingis Quair* (The King's Book) is frankly autobiographical. It is set (and probably at least partly written) in one of the castles in which James was imprisoned, where he writes a moving account of his life up until the moment when he sees a beautiful girl through his prison window. The proem and ensuing vision, like Chaucer's visions, draw on many sources, including Boethius' *Consolations*, the *Romance of the Rose* and its French imitations, and Chaucer's *Knight's Tale* and *Parliament of Fowls*. Thus, having fallen in love with the damsel, James wonders (like Palamon in the *Knight's Tale*) if she is a maid or a goddess, and feels himself to be more of a prisoner of love than of the English. After lying awake all night thinking of this maiden, he falls asleep and dreams of a Boethian ascent through the spheres (the supposed orbits of the Planets around the Earth) to the sphere and Temple of Venus. There he sees many mournful lovers (as Lydgate had in the

Temple of Glass), but, much more originally, he also sees (624ff.) different kinds of people of different ages for whom love has been a painful experience. These include those whose beloved has died, and those who have been separated from their lover by a restrictive marriage. These are perhaps familiar literary situations, but more startlingly realistic are the complaints of those who have been tricked into a celibate life, or into a marriage where their hearts could not be contented:

> Sum bene of thaim that haldin were full lawe
> And take by frendis – nothing thay to wyte –
> In youth from lufe into the cloister quite: ...
>
> And othir bene amongis thame also
> That cummyn ar to court on Lure to pleyne,
> For he thair bodyes had bestowit so:
> Quhare bothe thair hertes gruch[en] there ageyne. (626–34)

The dream ends with James appealing to Venus, who offers Good Hope to help him; at the end of the poem Fortune allows him to achieve his love. James was in fact released in 1423 back to Scotland, and married Joan of Beaufort on his way – a marriage which was apparently very happy until he was murdered in 1437.

Fifty years later another Scottish poet, William Dunbar, had established an important position for himself at the court in Edinburgh. His *Thistle and the Rose* is a political dream as much as a Love Vision, for it recounts the union in 1503 of Margaret Tudor (the Rose) towith James IV King of Scotland. It too is modelled on the *Parliament of Fowls*, though Nature now crowns the Thistle (James) as king of the plants and tells him to love none but the Rose (Margaret). It was often the Scottish Chaucerians who took up Chaucer's challenge not just to write in the new love idiom of Europe, but to do so in an original and unexpected way. This is particularly true of Dunbar's contemporary Robert Henryson (fl. 1460–1500), who wrote a sequel to Chaucer's *Troilus and Criseyde*, *The Testament of Cressid*, which will be discussed at the end of the next section.

(d) English and Scottish Love Romances

I will now turn to what we might call 'romantic fiction' and look at texts which tell the stories of lovers in sophisticated and ground-breaking ways. I have looked at the Sentimental Romances and Breton Lays already in Chapter 6, and will look in detail at Chivalric Romances in Chapter 8. But now I want to look at the Love Romances of Geoffrey Chaucer and his admirer Robert Henryson. This is not to say that their heroes never display the chivalry, truth and other virtues typical of the Chivalric Romances, or indeed that those Chivalric Romances do not include love stories at their very centre. As we will see in the next chapter, the most famous lovers of the Middle Ages – Lancelot and Guinevere, and Tristan and Isolde – are part of Arthurian Romances. But their love stories are not told simply for their own sake, but to put to the fore the qualities and values of the heroes and heroines in their chivalric communities. Chaucer's focus on *fin amour* and the philosophy of love, described in section (a) of this chapter, gives his Romances a different value-system from that of the Chivalric Romances. Furthermore, he is trying out new techniques of realistic narrative and dialogue which he had learnt from his European models, particularly Boccaccio (Malory is also moving towards realism, but by a different route). So although there is considerable overlap in theme and interest between the courtly Romances discussed in these last two chapters of this Guide, it is appropriate that Chaucer should dominate this one.

It may have been to give himself the freedom to move away from the chivalric values and narrative styles, that Chaucer and his followers chose Classical stories rather than the 'Matter of Britain'. The 'Matter of Thebes and Troy', which Boccaccio had mined in the 1330s and 1340s, gave them new opportunities and quite different models to follow from the Arthurian tradition. Boccaccio got the stories from the twelfth-century French writer Benoit de St Maure, who had written a *Roman de Troie* (the basis for Boccaccio's *Filostrato*) and a *Roman de Thebes* (the basis for Boccaccio's *Teseida*, and also his *Filocolo*, which Chaucer uses in the *Franklyn's Tale*). Chaucer had probably encountered Boccaccio's work during his travels in Italy in the 1370s, and he freely adapted these three Romances to make new English poems, packed with his wide reading in the European philosophy of love. My Example Text for this section is his *Troilus and Criseyde*, and I will then go on to discuss a poem that this Romance inspired: Henryson's *Testament of Cressid*. Henryson takes the story back towards the old Homiletic Romance tradition, but he also explores the new ideas about narrative, narrator, and plot that Chaucer had introduced into the genre. I will, however, begin with a few words about Chaucer's first experiment in this new Romance form: the *Knight's Tale*.

Chaucer's first such experiment in adapting a Boccaccio Romance is from the 'Matter of Thebes', the *Teseida*. Chaucer wrote his *Knight's Tale* probably in 1381–2, at about the same time as he was working on the *Parliament of Fowls*, which also uses part of it (see p. 213, above), and *Troilus and Criseyde*. This was at least ten years before the project of writing the *Canterbury Tales* was begun, but that, too, uses a Boccaccio text, the *Decameron*, as a model. The *Teseida* tells the story of two Theban knights, and Chaucer adds a substantial philosophical underpinning chiefly provided by Boethius. Indeed, the *Knight's Tale*, though full of chivalric language and detail, is structured as a kind of Boethian test case for God's providence, showing how it gives different destinies in love to similar people. The two knights, Palamon and Arcite, are alike in every way, including in their love for the beautiful Emily whom they see from their prison window while they are captives of Theseus in Thebes. Their actions thereafter are dictated by their love rivalry, which culminates in a huge tournament held under the governance of the pagan gods Mars, Venus and Diana. Chaucer can thus set up a series of descending circles of causality, in which the true God ('almighty Jove') directs events through the workings of these orbiting planetary Gods, and down through the turning of Fortune's wheel to the helpless protagonists, with the curiously balanced result that the knight who wins the battle between them is not the knight who wins the lady. The poem, though magnificent, is far from being realistic, and it contains little sentiment although love is at its centre. It shows, to my mind, Chaucer's first attempt to extend a Boccaccian narrative into a completely new area of significance, and to set human love, as he had in the *Parliament of Fowls*, in a Boethian cosmic context. The *Knight's Tale* may therefore be read as a preparation for Chaucer's even more original use of the new contextualisation of a given narrative in his *Troilus and Criseyde*.

Example Text: (i) Chaucer's *Troilus and Criseyde*

Chaucer wrote this narrative poem in the rhyme royale he had used for the *Parliament of Fowls* between 1382 and 1386, during most of which he was occupied all day with receiving the King's customs. He used Boccaccio's *Filostrato* (written in Italian in about 1335) as his main source. Boccaccio wrote his detailed and realistic poem from an episode in the *Roman de Troie* by the twelfth-century French writer Benoit de St Maure, and his thirteenth-century Latin paraphrase Guido de Colonnis. Benoit's account of the Trojan lovers, or rather of Troilus' love and Briseida's inconstancy, is made even more anti-feminist in the work by Guido, who adds other lovers before Troilus. It is in this tradition, a mixture of courtly love and misogyny, that Boccaccio presents his renamed Criseida as both flirtatious and calculating, though he also gives her charm, warmth and vulnerability. Chaucer generally refers to his main source not as Boccaccio, but as Lollius, a word associated with lying, but possibly also a name mistakenly given to a Latin historian. Why does Chaucer never acknowledge Boccaccio as his source, here or in the other places where he uses him extensively (such as the *Parliament of Fowls*, and the *Knight's Tale* and *Franklyn's Tale*)? And how does he use the figure of *myn auctor*, which he has so carefully and misleadingly constructed?

Whatever he calls its author, Chaucer is clearly responding to the Italian text throughout his story, sometimes translating it closely, more often using it as a basis for his own account of the same scenes, sometimes writing new ones to replace others he has cut, and occasionally developing completely new plot-lines. His greatest expansions to the narrative are to the second half of Book 2, where he describes how the relationship between the lovers developed before they consummated their love (in Boccaccio's text, their first real meeting is in the bedroom), and to the last two Books, where Criseyde's unavoidable betrayal and Troilus' misery are drawn with a much greater sense of compassion and tragedy than in the *Filostrato*. Most strikingly, these changes allow Chaucer to develop his Criseyde into a much more complex and sympathetic figure than she had hitherto appeared in Boccaccio. In fact, Chaucer transforms the story into something quite different from the *Filostrato*, and it seems possible that Shakespeare characterised her under the influence not so much of Chaucer's poem, as of Henryson's (see p. 230, below).

In at least one respect, however, Chaucer is developing Boccaccio's lead: he makes his story extraordinarily realistic and contemporary, an effect enhanced by his use of a dialect akin to modern English in its vocabulary and colloquialisms. It is interesting to work out how this realistic effect is achieved (see Wimsatt 1968, for some ideas). One approach is to look at Chaucer's use of dialogue, the play of conversation which seems to run effortlessly through the rhymed stanzas, and the suggestion of thoughts that may be at variance with the words spoken, such as when Criseyde *Thought, 'I shal felen what he meneth, y-wis'* (2.386–7). Another approach is to look at Chaucer's use of setting, his re-creation of a contemporary city, complete with the luxuries of aristocratic life-style, and the subtle social pressures that are brought to bear on young people who live such a life. For example, Criseyde is hopeful that her father will let her return to Troy to collect their valuable *moebles* (furniture), but underestimates the complete power he has over her as a father when he insists she stay safely out of Troy. A third approach is to look at how Chaucer develops a believable relationship between the lovers. For example, Troilus promises to obey Criseyde (as she insists, *ye shal namore han souereignete / Of me in loue* 3.171–2), and he remains true to this promise even though it goes against his own interests, for he allows her to decide whether or not they elope (*if that ye wol assente* 4.637 and 4.1526), and she decides against it (4.1527–96). This seems to vindicate Criseyde's praise of Troilus as *The gentilest, and ek the mooste fre* (2.1080) of knights. Aers sees Chaucer 'developing a social psychology which contributes to the inter-relations between ... individual responsibility and given social circumstances and ideologies' (Aers 1979, pp. 128–9). The poem develops a complex psychological realism similar to the realism we encounter in Chaucer's comic tales, written during the following decade.

But even while Chaucer was enhancing the realism he found in Boccaccio, he was also elevating his story by the use of Classical Epic, of the love religion from the *Romance of the Rose*, and the Boethian philosophy of Love, even though these pull the poem away from realism and towards a more symbolic truth. As he was writing a *tragedie* he gives the poem some of the trappings of Classical epic like those of Virgil and Statius. Books 1–3 have Proems which are addressed to different Muses, important warriors are named, battles recounted, and destiny invoked (see Kelly 1997, ch. 3, for a full discussion of *Troilus* as tragedy). Idealisation of another kind is achieved by the increased use of Romance motifs. Chaucer adds to the borrowings from Classical Epic many new borrowings from the *Romance of the Rose* to place his story well within the tradition of *fin amour*. Boccaccio had already used the 'off-stage' scene of Troilus as the lover weeping in the garden (which Chaucer recounts at 2.507–53), but Chaucer adds the figure of the God of Love himself, shooting an arrow through Troilus as he sees Criseyde in the Temple (1.206–8), and develops Troilus' ensuing commitment to obey the laws of Love (1.458–62). Chaucer also makes love incapacitate Troilus far more than Boccaccio does. Love sickness and swooning at inopportune moments are commonplaces of the French Romances written in the shadow of Guillaume's *Romance* (see, for examples, Mieszkowski 2008, pp. 49–51). Indeed, C. S. Lewis, in his detailed essay of 1932, sees Chaucer's revisions to Boccaccio as first and foremost a process of medievalisation' (56) in which he reaffirms the values and ideals of *fin amour* (which can only seem comic in the context of Chaucer's otherwise realistic depiction of social life).

As Lewis demonstrates, Chaucer enhances but also justifies Troilus' total obedience to the God of Love by making that deity Troilus' pagan understanding of a much more profound and cosmic force, that of Boethian Divine Love. Chaucer had recently translated his *Boece* and he uses it in other contemporary works, most notably the *Knight's Tale*. *Troilus and Criseyde* is full of Boethian phrases, analogies and ideas and includes several passages of close adaptation, such as Criseyde's speech about *fals felicity* (3.813–40, derived from *Consolation* 1 *prosa* 4), and the many descriptions of Fortune's temporary power over women and men (e.g., 5.1541–5; see Windeatt 1992, pp. 96–109, for a full list of parallels). If Fortune seems particularly associated with Criseyde (as I will discuss below), then the predestined purpose of God (His Providence) seems to be what Troilus accepts so uncomplainingly when he receives Love's arrow. Windeatt also summarises the manuscript evidence which suggests that

Chaucer added three very significant Boethian paraphrases at a relatively late stage of composition, two of which have been 'doctored' to enhance the arguments for predeterminism, and diminish or delete the arguments for free will. When Troilus uses these passages he reveals himself to be a determinist, who accepts God's Providence patiently and without apparently involving his own will. The first such passage is Troilus' Hymn to Love (3.1744–71, derived from *Consolation* Bk. 2 *metrum* 8), which in his version fails to include the tragic distinction that Boethius makes between the world of Nature (which is ruled by Divine Love) and of Mankind (which is not). Both at the beginning and at the end of Book 3, Troilus declares that lovers at least are obedient to the Divine rule of Venus or Love. This is the culmination of Troilus' happiness; the second 'doctored' passage is at the beginning of his fall. This is Troilus' soliloquy on predestination (4.953–1085, derived from *Consolation* Bk. 5 *prosa* 2 and 3), but which Philosophy will counter by insisting that God does not know or act within Time and so does not 'fore-know' or 'pre-determine' anything. Troilus, on the other hand, stops the argument half-way through, when he has proved to himself that he cannot escape his cruel fate. A third passage, which seems to have been added to the text when the other two were, describes Troilus' ascent to the spheres (5.1807–27, based on *Consolation* Bk. 4 *metrum* 1). In the *Consolations* such an ascent towards the God who rules the Universe would only be within the reach of those who practise reason and virtue; Troilus, however, seems to ascend to the sphere of the fixed stars simply because he was a true lover (*Swich fyn hath, lo, this Troilus for loue*: 5.1828). The effect of these three passages, together with Chaucer's use elsewhere of Boethius and the *Romance of the Rose*, is to make Troilus seem to be a martyr for Love; having once exercised his choice to *fully assente / Criseyde for to loue and nought repente* (1.391–2; 1.421–34), he gives up any freedom *To vnlouen [her] a quarter of a day* (5.1698), even when he knows he has lost her. His total passivity, his reliance on the actions of Pandarus and Criseyde to work out his Fate, like his one-sided view of the Providence of the only God he knows, both enobles him and renders him comic to his own (and our) more enlightened eyes (5.1821–2; and see Bloomfield 1957, for a discussion of Troilus' determinist position). Yet Troilus' obedience to the Divine Will means he himself imitates God's faithfulness – as he prays in the Hymn to Love at the end of Book 3:

> Loue that of erthe and se hath gouernaunce,
> Loue, that his hestes hath in heuenes hye ...
> Bynd this acord that I haue told and telle. (3.1744–50)

At first Criseyde can also be seen as being moved by Divine Love, at least when she loved Troilus. Indeed, when Criseyde first sees him at the window after hearing of his love, and feels the possibility of being sustained by him (*'who yaf me drynke?'* 2.651), Chaucer adds a stanza pointing out the influence of Venus:

> And also blisful Venus, wel arrayed,
> Sat in hire seuenthe hous of heuene tho,
> Disposed wel, and with aspectes payed,
> To helpen sely Troilus of his woo. (2.680–3)

Criseyde and Troilus' love can therefore be seen as helped by Fortune as the *executrice of wyerdes* (enacter of Fate), and by the *influences of thise heuenes hye* (2.617–18). But unlike Troilus, Criseyde never resigns control of her own will, and after this auspicious start, can be seen spending some two hundred and sixty lines (650–812 following Boccaccio), debating inwardly whether to accept Troilus' love or no. This does not suggest a soul willing to be moved by the Divine, but the calculating heroine of the *Filostrato*. Moreover, Chaucer goes out of his way, abandoning the *Filostrato* to do so, to explain that this was not *a sodeyn loue* (2.667), but took many meetings, one of which he describes in detail (at Deiphubus' house, which is not in *Filostrato*, where their first conversation is in the bedroom). This seems to indicate a process which required considerably more than a single epiphany like that of Troilus (see Mann 1991). Criseyde herself later claims that her love was a matter of judgement and moral approval, and not of an impulse of the blood:

> But moral vertue grounded vp-on trouthe,
> That was the cause I first hadde on yow routhe. (4.572–3)

But in relying on her own judgement and choice, Criseyde unwittingly puts herself under the control of Fortune, the uncertain and unfeeling goddess with whom she is associated while Troilus is accepting the will of Providence. Fortune can only grant *fals felicitee*, as she explains learnedly to Pandarus (813–36, derived from *Consolation* Bk. 1 *prosa* 4) when he claims that Troilus believes she has betrayed him for Horaste (which is, ironically, part of his plot to get her and Troilus true felicity). According to Boethius, Fortune does not really exist, but is the name we give to God's incomprehensible Providence, but for Chaucer's narrator Fortune is a cruel force who deliberately turns her wheel to bring Troilus first up and then down, and Criseyde is her agent. The changeableness of women (including Fortune) was, of course, a medieval commonplace, and every reader must decide how far Criseyde is responsible for betraying Troilus. Chaucer shows this as a series of steps: she refuses to elope with Troilus before the exchange; she fails to escape from her father's tent in ten days after the exchange, as she had promised; she accepts, though does not necessarily return, the 'love' of Diomedes. One explanation for this descent is to show her as weak: 'Criseyde is, in fact, *slydynge of corage* (5.825; see Barney 1992, p. 1). Her pragmatic responses to her changing Fortune can be seen more sympathetically, however, as forced on her by her gender and the vulnerability of her position, particularly when she finds herself in the all-male Greek camp (see Aers 1979, pp. 42–3). However, Weisl finds this approach makes Criseyde uninteresting, and goes so far as to say that 'in choosing Diomedes' protection, Criseyde, within a feminised context, plays a "mannes game" with a "mannes herte"' (2008, p. 130). It is up to the individual reader to consider whether Criseyde is so constrained by circumstance that Diomedes alone can be seen as guilty, or whether she is an agent with power to chose between faithfulness and betrayal – and so open to the charge of faithlessness.

It seems then that the text of *Troilus and Criseyde* suggests different approaches to Criseyde's love for and betrayal of Troilus. As Salter puts it (1991, p. 107), Chaucer refuses to present us with a 'unified whole'. Instead, he allows us to experience the ambiguities of the poem for ourselves:

The simultaneous awareness of the real validity of human values – and hence our need to commit ourselves to them – and of their inevitable transitoriness – and hence our need to remain uncommitted – represents a complex, mature, truly tragic vision of mankind. (Donaldson 1991, p. 56)

Questions on *Troilus and Criseyde*

- Do the courtly love elements in Troilus' love intensify the tragedy, or do they increase the comedy of a story in which only one character consistently inhabits the world of *fin amour*? (You might find discussion of Troilus' swoon by Mann 1991, and Mieszkowski 2008, helpful.)
- How far can Criseyde exercise judgement? Does she appear to do so with regard to Diomedes? Chaucer allows for a detailed comparison between the two; is Troilus' superiority visible only to the reader?
- Troilus' reliance on Pandarus to woo Criseyde for him, and to take on all the opprobrium of the seducer so that he can remain as innocent a victim of his machinations as Criseyde is, has provoked many critics to debate the question of his manliness. Even Criseyde herself asks '*Is this a mannes game? / What, Troilus, wol ye do thus for shame?*' (3.1126–7). Can you defend him from the charrges summarised by Mieszkowski (2008, p. 45):

> Since the mid-1990s, more and more commentators have characterized Troilus as effeminate, emasculated, even impotent, and based their judgment on his 'feminine' passivity ... ?

Example Text: (ii) Henryson's *Testament of Cressid*

Little is known about Robert Henryson's life (c. 1436–1503), but he appears to have been a leading schoolmaster (and therefore a cleric) in Dunfermline. He seems also to have acted as their Notary Public (unless that was a namesake), in which case he must have taken a degree in law as well as in theology. His works include a collection of

Fables and a retelling of the story of Orpheus and Euridice; all of these are available on-line and there is in addition an excellent verse translation by Seamus Heaney. But it is for his sequel to *Troilus and Criseyde*, the *Testament of Cressid*, that he is most remembered. It focuses not only on the fate of Cressid, but on the questions of her guilt, and of possible reader responses to it. Henryson himself takes an ambiguous role as narrator, and is self-conscious about his relation not only to the story he has inherited from Chaucer, but to the whole idea of 'truth' in the story (*Quha wait gif all that Chauceir wrait was trew?* Who knows if all that Chaucer wrote was true? 64).

Henryson indicates his half-antagonistic relationship with Chaucer from the first, by writing the poem in the same rhyme-royale stanza as Chaucer's, but starting his 'tragedie' with an anti-spring Prologue which almost anticipates the beginning of T. S. Eliot's *Wasteland*:

> Ane doolie sessoun to ane cairfull dyte
> Suld correspond and be equivalent
> Richt sa it wes quhen I began to wryte
> This tragedie, the wedder richt fervent
> Quhen Aries in middis of the Lent
> Schouris of haill gart fra the north discend
> That scantlie fra the cauld I micht defend. (*Testament* 1–7)
>
> *doolie*: gloomy; *dyte*: poem; *quhen*: when [Henryson often uses *q* where we would use *w*); *Aries ... Lent*: the Ram (mid-March), spring; *gart*: fall

As we continue reading this tightly-structured poem we discover how relevant the paradox of frost in spring is to the story as a whole. It depends on one medieval idea of tragedy as unexpected misery in the midst of good fortune, and it anticipates the cold malignancy of Saturn, who is to inflict leprosy on Cressid (311, 334), after she has been rejected by Diomeid. But the *cauld* will not be able to overcome the warmth of Troilus' love. He sees Cressid in her misery, and although he does not recognise her, she reminds him of *his awin darling* (504), and in her memory he gives this leper-beggar his valuable jewelled girdle. It is this wealth which is to be distributed by her 'Testament' at the end of the poem, when she is overtaken not only by the coldness of death but by the warmth of her repentance to Troilus, symbolised by the *rubie reid* (582) she leaves him (for a detailed analysis, see Gray 1979, ch. 5; see also Mapstone 2009, pp. 205–16).

The action of the story is interrupted by a series of set-pieces, usually showing Henryson's knowledge of European traditions. In the first (78–91) the narrator debates the facts of Cressid's fate with himself, and concludes, at least according to Kelly, that it was only slanderers (*sum men sayis* 77) who suggested she became a whore, and that she herself was so ashamed of being rejected by Diomeid that she only wanted to hide herself with her father (1997, pp. 227–34). This is by no means the only possible interpretation of this passage. Shakespeare almost certainly read Henryson's *Testament* as the (then unacknowledged) sixth Book of Chaucer's *Troilus and Criseyde*, and it is tempting to think that he developed his more raunchy Cressida from lines of Henryson such as these:

> O fair Creisseid the flour and A per se
> Of Troy and Grece, how was thow fortunait
> To change in filth all thy feminitie
> And be with fleschelie lust sa maculait
> And go amang the Greikis air and lait
> Sa giglotlike takand thy foull plesance!
> I have pietie thee suld fall sic mischance. (78–84)
>
> *flour and A per se*: flower and unequalled (= A on its own); *fortunait*: unfortunate; *maculait*: stained; *air and lait*: early and late; *giglotlike ... plesance*: taking thy foul pleasure like a strumpet

The next set-piece is Cressid's apostrophe to Cupid and Venus (125–140, blaming him for betraying her (indeed the poem is a series of betrayals, from which Troilus is the shining exception):

> O fals Cupide, is nane to wyte bot thow
> And thy mother, of lufe the blind goddess (134–5)
>
> *wyte*: blame; *blind*: applies to Cupid, as Venus uses her eyes (231)

Using the imagery introduced in the Prologue, Cressid describes her beauty, the seed of love, as a flower destroyed by frost (139). She then experiences a Dream Vision in which all the planetary Gods process before Cupid their king, who commands Saturn to punish her blasphemy against his mother and himself by giving Cressid leprosy. It is clear that this is not a punishment for her infidelity or her promiscuity, but for blaming the gods for her own faults. However, the reader might feel that Venus', Cupid's and Saturn's deceptiveness or malignancy quite overshadow poor Cressid's fault, and her 'blasphemy' seems perfectly justified.

Cressid awakens with an *uglye lipper face* (372) and is taken by her father to the hospital at the town's end (there was one such lazar-house outside Dunfermline). Here she recites *The Complaint of Cresseid* (407–69), the next set-piece, which is in the form of an *ubi sunt* poem, lamenting the passing of worldly happiness (*ubi sunt* means 'where are they now?'). This theme is relevant to all people, not just to lepers, and here the character is clearly addressing the readers:

> Nocht is your fairnes bot ane faiding flour,
> Nocht is your famous laud and hie honour
> Bot wind inflat in uther mennis eiris;
> Your roising reid to rotting sall retour.
> Exempill mak of me in your memour
> Quhilk of sic thingis wofull witnes beiris . . .
> Fortoun is fikkill quhen scho beginnis and steiris. (461–9)
>
> *laud*: praise; *inflat*: blown; *roising reid*: red rosiness; *rotting sall retour*: return to rottenness; *wofull witnes beiris*: bear woeful witness to; *beginnis and steiris*: begins to take control of you

(We are reminded of the patient men and women who learn to 'steer their hearts'; see pp. 177, 180, above.) However, in spite of the *memento mori* element in this passage, Henryson does not lead us towards Cressid's death, but to the 'failed recognition scene' (501–25) which is the climax of the poem. It is crucial that neither Troilus nor Cressid should recognise each other as this would then involve some action and possibly avert the 'tragedie' which is Henryson's structure, and so he insists that *nevertheles not ane ane uther knew* (518). But it is also crucial that Troilus' partial recognition should prompt him to prove his continuing faithfulness by giving the beggar a valuable treasure because she has reminded him of Cressid, and thus demonstrating his refusal to change with the times, in contrast to Diomeid and Cressid. Cressid recognises this in her final set-piece (547–74), in which she contrasts herself with Troilus (*Fy fals Cresseid, O trew knicht Troylus!* 560; see also 435 and 555) and acknowledges her own guilt (*Nane but myself as now I will accuse* 974). She distributes Troilus' bounty and dies. Henryson's brief moral address to his female readers urges them to avoid *fals deceptioun* (613), but as Cressid explained in her lament, men are as likely to be deceptive as women. It is left to the reader to decide if the effect of the poem is to condemn Cressid as one who needs quite extraordinary punishment to bring her to an awareness of the truth, or to exonerate her as a victim of the duplicity of Diomeid, Cupid, Venus and Fortune – not to mention the evil rumour-mongers whom both Henryson and Chaucer blame rather disingenuously for ill reports of her character.

Questions on *Testament of Cressid*

- Look at the detailed description of Venus (218–38). What has she in common with Fortune or with Cressid herself and what is the effect of these parallels?
- Henryson was a cleric, but should he be seen as anti-feminist? Do you feel he is trying to wrench the older story into a different direction, and if so, is it to condemn Cressid more, or to increase our sympathy for her?
- How does the narrator of the *Testament* compare with the narrator of Troilus and Criseyde? What appears to be his attitude towards his sources (including Chaucer), and does he seem to be less constrained than Chaucer in abandoning them and inventing 'truth' for himself?

Texts, Sources and Further Reading

Texts of European sources

Halsall, Paul (ed.) (1996) *Alain of Lille's Complaint of Nature* (Medieval Sourcebook, http://www2.kenyon.edu/projects/margin/alain.htm).

Stahl, W. (transl.) (1952) *Commentary on the Dream of Scipio by Macrobius* (Columbia University Press).
Strachey, J. (1917; transl. 1995; repr. 2010) *Freud's New Introductory Lectures in Psychoanalysis* (Norton).
Sutherland, R. (ed.) (1967) *Romance of the Rose* (Blackwell Publishing).
Walsh, P. G. (ed. and transl.) (1982) *Andreas Capellanus on Love* (Duckworth).
Watts, V. (transl.) (1963) *Boethius: Consolation of Philosophy* (Penguin Classics). (Chaucer translation quoted from http://www.archive.org/stream/chaucersboece).

Texts of Lyrics

Brook, G. L. (1956) *The Harley Lyrics* (Manchester University Press).
Burrow, J. A. (ed.) (1977) *English Verse, 1300–1500* (Longman Publishing).
Cooney, H. (ed.) (2006) *Writings on Love in the English Middle Ages* (Palgrave Macmillan).
Davies, R. T. (ed.) (1964) *Medieval English Lyrics: A Critical Anthology* (Northwestern University Press).

Chaucer texts

(See Chapter 3 for texts of the *Canterbury Tales* and Collected Works.)
Fisher, J. (1989) *The Complete Poetry and Prose of Geoffrey Chaucer*, 2nd edn (Holt, Rinehart and Winston).
Parliament of Fowls (http://www.wwnorton.com/college/english/nael/noa/pdf/08Fowls_1_17.pdf). This is the text used for quotation.
Windeatt, B. (ed.) (1993) *Troilus and Criseyde* (Oxford Text Archive, http://quod.lib.umich.edu/c/cme/Troilus/1:3.2.3?rgn=div3;view=toc). This is the text used for quotation.

Chaucerian texts

Heaney, Seamus (transl.) (2009) *The Testament of Cressid and Seven Fables by Robert Henryson* (Jonathan Bate).
Mitchell, A. (2007) *John Lydgate: The Temple of Glass* (TEAMS, http://d.lib.rochester.edu/teams/text/mitchell-lydgate-temple-of-glas). This is the text used for quotation.

Parkinson, D. (2010) *Henryson: The Complete Works* (TEAMS, http://d.lib.rochester.edu/teams/text/parkinson-henryson-complete-works). This is the text used for quotation.

History and criticism on the European love tradition

Busby, K. and Kleinhenz, C. (eds) (2006) *Courtly Arts and the Art of Courtliness* (D. S. Brewer).
Cherry, J. (2005) *Medieval Love Poetry* (British Museum Press).
Heinrichs, K. (1990) *The Myths of Love: Classical Lovers in Medieval Literature* (Pennsylvania State University Press).
Kelly, D. (1978) *Medieval Imagination: Rhetoric and the Poetry of Courtly Love* (University of Wisconsin Press).
Lewis, C. S. (1936) *The Allegory of Love* (Oxford University Press).
Lewis, C. S. (1964) *The Discarded Image* (Cambridge University Press).
Taylor, P. B. (1996) *Chaucer's Chain of Love* (Methuen; Associated University Presses).

Criticism on English love lyrics

Duncan, T. G. (ed.) (2005) *A Companion to the Middle English Lyric* (D. S. Brewer).
Gray, D. (2005) 'Middle English courtly lyrics: Chaucer to Henry VIII', in Duncan, T. G. (ed.), *A Companion to the Middle English Lyric* (D. S. Brewer).
Moore, A. K. (1951; repr. 1970) *The Secular Lyric in Middle English* (University of Kentucky Press; Greenwood).
Pearsall, D. A. (1977) *Old English and Middle English Poetry* (Routledge).
Sadlek, G. M. (2004) *Idleness Working: The Discourse of Love's Labor from Ovid through Chaucer and Gower* (Catholic University of America Press).
Scattergood, J. (2005) 'The love lyric before Chaucer', in Duncan, T. G. (ed.), *A Companion to the Middle English Lyric* (D. S. Brewer).

English and Scottish Love Visions

Aers, D. (1981) 'The *Parliament of Fowls*: authority, the knower and the known', in Quinn, W. A. (ed.) (1999), *Chaucer's Dream Visions and Shorter Poems* (Basic Readings in *Chaucer and His Time*, Garland).

Benson, C. D. (1992) 'Critic and poet: what Lydgate and Henryson did to Chaucer's *Troilus and Criseyde*', *Modern Language Quarterly*, 53, pp. 23–40.

Benson, C. D. (2006) 'Civic Lydgate: the Poet and London', in Scanlon, L. and Simpson, J. (eds), *John Lydgate: Poetry, Culture and Lancastrian England* (University of Notre Dame Press).

Calabrese, M. A. (1994) *Chaucer's Ovidian Arts of Love* (University of Florida Press).

Edwards, R. R. (1989) *The Dream of Chaucer: Representation and Reflection in the Early Narratives* (Duke University Press).

Fumo, J. C. (2010) *The Legacy of Apollo: Antiquity, Authority, and Chaucerian Poetics* (University of Toronto Press).

Muscatine, C. (1957) *Chaucer and the French Tradition* (University of California Press).

Olson, P. A. (1980) 'Aristotle's *Politics* and the foundations of human society', in Quinn, W. A. (ed.) (1999), *Chaucer's Dream Visions and Shorter Poems* (Basic Readings in *Chaucer and His Time*, Garland).

Pearsall, D. (1970) *John Lydgate* (Routledge).

Quinn, W. A. (ed.) (1999) *Chaucer's Dream Visions and Shorter Poems* (Basic Readings in *Chaucer and His Time*, Garland).

Russell, S. (1988) *The English Dream Vision: Anatomy of a Form* (Ohio State University Press).

Scanlon, L. and Simpson, J. (eds) (2006) *John Lydgate: Poetry, Culture and Lancastrian England* (University of Notre Dame Press).

Spearing, A. C. (1976) *Medieval Dream-Poetry* (Cambridge University Press).

St John, M. (2000) *Chaucer's Dream Visions: Courtliness and Individual Identity* (Ashgate).

Williams, D. (2006) 'The Dream Visions', in Lerer, S. *The Yale Companion to Chaucer* (Yale University Press).

Wimsatt, J. I. (1968) *Chaucer and the French Love Poets* (University of North Carolina Press).

Criticism of Chaucer's *Troilus and Criseyde* and Henryson's *Testament of Cressid*

Aers, D. (1979; repr. 1991) 'Criseyde: woman in Medieval society', in Benson, C. D. (ed.), *Critical Essays on Chaucer's Troilus and Criseyde and his Major Early Poems* (Open University Press).

Barney, S. A. (1992) 'Troilus Bound', in Shoaf, R. A. (ed.), *Chaucer's Troilus and Criseyde: Subgit to alle Poesye: Essays in Criticism* (Medieval and Renaissance Texts and Studies).

Benson, B. H. (1999) 'The *Parliament of Fowls* revisited', in Quinn, W. (ed.), *Chaucer's Dream Visions and Shorter Poems* (Garland).

Benson, C. D. (ed.) (1991) *Critical Essays on Chaucer's Troilus and Criseyde and his Major Early Poems* (Open University Press).

Benson, C. D. (2006) 'Civic Lydgate: the Poet and London', in Scanlon, L. and Simpson, J. (eds), *John Lydgate: Poetry, Culture and Lancastrian England* (University of Notre Dame Press).

Bloomfield, M. (1957; repr. 1991) 'Distance and predestination in *Troilus and Criseyde*', in Benson, C. D. (ed.), *Critical Essays on Chaucer's Troilus and Criseyde and his Major Early Poems* (Open University Press).

Boitani, P. and Mann, J. (eds) (2003) *The Cambridge Companion to Chaucer* (Cambridge University Press).

Brown, P. (2000) (ed.) *A Companion to Chaucer* (Blackwell Companions to Literature and Culture, Blackwell).

Delaney, S. (1992) 'Techniques of alienation in *Troilus and Criseyde*', in Shoaf, R. A. (ed.), *Chaucer's Troilus and Criseyde: Subgit to alle Poesye: Essays in Criticism* (Medieval and Renaissance Texts and Studies).

Donaldson, E. T. (1991) 'Commentary on *Troilus and Criseyde*', in Benson, C. D. (ed.), *Critical Essays on Chaucer's Troilus and Criseyde and his Major Early Poems* (Open University Press). Originally published in 1958.

Edwards, R. (2006) *The Flight from Desire: Augustine and Ovid to Chaucer* (Palgrave Macmillan).

Fumo, J. C. (2011) 'Hating Criseyde: last words on a heroine from Chaucer to Henryson', *Chaucer Review*, 46, pp. 20–38.

Gray, D. (1979) *Robert Henryson* (Brill).

Hansen, E. T. (1992) Chaucer and the fictions of gender (University of California Press).

Inshaw, C. (1992) 'Reading like a man: the critics, the narrator, Troilus, and Pandarus', in Shoaf, R. A. (ed.), *Chaucer's Troilus and Criseyde: Subgit to alle Poesye: Essays in Criticism* (Medieval and Renaissance Texts and Studies).

Kelly, H. A. (1997) *Chaucerian Tragedy* (D. S. Brewer).

Lerer, S. (2006) *The Yale Companion to Chaucer* (Yale University Press).

Lewis, C. S. (1932; repr. 1991) 'What Chaucer really did to *Il Filostrato*' (Essays and studies), in Benson, C. D. (ed.), *Critical Essays on Chaucer's Troilus and Criseyde and his Major Early Poems* (Open University Press).

Mann, J. (1991) 'Troilus's swoon', in Benson, C. D. (ed.), *Critical Essays on Chaucer's Troilus and Criseyde and his Major Early Poems* (Open University Press).

Mapstone, S. (2009) 'Robert Henryson', in Scanlon, L. (ed.), *Cambridge Companion to Medieval English Literature 1100–1500* (Cambridge University Press, also available as Cambridge Companions Online).

Mieszkowski, G. (2008) 'Revisiting Troilus' faint', in Pugh, T. and Marzec, M. S. (eds), *Men and Masculinities in Chaucer's Troilus and Criseyde* (D. S. Brewer).

Olson, P. A. (1980) '*The Parlement of Foules*: Aristotle's *Politics* and the foundations of human society', *Studies in the Age of Chaucer*, 2, pp. 53–69.

Pugh, T. and Marzec, M. S. (eds) (2008) *Men and Masculinities in Chaucer's Troilus and Criseyde* (D. S. Brewer).

Quinn, W. (ed.) (1999) *Chaucer's Dream Visions and Shorter Poems* (Basic Readings in Chaucer and his Time, Garland).

Rose, D. M. (1981) *New Perspectives in Chaucer Criticism* (Pilgrim Books).

Salter, E. (1991) '*Troilus and Criseyde*: a reconsideration', in Benson, C. D. (ed.), *Critical Essays on Chaucer's Troilus and Criseyde and his Major Early Poems* (Open University Press). Originally published in 1966.

Salu, M. (ed.) (1979) *Essays on Troilus and Criseyde* (D. S. Brewer).

Saunders, C. (ed.) (2006) *A Concise Companion to Chaucer* (Blackwell Publishing).

Scanlon, L. (ed.) (2006) *Cambridge Companion to Medieval English Literature 1100–1500* (Cambridge University Press, also available as Cambridge Companions Online).

Shoaf, R. A. (ed.) (1992) *Chaucer's Troilus and Criseyde: Subgit to alle Poesye: Essays in Criticism* (Medieval and Renaissance Texts and Studies).

Simpson, J. (2006) 'Chaucer as a European writer', in Lerer, S. (ed.), *The Yale Companion to Chaucer* (Yale University Press).

Taylor, P. B. (1996) *Chaucer's Chain of Love* (Methuen Associated University Presses).

Weisl, A. (2008) '"A mannes game": Criseyde's masculinity in *Troilus and Criseyde*', in Pugh, T. and Marzec, M. S. (eds), *Men and Masculinities in Chaucer's Troilus and Criseyde* (D. S. Brewer).

Wimsatt, J. I. (1973; repr. 1991) 'Realism in *Troilus and Criseyde* and the *Roman de la Rose*', in Benson, C. D. (ed.), *Critical Essays on Chaucer's Troilus and Criseyde and his Major Early Poems* (Open University Press).

Windeatt, B. (1992) *Oxford Guide to Chaucer: Troilus and Criseyde* (Oxford University Press).

Chapter 8

Chivalric Romances

This final chapter will look at the tradition of courtly Chivalric Romance characteristic of 'The Matter of Britain', which in the fourteenth and fifteenth centuries generally meant tales of King Arthur and his court. This will be my main focus but I will look more briefly at Lydgate's contributions to the other main chivalric tradition, 'The Matter of Antiquity', or of Greece and Rome. (The non-courtly or Popular Romances have already been discussed in Chapter 6, and Chaucer's contributions to 'The Matter of Antiquity' were discussed in Chapter 7.) Arthurian stories were the more popular because England was at war during this period, the Hundred Years War with France reaching from 1342 until 1453, and the Wars of the Roses continuing the fighting at home until 1485, for the ancient story of the Death of Arthur includes both foreign invasion and civil war. Thomas Malory, the author of the most important collection of Arthurian stories, was himself involved in these dynastic wars, and it is tempting to conclude that his *Morte Darthur*, completed in prison in 1470, was shaped not only by the texts of the Arthurian tradition from France and England, but also in the heat of his own experience of war.

Who were the readers of these late Middle English Romances? One group would have been the nobility, who had been reading French Romances, often in the original language, since the twelfth century. However, the nobility were themselves in an increasingly troubled state in the fifteenth century, as failure in the French wars and the bloodshed of the Wars of the Roses divided and weakened them. Their power was being steadily encroached on by the 'gentry class', the increasingly wealthy knights, untitled landowners and propertied townsmen, who were powerful in local politics, and becoming more influential at court or in Parliament (as MPs) than their high-born betters. Edward IV, recognising their value, made 30 per cent more knights from this class than his predecessors, holding mass knightings for men who had distinguished themselves in peacetime rather than in military service, or whom he thought would be useful to his court or household as 'esquires'. Radulescu gives evidence from letters and manuscript collections that this class shared the values and preoccupations they would encounter in Arthurian romances:

> The concepts of worship, friendship, lordship and fellowship informed fifteenth-century gentry attitudes, irrespective of the area the gentry lived in, as these concepts formed the basis of their relationships and interaction with one another and with their magnates. (Radulescu 2003, p. 13)

Although the more sophisticated and aristocratic readers found the 'Matter of Britain' out-of-date and provincial, and preferred the ornate and learned offerings of Lydgate, there were plenty of the aspiring gentry class who enjoyed Arthurian Romances. Some of the Arthurian stories were derived at least partly from British sources, like the elaborately courtly *Morte Arthure* and *Sir Gawain and the Green Knight*, but the majority were adapted from French romances. The translators often tailored their versions for the English market; they reduced the elaborate manners of courtly love and courtesy and the descriptions of a princely life-style of feasting and hunting, which they found in their sources. They focused instead on divided loyalties and political crisis, where the painful experience of love is important not for its own sake (as in the stories discussed in the previous chapter) but for the effects it has on the fellowship of knights and the chivalric code. They focused on knightly adventures and the values of loyalty and honour. It was therefore a considerable readership, which William Caxton, England's first printer, quite deliberately targeted when he published Malory's *Morte Darthur* together with two Romance histories and a book on chivalry (see below, p. 261). Malory's Arthurian Romance was one of the very first texts to be published not as a series of handwritten manuscripts (though one manuscript does survive) but, in 1485, as a printed book. Although Malory was already dead, it is striking how widely his matter-of-fact style, his dramatic action, and his realistic characterisation must have extended his readership through all classes of men and women, then as now.

I will begin by looking at England at war, go on to describe some of these Arthurian sources, and then look at some of the important fourteenth-century Romances written in this tradition: *Ywain and Gawain*, the *Stanzaic Morte Arthur* and *Alliterative Morte Arthure*, and my first Example Text: *Gawain and the Green Knight*. Finally, I will turn to the fifteenth century, briefly introduce Lydgate's Classical Romances, and then look in detail at Malory's 'definitive' version of the story of Arthur, and discuss his conclusion to his *Morte Darthur* as my second Example Text. The printing of this text by Caxton takes us not only into the fifteenth century but to a new and enormously increased reading public, and so will be a good place to end this Guide.

(a) England at War

For most of the period covered by this Guide, England was intermittently at war with France (the 'Hundred Years War', 1342–1453), or enduring, again intermittently, its own war of royal succession (the 'Wars of the Roses', 1452–87). But what might have seemed a constant opportunity for performing deeds of honour became increasingly the reverse. At first the war in France seemed glorious and profitable. Edward III's early conquests with the Black Prince at Crecy and Bretigny (1346, 1359) brought prestige and validity to the English claim to the crown of France. They also brought a good deal of booty and ransom money – including a huge sum for the captured French king John II. The French writer Froissart (see p. 205, and excerpts printed in Allmand (ed.), *Society at War*, 1998, pp. 22–5) described the English nobility with magnanimous admiration as epitomes of chivalric knighthood. But the battles were interspersed with *chevauchées*, long marches designed to bring devastation to the French countryside, and with sieges, bringing starvation to the French towns. This disillusioned many Englishmen with the war, and the next king, Richard II, preferred a cheaper peace policy in spite of occasional invasion scares, justifying it in 1397 because 'war causes great harm and unnecessary destruction to both kingdoms' (Allmand, *Hundred Years War*, 1998, p. 24). His successor Henry IV went doggedly on with the war in spite of popular feeling against it, but Henry V briefly revived its image by his clear (if hardly untainted) victories at Harfleur and Agincourt in 1415; for a brief period the English king also wore the French crown. However, Henry's death in 1422 and the accession of his nine-month-old son Henry VI was to spell the end of the war. The last time the barons of England came in any numbers to fight in France was in 1429, when 'la pucelle', Jeanne d'Arc, raised the siege of Orleans in spite of them, and led Charles (the dauphin forbidden by Treaty to take his throne) to be crowned King at Rheims. Even after Jeanne was captured and burned in 1431, and Henry crowned in Paris, Charles maintained the impetus to drive the English ignominiously from almost the whole of France by 1453.

Although there are many poems urging war in the fourteenth and fifteenth centuries (see Robbins 1959), the major poets of the period seem united in a desire for peace. The poet Langland claimed it was promoted by Meed or personal reward, and showed how disbanded soldiers were a scourge to villagers (see Passus 3–4, 6). Chaucer (notably in the *Tale of Melibee*), Gower (in *In Praise of Peace*), Hoccleve (in the *Regiment of Princes*) and Lydgate (in *The Debate of the Horse*, and *The Goose and the Sheep*), among many others, urged the king to make peace. The Lollards were particularly associated with hostility to any war between Christians (see Swindeby's spirited sermon excerpted in Allmand (ed.), *Society at War*, 1998, pp. 10–11). More orthodox critics used the principles of the 'just war' to argue against this particular war as well as against war in general. In fact the Roman lawyer Justinian, the twelfth-century writer on war Vegetius (much quoted by Giles of Rome), and the fifteenth-century French author Raymondus Lull, all explained that the principles of law took precedence over the principles of honour or mere aggression. As I will be showing, it seems the last two 'books' of the *Morte Darthur* are making the same point (see p. 266).

Henry VI's long minority also allowed opposition to develop at home, and, in the coups and counter-coups between the Houses of York and Lancaster (not to mention popular rebellions like that of Jack Cade in 1450), there was even less scope for honour and chivalry. The fighting armies, in a system developed for the French wars, were generally groupings of the noble households with their retinues of aristocrats and tenants, plus associated local gentry, and professional soldiers under contract. These groupings could not be relied on to obey the basic chivalric principle of loyalty, but changed their political allegiance at crucial moments. In early 1461, for example, fourteen of the forty peers then involved in the war changed sides to follow Richard Duke of York against the reigning monarch Henry VI. The soldiers they commanded were also inclined to run away, particularly when confronted by large 'public' forces mustered by the king's 'commission of array' from local towns and country. Richard Neville, Duke of Warwick, who had recently himself changed sides to follow Richard of York, was defeated in March 1470 by the enormous army that Edward IV commissioned at Lincoln Field (Empingham); the courageous sallies of some of Warwick's forces proving more disastrous than simple flight from the field – hardly a triumph for chivalry. (Warwick returned with Henry VI's wife Margaret to defeat Edward IV in October.) Thus some phases of the war involved far more of the populace than others, and so caused more widespread harm. As the war progressed, the peers became less and less interested in joining the dynastic struggle, and the Battle of Bosworth Field, which ended the reign of Richard III and brought Henry Tudor the crown, was fought with small forces. There was now little pretence that these largely professional soldiers were pursuing any kind of chivalric ideal. See the text-box on p. 261 for an account of Malory's participation in these troubled wars; it is an open question whether the *Morte Darthur* describes a fictional world into which its author and readers might escape from the horrors of the real one, or imports into that world some of the experience of a current civil war.

(b) The Principal Sources for English Arthurian Romance

(i) Geoffrey of Monmouth

In 1130–6 Geoffrey, an Oxford historian from Wales, wrote down some of the myths already associated with King Arthur in Celtic legend, in a 'history of the kings of Britain' which was to become 'one of the most influential books ever written', with about 200 manuscripts still surviving plus those of French and English translations (Pearsall 2003, pp. 6–13). For Geoffrey, Arthur epitomised the nation of Britain, founded by the Trojan hero Brutus, and he and his prophet-advisor Merlin have more prominence than any other king described.

Geoffrey tells of his accession, which requires several battles against the Saxons, his marriage, his battle with the giant at Mont St Michel, his invasion of France and Rome, and his final battles against his treacherous nephew Mordred, ending with his burial (supposedly in 542) on the isle of Avalon. His successors are unable to prevent Britain from passing to the Saxons. Of the late medieval texts discussed below, the *Alliterative Morte Arthure* is the closest to Geoffrey's work and it is interesting to reflect that although Malory included some of that poem, Caxton removed some of this material from his edition.

Geoffrey's work was soon translated into French, the version by Wace known as the *Roman de Brut* (1155) soon becoming the most widely known. Like the *Roman de Troie* (see above, p. 222) this expanded the old story with new ideas about courtesy and the emotional side of chivalry, and briefly introduced the Round Table, though he added little about love. The more heroic and national *Brut* written by Layamon in the middle of the thirteenth century in vigorous alliterative rhyming verse, reversed some of these changes. His Arthur is not only a ferocious fighter, but the establisher of peace, using the Round Table to encourage loyalty and equality among Arthur's knights (see Pearsall 2003, pp. 13–20, for discussion of these texts).

(ii) Chrétien de Troyes and his immediate imitators

It was Chrétien de Troyes (1136–83), writing in the sophisticated court of Queen Marie de Champagne, who promoted Lancelot into Arthur's chief knight, and made him the lover of his queen, Guinevere. This was a significant move in the 'romancing of the Romances', for it allowed the new 'religion of love' found in lyrics, dream poetry and handbooks (see Ch. 7, pp. 202–4) to permeate the growing genre of Romance. Chrétien's other Arthurian Romances also include love, and I will look briefly at one of these (*Yvain*), as it was translated into Middle English verse in the early fourteenth century. But it is *Knight of the Chariot* (the first Lancelot and Guinevere story, which Chrétien says was suggested to him by the Queen herself) which pre-eminently describes the passionate, adulterous love of *fin amour*. Chrétien also demonstrates how virtues like purity, constancy and courtesy, the effects of love, can co-exist with the more 'masculine' virtues of prowess and loyalty which had already become a part of the knightly code of behaviour.

Chrétien was also the first writer to introduce into Arthurian romance the Celtic motifs of the Grail Legend. Modern research has uncovered some of the fascinating early versions of the Grail Legend, relating the Grail itself (the cup with which Jesus was supposed to have celebrated the first Eucharist, or in which his blood was caught) to the Welsh and Irish legends of a horn or dish of plenty, and finding ancient antecedents for the legends of the bleeding lance and of the Fisher King whose phallic wound laid his land waste. Towards the end of his life, Chrétien, who was a cleric, turned some of these Celtic stories into the two parts of his *Perceval*, leaving the second part unfinished. Perceval's quest to find the meaning of the Grail and heal the Fisher King is contrasted with that of the lascivious Gawain. The story inspired four continuations (the first of which may have suggested the plot of *Gawain and the Green Knight*; see below, p. 252), and was freely translated and extended by Wolfram von Eschenbach in Middle High German as *Parzival* (c. 1210). At about the same time and in the same language, Gottfried von Strasburg (1225–35) was writing a version of the Old French story of Tristram and Isolde, which, like Chrétien's *Lancelot*, was a story of an adulterous but very refined love between a knight and a queen.

(iii) The French Vulgate Cycle and beyond

After the success of Chrétien de Troyes there was an explosion in French Romance writing, including both the Homiletic Romances which became so popular in England, and the stories developing the characters and plots of Arthurian romance. In the early thirteenth century a group of writers inspired by Cistercian monasticism collected these and shaped them into what became known as the French Vulgate Cycle. This huge prose compilation gave the whole corpus an arch-structure, in which Arthur's conquests establish his power and prestige, and the Quest for the Grail represents the high point of Arthur's ideal of Christian knighthood. The final dissolution of the Round Table fellowship is caused by failures in upholding that ideal, notably by Arthur, whose illicit and incestuous love for his half-sister is now discovered to have created the treacherous Mordred, and by Lancelot, who fails to keep his Grail Quest vow to end his adulterous relationship with the queen. The moral is clear: chivalry which does not serve God will destroy society. The stories of individual knights are interlaced, making them hard to follow, and the religious message was not to everyone's taste (Grail stories are practically unknown in English before Malory's highly abbreviated version). But the French Vulgate Cycle's overall structure was of immense help to any adaptor who tried to make sense of this mass of stories, and both the author of the *Stanzaic Morte Arthur*, and to a much greater extent Malory himself, used it to shape their plot, even if they disentangled the interlacing and detached themselves from its monastic ethos.

The Vulgate Cycle comprises:

- *Estoire de Sainte Grail*, *Estoire de Merlin* and the somewhat later *Suite de Merlin* (Joseph of Arimathea's bringing of the Grail to England, and the early life of Arthur, the sword in the stone, his establishment as King, and the incestuous conception of Mordred)
- Lancelot Cycle
  - *Prose Lancelot* (Chrétien's story of the love between him and Guinevere but enormously expanded and with additions of many adventures for Lancelot)
  - *Perceval* or *The High History of the Grail*
  - *La Queste de Saint Grail* (the version used by Malory in which Galahad, Lancelot's son, with Parsifal and Bors, achieve the Grail)
  - The *Morte Artu* (using Geoffrey of Monmouth's story of Arthur's expedition to Rome and Mordred's treachery)
- *Tristram* (another tale of adulterous love but from a different source which vulgarises and significantly changes Gottfried von Strasburg's story; unfortunately this was what Malory used).

The *Stanzaic Morte* uses the *Morte Artu*, and Malory recounts what he feels to be the essentials of the *Suite de Merlin*, the *Lancelot* and *Tristram* sections, and also makes considerable use of both the *Alliterative Morte* and the *Stanzaic Morte*. (Malory also used the English Arthurian prologue to the mid-fifteenth century *Chronicle of John Hardyng*, which includes an account of the Grail Quest, and seems to have known several of the fourteenth-century English Arthurian romances.)

(c) Fourteenth-century English Arthurian Romance

Most fourteenth-century Romances are Homiletic and sentimental stories, or Breton Lays and marvellous stories of the Constance type, and I have discussed them above in Chapter 6; they generally survive in only a single copy. Somewhat more numerous are the non-courtly 'Matter of Britain' Tales discussed on p. 167 above, such as *Athelston* (the supposed history of an Anglo-Saxon king) and *Gamelyn* (a Robin-Hood type of story which survives in 26 manuscripts because it was attached to the Canterbury Tales as the *Cook's Tale*), and *Sir Degrevaunt* (a story about a Yorkshire countryman and his legal disputes with his neighbours; for all these, see Pearsall 1977, pp. 143–4). There can, however, be found a few genuinely Courtly Romances, mostly adapted from French originals. Some of these concern 'The matter of Antiquity', such as *Ipomadon*, and the 'history' of King Alexander the Great, mostly derived from the Latin *Historia de Preliis*. Several Middle English versions of this survive, including three long alliterative 'fragments', of which the most successful and complete is the alliterative chronicle known as *The Wars of Alexander* or *Alexander* (mid-fifteenth century); there is also a prose *Life of Alexander* copied by Robert Thornton in 1440, which translates the same Latin source (see Pearsall 1977, pp. 167–9). But the most 'literary' group, which I will now discuss, are the courtly 'Matter of Britain' stories about King Arthur and members of his court. These use many of the Arthurian sources described above, and include:

(i) *Yvain*, an early fourteenth-century unique translation of one of Chrétien's romances
(ii) the mid-fourteenth-century *Stanzaic Morte Arthur*, adapted and shortened from the French *Morte Artu*, which concludes the *Vulgate Cycle*

(iii) the *Alliterative Morte Arthure*, which tells the basic 'history' outlined by Geoffrey of Monmouth, giving it all the 'rise and fall of princes' shape characteristic of the Vulgate Cycle but without any reference to the Grail or to the adultery of Lancelot, who is not mentioned

(iv) *Sir Gawain and the Green Knight*, which, like Geoffrey's *History* and the *Alliterative Morte*, is focused on Gawain rather than on Lancelot, and which, like the Grail material which may be among its sources, is focused on Christian as well as chivalric virtues. This will be my Example Text for the section, although it is so outstanding an example of the tradition as not to be really characteristic of it, but I will now say a little about the other texts in this group.

(i) *Yvain*

The first of these is an early fourteenth-century and unique translation of a Chrétien story, his *Yvain* or *Le chevalier au Lion*, a tale of a knight's long penance for his failure to keep his word to his lady. It is retold in rhyming couplets, as is usual with early romances from the French, with several decorative uses of linked words and rhymes (see the text-box on p. 206). The translator has stressed the need to keep 'truth', which is also key to many other romances including *Sir Orfeo* (discussed on p. 168, above), and *Sir Gawain and the Green Knight*, perhaps because it is a virtue common both to the old values of chivalry and to the newer and softer values of love and courtesy (see Chapter 7). However, neither of the protagonists seems capable of a genuine emotional faithfulness. The Lady turns in a matter of hours – and without apparent reproach from the narrator – from her first husband to the man (Yvain) who has killed him, and Yvain himself, once he has married her, seems to forget her completely when he is away from her. Each of them has to learn to miss and then truly win the other, instructed by the Lady's servant, the sharp and perceptive Lunette, who is easily the most interesting character. It is she who finally tricks the estranged couple into a reconciliation. (The text is printed in Schmidt 1980, Vol. 2.)

(ii) The *Stanzaic Morte Arthur*

This is a significant mid-fourteenth-century adaptation made from the last book of the *Vulgate Cycle*, the French prose *Mort Artu*. This had added the story of the exposure of the relationship between Lancelot and Queen Guinevere, to Geoffrey of Monmouth's history, which does not mention Lancelot, but blames Arthur's fall entirely on the treachery of his nephew Mordred. The poet reduces this double story to a fifth of its length, and gives a wonderful sweep and inevitability to the plot, which Malory (who clearly knew the poem) will refine and clarify and bring to even greater life. The poet writes, like many early English adaptations of French narratives, in octo-syllabic lines, which he groups not in couplets but into 8-line stanzas with two alternating rhymes. This is an easy form to remember, suggesting an audience of listeners as well as readers. But it is a hard form to write, and the poet uses repeated rhymes, imperfect rhyme and some special effects to help him convey the action, including plenty of alliteration. It is capable of vivid effects, as here where the poet describes the devastation of war:

> Though we might with worship win,
>   Of a thing mine herte is sore:
> This land is full of folk full thin,
>   Batailes have made it full bare;
> Wite ye well it were grete sin
>   Cristen folk to slee thus more
> (*Stanzaic Morte* 2596–601; see also 4360–4)
> *Wite ye well*: you should know well

It is extremely illuminating for students of Malory to compare the last two Books of his *Morte Darthur* (Caxton ed., 20–21) with the equivalent passage in the *Stanzaic Morte* (1672ff.). Benson does this (1996, pp. 221–38), focusing particularly on structure and characterisation. One can also look at the difference between the form of each text. What difference does it make that Malory writes in prose rather than in rhymed verse? Are there any effects that Malory cannot achieve in prose? Does the dialogue between characters show the development of realistic prose? One can also explore the difference in attitude to women's roles between the earlier and later texts, which are about a century apart (although both using the same thirteenth-century source). Here the figure of Elaine is very interesting; do you think that she chooses death as an act of will in both texts, or only in the later one?

(iii) The *Alliterative Morte Arthure*

Dating from even later in the fourteenth century than the *Stanzaic Morte Arthur*, the *Alliterative Morte Arthure* is much more consciously nationalist. It is based on Geoffrey of Monmouth's *History* of Arthur, and it uses the old alliterative metre of Layamon's *Brut*, though without his Frenchifying rhyme or plot additions. The *Alliterative Morte* describes Arthur's establishment of himself as king in Britain with his company of knights, of whom Gawain is the chief, and his invasion of Rome and France including his battle with the giant on St Michael's Mount. His absence allows Mordred, his nephew and warden of England, to seize the throne and his queen, and the story ends with the death of Arthur and almost all his knights in defeating Mordred. The poet makes significant additions to the detail of his given story. Thus while following Geoffrey in its interest in heroic battles, often involving chivalrous tourneys between individual knights, the alliterative writer shows awareness of the suffering that such battles cause, not so much to the inhabitants of conquered lands as in the *Stanzaic Morte*, as to the knights and people of Britain themselves. The poet's tone of lament for his unhappy kingdom can be seen, for example, in Arthur's words to his dead knights:

> than remys the riche kyng with rewthe at his herte,
> Hewys hys handys one heghte and to the heuen lokes:
> 'Qwythen hade Dryghttyn destaynede at his dere will,
> that he hade demyd me todaye to dy for yow all;
> That had I leuer than be lorde all my lyfe tym
> Off all that Alexandere aughte qwhills he in erthe lengede.'
> (*Alliterative Morte* 4155–60)
>
> *rewthe*: pity; *Hewys*: heaves; *Qwythen hade Dryghttyn ... to dy for yow all*: Why did God's dear will not allow me to die for you all; *leuer than*: rather than; *aughte qwhills he in erthe lengede*: owned while he lived on earth

These sufferings are chiefly caused by Mordred, whose adultery with Guinevere (Waynore) is only one of a list of his crimes against king and country recounted by one who has suffered them:

> He has castells encrochede and corownde hym seluen,
> Kaughte in all the rentis of the Rownde Tabill;
> He devisede the rewme and delte as hym likes ...
> They robbe thy religeous and ravische thi nones,
> And redy ryddis with his rowtte to rawnsone the pouere ...
> He has weddede Waynore, and hir his wieffe holdis ...
> And has wroghte hire with childe, as wittnesse tellis.
> Off all the wyes of this worlde, woo motte hym worthe,
> Thus has Sir Modrede merrede vs all! (*Alliterative Morte* 3525–655)
>
> *encrochede*: captured; *Kaughte in*: appropriated; *devisede*: divided; *religious*: monks and friars; *redy ryddis with his rowtte to rawnsone*: he is ready to ride with his gang to rob; *wyes*: men; *woo motte hym worthe*: let woe come to him

Is the poet thinking of the troubles of the land under the tyranny of Richard II when the king's favoured aristocracy protected criminal gangs?

The poem is also suffused with a medieval sense of tragedy (see Schmidt 1980, 'Introduction'). Arthur's final battle is lost not through his personal fault but in obedience to the turning of Fortune's wheel. Arthur's dream of the wheel is in the French source used by the *Stanzaic Morte*, but now it is much developed to give the story an archetypal inevitability. The shape of Arthur's rise and fall is that of the princes of medieval historians, increasing the sense that Arthur was a real national hero.

(iv) Example Text: *Sir Gawain and the Green Knight*

Contemporary with the *Alliterative Morte* is the most celebrated alliterative verse romance in Middle English: *Sir Gawain and the Green Knight*. This is now thought to have been written by a member of a noble household from the North-West Midlands, as both the dialect and some of the specialist vocabulary of geographical features suggest close familiarity with the Wirral (see Elliott 1997). However, he need not have been resident there when he wrote the poem, and several critics have suggested that he was a cleric to a noble retinue, perhaps from Cheshire, stationed at Richard II's court. He himself was probably a cleric rather than a knight, as the other three poems in the manuscript are probably also by him, and these are religious (see text-box on the *Pearl*-poet at p. 175, and Andrew 1997). The poem is written in astonishing alliterative verse, whose virtuosic diction is enhanced by a tight control of metre and structure. The poem is written in alliterative long line (see text-box on p. 25), each stanza being completed by a 'bob' (single-stressed line) and rhymed 'wheel' of four short lines. The subtlety and dry wit of the specialist alliterative and regional language is vividly translated by Simon Armitage (2009), though it is to be hoped that this will then send readers to sample at least their favourite passages in the original tongue in a well-glossed edition.

This poem shares with Chaucer's *Troilus and Criseyde* the richness and ambiguity occasioned by using several different and conflicting traditions, which I shall sum up as folk tale, Arthurian Romance, religious traditions, and realism with humour. One way of approaching the poem is to look at the fault-lines between these different traditions as they appear in it, and to try to resolve the contradictory interpretations that each tradition seems to demand. I will therefore recount the story under headings suggested by different groups of sources, and suggest the kinds of issues each part of the story seems to raise. How can the poem feel so unified and what does it really mean?

The folk-tale tradition (Celtic and Breton stories)

The framing narrative of the story is a version of the 'Beheading Game' also found in the Middle-Irish *Bricriu's Feast*, where the hero is Cuchulainn, and the Breton story of Carados (reproduced and discussed in E. Brewer 1973, pp. 9–46, and reprinted in her 1992 collection of sources); as we will see in the section on Religious Traditions (p. 257), the poet probably learned the story from a later Grail narrative. In our poem a Green Knight appears at Arthur's court and demands a *Crystemas gomen* (Christmas game, 283) in which he will allow a knight to strike a blow at him in return for a blow which he will strike a year later. Arthur accepts the challenge but Gawain begs to take it instead, strikes the blow and beheads the Green Knight, but the Green Knight simply recovers his head from the floor and tells Gawain to meet him at New Year the following year in the *Grene Chapel* (451). The name of the rendezvous, and the appearance of the *aghlich mayster* (ugly master, 136) carrying a *holyn bobbe* (holly branch, 206), suggest an origin in the folk figure of the Green Man characteristic of ancient 'vegetation myths' (see Spiers 1957, pp. 215–51, and other references below). This underlying symbolic meaning is reinforced by the various cycles which occur in the poem, such as the passing of the year, the repetition of three hunts, three temptations and three blows, or the appearance of youth (Gawain / Lady), middle age (Bertilak) and old age (Morgan le Fay) at different points in the poem. These and other patterns are explored by Sadowski, who explores the 'cosmological, mythological, historical, seasonal, christological, social, and individual layers of meaning' (1996, p. 53). This mythic rationale for the poem does not require either believable characters or convincing causality of events to work, and so it conflicts with the presence of these realistic elements in the poem. Is the powerful and sardonic presence of the Green Knight really conveyed by interpreting him as a Green Man?

The Arthurian Romance tradition

Geoffrey of Monmouth had made Gawain fellow-hero with Arthur in his *History of the Kings of Britain*. As we have seen (p. 244), Layamon's alliterative versification of the *History* had inspired alliterative heroic Romances, of which the *Alliterative Morte* and *Gawain* are two surviving examples. Both poems appeal to the English taste for a national tradition of poetry, but *Gawain* is also very much in the tradition of French Arthurian Romance, which Putter sees as pre-eminently civilising:

> the best French Arthurian romances ... expose and explore the tensions between love and duty, conscience and worldly glory, obligation and self-interest ... Their concern with the cultivation of a new kind of Sensibility also informs ... the heroic ideal which Chretien, his continuators, and the *Gawain*-poet put forward, namely, the ideal of the 'courtly knight' who combines chivalry with clerical restraint, discipline, and scruples. (Putter 1996, pp. 6, 8)

The key principles against which this 'courtly knight' Gawain seems to be tested are truth (meaning faith-keeping) and courtesy – principles which are ultimately incompatible. In the central section of the poem, Gawain, now armed for his fight with the Green Knight, goes to seek the Green Chapel. On Christmas Eve he finds himself at a castle apparently only two miles from his destination, and spends the holidays there as his appointment is for New Year's Day. Here he is subjected to two tests: three attempts by the wife of Bertilak, his host, to seduce him, and three exchanges of the day's winnings with Bertilak, who spends the time out hunting. Both of these are essentially tests of truth – loyalty to the host in not sleeping with his wife, and faith-keeping in the exchange. As we have already seen from the English romances already discussed, in *Yvain*, or the *Stanzaic Morte*, the failure to keep faith to a promise or a liege-lord is catastrophic, and in *Gawain* the whole quest has been a test of his truth to the promise made to the Green Knight in Camelot.

Gawain does keep his *forwarde* (promise) to the Green Knight, but he fails to keep another *forwarde*, one made to Bertilak to swap at evening any gains he has made during the day (the kisses, and then the girdle, given him by Bertilak's wife). However, Bertilak judges him to have wonderfully succeeded in the test of keeping his *forwarde* to receive a potentially deadly return blow, and that this has saved the reputation of his king and court. Moreover, Gawain's refusal to sleep with his host's wife is – in Bertilak's words – another proof of his *grete traweth* (2470, recalling 403). However, Bertilak reveals that Gawain has failed in truth – a little – by retaining what he believes to be a magic girdle, which the Lady has given him (see Martin 1997). Pearsall (1997, p. 357) sees Gawain's embarrassment at this point as being caused not by guilt but by shame that his slippage of moral standards is now public, polluting the honour of Arthur's court. Such an interpretation recalls the feudal origins of knighthood, and its expression of ideals in chivalric action. However, it conflicts with the Christian interpretation of the poem, which I shall offer in the next section, which sees Gawain's self-reproach as guilt for a failure in his own internal standards, integral to his own sense of identity, and to the moral fabric of his society.

Gawain is also tested for his courtesy, another virtue which has both an outward and an inner aspect. If Truth represents the more masculine and military side of chivalry, courtesy can be seen as the standard by which to judge peace-time pursuits of hunting, feasting and love-talking. In the pentangle on Gawain's shield, which encapsulates the virtues he should uphold, courtesy plays an important part in the fifth group of virtues:

> the fyft fyue that I finde that the frek vsed
> Watz fraunchyse and felaghschyp forbe al thyng,
> His clannes and his cortaysye croked were neuer,
> And pité, that passez alle poyntez, thyse pure fyue (*Gawain and the Green Knight* 651–4)
>
> *frek*: man; *forbe*: above; *pité, that passez alle poyntez*: and compassion / piety which surpasses all qualities

Franchise (generosity), fellowship (loyal friendship) and courtesy (good manners) are all characteristic of the Romance virtues exercised in the chivalric court, or (as we saw in the last chapter) in the garden of Love. Both Cleanness and Pity can also be used in a courtly sense to represent good behaviour. Many critics have explored the importance of courtesy to Gawain (e.g., Brewer 1966), focusing, for example, on his humble politeness in taking the original challenge although *the wakkest, I wot, and of wyt feeblest* (354), and his welcome at Bertilak's castle as the *fader of nurture* (919). Does his anxiety not to fail in courtesy – and simply tell the Lady to leave – itself become a source of danger?

> He cared for his cortaysye, lest crathayn he were,
> And more for his meschef yif he schulde make synne,
> And be traytor to that tolke that that telde aght.
> 'God schylde,' quoth the schalk, 'that schal not befalle!' (*Gawain and the Green Knight* 1774–7)
>
> *crathayn*: churlish; *tolke that that telde aght*: the man who owned the dwelling; *God schylde*: God forbid!; *schalk*: man; *befalle*: happen

Here we can see clearly that for Gawain, being merely courtly (retaining his *cortaysye*) risks making *synne*, and being a *traytor*. In the bedroom, courtesy in speech is not always truthful, but is always elegant and witty. Does Gawain fail in courtesy in even accepting the girdle when he has no *tokenez of trweluf craftes* (1527) to offer in exchange? Does the poet celebrate or warn against the expensive life-style he so flamboyantly described in the feasting and hunting scenes? Does such a life-style not conflict with the poverty and patience he upheld in *Patience* (see Chapter 6), or is he looking for beauty and perfection wherever it can be found?

Religious traditions

Critics from Benson in 1965 to Putter in 1995 have noted that the poet probably learned the story of the beheading-game through *The Quest for the Holy Grail*, which is the first continuation of the *Perceval* by Chrétien de Troyes (see L. Benson 1965, Appdx. B; Mills 1968, p.85–198; Putter 1995, p. 41; relevant parts of this text are reprinted in E. Brewer 1992). As Mills explains in some detail, such texts abound with marvels and temptresses, which test the Christianity and moral resolve of the hero. Such a context would allow for an allegorical interpretation of Gawain's arming as a Christian knight in Fitt 2, where his shield in particular seems to suggest a well-known passage from Ephesians 6:13–16:

> Wherefore take unto you the whole armour of God, that ye may be able to withstand in the evil day ... having your loins girt about with truth, and having on the breastplate of righteousness ... Above all, taking the shield of faith, wherewith ye shall be able to quench all the fiery darts of the wicked.

Two of the five 'fives' represented by the pentangle are indeed evidence of Gawain's religious faith (his trust in the five wounds of Christ and in the five joys of Mary). Two concern his physique (the five fingers and his five wits or senses), which, as Twomey shows (2009, p. 75), are intimately connected to his spiritual life. The fifth five need not be interpreted as Romance virtues, but as virtues which concern Gawain's relationship to God or to the Virgin, painted on the inside of his shield. Does the entire pentangle, as Green argued in 1966, represent an abstract perfection, in which human beings cannot but fail? Or is it too ambiguous, too self-conflicting, to suggest the Divine protection which surrounds a Galahad or a Perceval and makes them un-temptable?

Although an allegorical interpretation may seem too blunt an instrument to dissect the subtleties of *Gawain*, there are many ways in which the poem is illuminated by Christian teaching. Scattergood (1981) argues that Gawain's lazy days in Bertilak's castle encourage gluttony, lechery and above all, the sloth which tempts him to neglect his promise to exchange his winnings. Lechery is a much more obvious temptation and Rooney (1997) has given several useful analogues to the theme of sexual temptation of the Christian knight – often involving a husband absent on a hunt. During the third temptation scene, we are told that he has felt physically drawn to the Lady and was only restrained by the Virgin Mary for *Gret perile bitwene hem stod, / Nif Maré of hir knygt mynne* (had not remembered; 1768–9). The element of physical temptation continues when he accepts the green girdle, because he feels it might save his life when he confronts the Green Knight in the morning. Accordingly, when his deception is exposed, he castigates his failure as a sin as well as a failure in courage:

> 'Corsed worth cowarddyse and couetyse bothe!
> In yow is vylany and vyse that vertue disstryes.' (*Gawain and the Green Knight* 2374–5)

The Green Knight adopts the same Christian language, assuring Gawain that he has now confessed and done penance for the sin by receiving a nick on the neck from his axe (see Burrow 1966):

> thou art confessed so clene, beknowen of thy mysses,
> And hatz the penaunce apert of the poynt of myn egge (*Gawain and the Green Knight* 2391–2)
>
> *beknowen of thy mysses*: cleared of thy fault; *apert of the poynt of myn egge*: openly at the point of my weapon

The Green Knight then praises Gawain's resistance to the Lady as that of the purest of knights (*a perle bi the quite pese* 2364), almost as if Gawain were comparable with the *Pearl*-maiden herself. But Gawain will not be comforted and goes back to Camelot wearing the girdle as a badge of his imperfection. We, like the Green Knight and the court, may laugh at his discomfiture. But in the context of a Christian interpretation, his replacement of the perfect pentangle by the deceptive girdle does seem to epitomise sin, however excusable Gawain's motives (see Howard 1964). Do you find this kind of interpretation sufficiently inclusive, or does it exclude too many of the other values which seem to be celebrated in it?

Realism and humour

At first reading, *Gawain* may appear far from realistic. Not only is the language and the setting highly wrought, and the story structured in a series of contrasts and balances, but it is permeated with the marvellous. Yet the impression left on the reader, as with *Troilus and Criseyde*, is of the reality of the characters, the accurate detail of the courtly life, and the vivid realisation of nature. Does this realism undercut the other traditions we have been looking at – of the folk myth, or the elevated romance, or the religious absolutes? Perhaps the only way to resolve these tensions is to look at local effects through close analysis, as Putter does in his Introduction (1996). This is certainly a good way of appreciating the realism of his characterisation, for example the poet uses the passive voice to describe how Gawain both does and does not accept the green girdle (1996, pp. 91–3, referring to 1855–65), suggesting the moral slippage in his failure to resist. In a section on 'romance and realism' (45–75) Putter includes an examination of the picturing of the landscape as Gawain rides across the Wirral. This passage is also analysed by Stanbury (1991, pp. 105–7), who sees how the viewer's eyes realistically focus on the near and the far. She applies this notion of perspective to the narrator's judgement as well as his gaze, allowing us both to share and to assess Gawain's or the court's viewpoint. This is the source of much of the humour generated by the poem. What is the point of the courtly accoutrements of armour and fine embroidered cloth when the real enemy is the cold? Why should one keep one's oath to a knight who has not explained that he can manage without his head? What is wrong with taking a magic girdle in a world where magic knights are sharpening their axes?

Our widening view can take in all four of the traditions I have been outlining, simultaneously. It is indeed the clash of all these levels of meaning – the marvellous, the Romance, the religious, the realistic – which makes the poem essentially a comedy – perhaps even a parody of the high style in which it is written. At any rate this extraordinarily complex poem resists a single interpretation, and mirrors the contradictions of real life.

Questions on *Gawain and the Green Knight* and other fourteenth-century Chivalric Romances

- How does Arthur's characterisation as a public figure, kingly and responsible hero of the *Alliterative Morte Arthure*, contrast with his portrayal in the *Stanzaic Morte Arthur* or in *Gawain and the Green Knight*?
- Compare Bertilak's wife in *Gawain and the Green Knight* with Guinevere in the *Stanzaic Morte*. Is she any more than a temptress in *Gawain* and does she have any aspects of the temptress in the *Morte*? How closely does your interpretation relate to the traditions from which each text derives?
- Look at how the poet of the *Alliterative Morte* conveys the mysterious wood of Arthur's dream (3218ff.), and contrast it with the wood described in *Gawain and the Green Knight* 740–62 (see Stanbury 1991, for perception in dreams).
- Compare the *Stanzaic Morte* passage 3446–525, in which Arthur gets Bevedere to return his sword to the lake, with the passage in Malory 21.5, which it has clearly inspired, and to the use of the axe in *Gawain*. In none of these texts is the weapon simply a weapon.

(d) The Fifteenth Century: Lydgate and Malory

Lydgate's extraordinary popularity did much to ensure that Chaucer's European kind of poetry continued to be the principal path for English writers to follow. His two long Romances, the *Troy Book* (1412–20) and the *Siege of Thebes* (1420–2) followed Chaucer's lead in every essential (apart from humour and the power to outlast time). The *Troy Book*, like *Troilus and Criseyde*, is based on Guido delle Colonne's version of the Troy story, though unlike Chaucer, Lydgate does not focus on the lovers, or use Boccaccio. Instead he gives a detailed translation of Guido, amplified into 36,000 lines by long digressions, so that in Pearsall's words, 'it is a homily first, an encyclopaedia second and an epic nowhere' (1970, p. 129). It was, however, commissioned by Henry V and read by the aristocracy and many others (23 manuscripts survive, one or two very lavish). The *Siege of Thebes* is only 4,716 lines long, and it takes its inspiration from Chaucer's *Knight's Tale*, this being supposedly a tale told by Gower himself who has joined the pilgrims for the return journey from Canterbury (there is a eulogy to Chaucer in the Prologue 39–57). Lydgate reminds his listeners occasionally that they have heard part of the story already from the Knight, but unlike the Knight, he does not take his tale from Boccaccio's *Teseida* but directly from Benoit's twelfth-century *Roman de Thebes* (a companion text to the *Roman de Troie*), through a French prose redaction. The poem is in rhyme royale and is more thematically unified than the *Troy Book*, suggesting a less grandiose purpose; it was not a royal commission but written by Lydgate for himself. It does have a relevance to the king, however, for it includes much 'Mirror for Princes' material, attacks war, and praises peace; 1430 was the year in which Henry V had apparently resolved the war in France by the Treaty of Troys. This must have helped to make it popular with the kind of wealthy and aristocratic audience likely to have owned the twenty-nine carefully-produced surviving manuscripts. Simpson suggests that, as England slipped into civil war, this Tale of a struggle between the two sons of Oedipus as to who should rule Thebes may have seemed increasingly relevant (Simpson 2009).

It was against the background of that civil war that Malory produced the most significant Middle English addition to the tradition of Arthurian Romance: the *Morte Darthur*. Its publication history is itself of great interest. 1485, the year of the accession of Henry VII which ended the Wars of the Roses, was the year in which William Caxton first printed it. He was in the middle of a publishing project that he hoped would prevent the English from ever becoming embroiled again in such a base conflict. He had been printing books in his Westminster Press for about eight years, and had already secured a huge readership in comparison with the bookshops, which could only produce handwritten manuscripts, so he was entitled to think that he had real influence. The four books of his new project were designed to inspire the reader to return to the virtuous warfare of the past, represented by three long accounts of three worthies – 'Godefroy of Boloyne' (a crusading knight), 'Charles the Grate' (Charlemaigne) and 'King Arthur', together with the chivalric and Christian principles outlined in Caxton's own translation of Lull's *Book of the Ordre of Chyualry*. It was certainly an ambitious project, but it was a publishing success, particularly the history of the British King Arthur, offered as Malory's translation of the French Arthurian legends that he had completed some fifteen years earlier (see Goodman 1985). Caxton's *Preface* to this work indicates his hopes for the effect that he hopes it will have on the English upper classes:

> Sir Thomas Malorye did take out of certain books of French, and reduced ... into English. And I, according to my copy, have done set it in imprint, to the intent that noble men may see and learn the noble acts of chivalry, the gentle and virtuous deeds that some knights used in those days, by which they came to honour ... humbly beseeching all noble lords and ladies ... of what estate or degree they been of. ...
> Do after the good and leave the evil, and it shall bring you to good fame and renown.

Thomas Malory

If he was the Thomas Malory of Newbold (b. 1416?–17), Malory had a turbulent and self-conflicted life. In the 1430s and 1440s he was, on the whole, a respectable member of the country gentry, inheriting his father's lands in Warwickshire in 1433 and receiving his knighthood in 1440, possibly serving in Gascony in 1442, and acting as MP for Warwickshire in 1445 when he also married Elizabeth Walsh. However, during this period he also began a career of violent politics and violent crime, interrupted by periods in prison. At first a Lancastrian and follower of Buckingham, he turned against him and eventually tried to kill him in 1451. He was imprisoned in 1452–8 and then he joined Warwick as a Yorkist and fought in Edward IV's army in 1462. Though Edward reigned (for the first time) from 1461 to 1470, the tide was turning against him – as was Warwick – at the end of his first reign, and possibly in consequence Malory was accused of a variety of further crimes of violence, including taking part in a Lancastrian plot, and was imprisoned again in 1468. He finished writing the *Morte Darthur* in 1470 and was released. He died at home in 1471.

See Riddy (1987, and references on p. 3); and Field 1993.

For some of the many years that Malory may have spent in prison he must have been researching and writing the *Morte Darthur*, which Caxton says he 'reduced' from French books. Though far shorter than his main source, the immense French *Vulgate Cycle*, the *Morte Darthur* is far from being a mere précis and translation, and it uses English as well as French sources, notably the *Alliterative Morte* and *Stanzaic Morte*, and the Prologue of the *Chronicle of John Hardyng*. Modern scholars are revealing just how original his work is, for he did not merely cut and disentangle and translate, but also reshaped his material to make it more dramatic, to convey his feeling about the characters, and to suggest general themes such as the flaws within chivalry. Caxton changed his text a little more by dividing it into twenty-one books, each with at least a dozen chapters; he also significantly cut Book 2, about Arthur's Roman campaign, presumably because he did not like the alliterative borrowings from the *Morte Arthure*. In 1934 a fifteenth-century manuscript of the *Morte Darthur* was discovered in Winchester School, with quite different divisions by modest rubrics into eight Books, a much longer Book 2, and other differences from Caxton's text, including several details of plot which are in the source but not in Caxton. Vinaver published this as Malory's 'authentic' text. It is certainly earlier than Caxton's, and it is the text in which the book is read by scholars (the Penguin edition, Cowen 2004, uses Caxton), but the Winchester Manuscript is now not generally seen either as Malory's autograph, or as Caxton's base text, in spite of the traces of printer's ink on the pages. Field (1998) places both the manuscript and Caxton's text independently at one remove from Malory's original, but apart from Book 2, both seem to be pretty close to that original. In what follows, I will use Vinaver's more authentic text, but as this is available in several editions, will give references to Caxton's sub-divisions into Books and Chapters, since virtually every edition gives these references throughout their text.

The choice of what histories to include in his 'Grete Booke', or chivalric anthology, is interesting. He abridges and rewrites, but uses all kinds of material on Arthur, including the story of his Roman wars taken from the *Alliterative Morte Arthure* (which he sometimes transcribes almost unaltered), on Lancelot and Guinevere, on Sir Gareth, on Sir Tristram, and (greatly abbreviated) on Sir Galahad and the Grail Quest. However, he changes the focus and direction of much of this material, adding new scenes and enormous amounts of dialogue. In spite of Caxton's hope that his publishing project would inspire a new crusade against the Turks, Malory does not follow the Grail Cycle in centring his book on the Grail Quest and its depiction of Christian chivalry. He limited the Grail Quest itself to five short books (13–17 in Caxton's edition), and does not allow its Christian ethos to undermine the secular values upheld by Arthur and his best knights in the rest of the book, the values of honour or *worship*, loyalty, courtesy and prowess (see Barber 1996). In the *French Vulgate Cycle* Arthur and Lancelot have contaminated the purity of the Round Table Fellowship long before its tragic fall. The late *Suite de Merlin* compounds Arthur's sin of the adultery which engendered Mordred, by saying it was also incest with his half-sister Morgawse, and that Arthur then attempted to kill the baby as it was prophesied he would slay him (see 'Mordred', in Field 1998). Malory uses these plot elements but focuses on the wickedness of Mordred rather than the failings of Arthur. The *Prose Lancelot* portrays the long liaison between Lancelot and Guinevere as explicitly adulterous from the first, whereas in Malory's version there is only one very late scene in Book 19 when they are actually said to be in bed together. It is the discovery of this adultery which prompts the downfall of Lancelot in both texts, so it cannot be said that Malory removes this causality of sin and resulting moral compromise from his story. But he transforms it by making the love between Lancelot and Guinevere not only the most believable, but in some ways the most idealistic relationship in the book. It certainly trumps the paper-thin moralities of the *Queste de Saint Grail*.

Furthermore, Malory enhances the tragic structure of his book, and thus suggests that the end of the Round Table is independent of any individual knight's sinfulness. He fits it within the medieval expectation that all kings must eventually fall by the turning of Fortune's wheel, using Arthur's dream of the wheel from the *Alliterative Morte Arthure* (see 21.3). Fate seems to be against Arthur, driving him to fight before reinforcements arrive, because one of the soldiers drew his sword to kill an adder and so precipitated the slaughter (21.4). Malory increases the sense of tragic inevitability by suggesting that there is an inherent flaw in the knightly code itself (rather as the *Gawain*-poet had suggested that knightly values contradict one another). This flaw is most clearly seen in the principle of prowess, that the knight who wins a battle is not only the strongest knight but also the best knight, and moreover has right on his side. The discussion of my Example Text – the last two Books of Malory's *Morte Darthur* – will indicate how much that principle is undermined and how this contributes to the tragedy of the whole (see Kelly 1997; Radulescu 2005).

Before I do this, however, I would like to include some discussion of Malory's women. There are strong female characters in all the stories apart from that of the Holy Grail, and it is illuminating to compare them, as several modern critics have done (see, for example, Archibald and Edwards 1996; Robeson 2005). Cherewatuk (2006, ch. 3) compares Elaine of Astolat, who falls in love with Lancelot in Book 18.8–20, with Lyonesse, the bride of Gareth in Book 7. Both women use words from the marriage ceremony to assert their claim over their knight, only in Elaine's case these are repudiated by Lancelot, who maintains he is not free to love her. Indeed, in a possible echo of Chaucer's *Franklyn's Tale*, he later tells Guinevere that *love muste only aryse of the herte self, and nat by none conareaynte* (18.20). Elaine, however, refuses to be constrained *not* to love, and expresses her power simply by accepting nothing but death either from her father or from Sir Lancelot himself, who offers to give her a large dowry to marry someone else. Elaine of Corbin (Books 11–12), who tricks Lancelot into fathering her son Galahad, and later nurses him back to health and lives with him in her castle, is an even clearer example of a woman who pursues her own goals in despite of her lover's wishes. Because of her association with the saintly Galahad she is not condemned, even by her father, and indeed, Lancelot's nephew Bors urges him to marry her. Thus both Elaines suggest an alternative future for Lancelot, one which would not inevitably lead to tragedy for him and his fellow-knights. Do such positive women darken the figure of Guinevere, whom Elaine of Corbin accuses of doing herself *grete dysnonoure, for ye have a lorde royall of youre owne, and therefore hit were youre parte for to love him* (11.7)? Or does it indicate that it is Lancelot himself who cannot change, and that neither the Elaines nor Guinevere have any real power to alter his feelings, though they can cause him pain? The relationship between him and Guinevere is at the centre of the tragedy to which I shall now turn.

Example Text: The closing Books of the *Morte Darthur*

The last parts of the *Morte Darthur* are named by Vinaver as *The Book of Sir Launcelot and Queen Guinevere* (Caxton's Books 18–19), and *The Most Piteous Tale of the Morte Arthur sanz Guerdon* (Caxton's Books 20–1).

Walsh (1985) and Benson (1996) give illuminating analyses of Malory's changes here to his sources, principally the French prose *Lancelot* and the *Stanzaic Morte Arthur*. These books cover the period from the end of the Grail Quest to the deaths of Lancelot and Guinevere. In the Grail Quest it is Lancelot's son, Galahad, rather than he himself, who achieves spiritual perfection. Lancelot blames his failure on his feelings for the Queen, and when he returns he makes determined efforts to end the liaison (for Walsh 1985, this is a real conflict between his spirit and his flesh) – or at least make it more discreet. He tries to conceal his particular love for her behind a general championing of all ladies, a manoeuvre which she condemns and then follows herself by inviting several knights (not including Lancelot) to a 'pryvy dynere'. In the course of the meal, Sir Patryse is poisoned by an apple which Sir Pyonell had in fact intended for Sir Gawain, and Guinevere is accused of murder. She is put on trial in an archaic way, by which the murdered knight's kinsman, Sir Mador, 'appeals' her of murder, and she has to find a champion to prove the rightness of her cause. At the last minute, Lancelot, whom she has banished from the court, appears and fights with Sir Mador, beating but not killing him, and the Queen is exonerated. (Later Nynyve, the Damsel of the Lake, testifies to her innocence.) Malory has established a pattern, which he will repeat twice more, by which the Queen is put on trial and then exonerated (or rescued) by Lancelot acting as her champion. In this, the first case, Guinevere really is innocent and Lancelot's success in battle endorses this.

However, Guinevere becomes increasingly guilty of the crime for which she is 'appealed', and so Lancelot's rescues become increasingly illegal and even criminal. They also become increasingly bloody. Presumably to achieve this effect of the successive defeat of law by mere prowess, Malory inserts the episode Vinaver calls *The Knight of the Cart* from its much earlier position in the *Vulgate Cycle*, at this point in the story. In this, the second of the trial situations, Guinevere has been accused by her would-be rapist, Sir Melliagaunt, of sleeping with one of the twelve wounded knights who guard her bedchamber, his evidence being the streaks of blood on her sheets. In fact it is Lancelot who has made these marks, because in coming (invited) into the Queen's bedroom he wounded his hand by wrenching out the iron bars of her window. The irony of the situation is striking: bloodied sheets are here not a sign of a wife's virginity but of her adultery, and the forced window suggests her violator (see Francis 2011, and Kelly 1985, for the symbolism of wounds). Melliagaunt 'appeals' (accuses) Guinevere of treason, and when Lancelot says he will fight to prove Guinevere's innocence, Melliagaunt warns him that he should

> beware what ye do; for though ye are never so good a knight, as ye wot well ye are renowned the best knight of the world, yet should ye be advised to do battle in a wrong quarrel, for God will have a stroke in every battle. (19.7)

(Indeed, all Arthur's knights had sworn not to fight in a wrong quarrel when he instituted the Order of the Round Table in 3.15: the 'Pentecostal Oath'.) However, God seems to be on Lancelot's side, apparently allowing him to defeat and kill Melliagaunt with one hand tied behind his back. This is one of many additions and changes that Malory makes to his immediate source for the story (the French prose *Lancelot*) and it is followed by an even more substantive change, in the insertion of a completely original episode into the story. The 'audacity of the story's placement' (Walsh 1985, p. 320) seems to have the purpose of proving to the reader that God still places him as the 'best knight of the world' in spite of his adultery and the 'wrong quarrel' with Melliagaunt. A wounded knight, Sir Urré, comes to Camelot to find the 'best knight of the world', who has been prophesied to cure him by his touch. Lancelot is most unwilling to take part in a public virtue competition, but after every other knight (including King Arthur) has failed to heal Sir Urré, he does search his wounds, which *fair healed* at once. Lancelot, confounded by his own sense of inadequacy, *wepte as he had bene a childe that had bene beatyn* (19.12). This moving episode seems to heal the earlier scene where Lancelot's own wound had been the cause of suspicion, deceit and death.

The characterisation of Lancelot and Guinevere, and their relationship, in all the episodes we have been discussing is quite masterly, and is conveyed through a strikingly dramatic use of prose dialogue. Malory's originality and skill goes even further in his account of *The Most Piteous Tale of the Morte Arthur sanz Guerdon* (Caxton's Books 20–1). As Hanks has demonstrated (Hanks 1992, pp. 78–90), Malory adds crucial incidents to the *Stanzaic Morte*'s account of Lancelot's catastrophic last days at Arthur's court, and enormously increases the proportion of dialogue. These changes enrich the characterisation of both Lancelot and Guinevere, and intensify the sense that their love is hallowed in spite of the damage it is doing to the court. Malory also adds realistic detail and drama, contrasting the tumult when the fourteen knights attempt to batter down the door and fight Lancelot, with the quiet inside the chamber after the slaughter has ended and Lancelot and Guinevere exchange rings and promises of fidelity:

> And than he kyste her, and ayther of hem gaff othir a rynge; and so the quene he lefte there, and wente untill hys lodgyng. (20.4)

(We are reminded of Troilus and Criseyde's first parting, when they also exchange rings and vow fidelity.)

Once more the Queen is placed on trial and once more Lancelot feels he must rescue her. He is supported in his decision by his kinsman Bors, who argues the case for continuing loyalty to Guinevere rather than to Arthur in a telling new insertion in 20.5–6. Malory develops the theme of the destructive effects of prowess, as Arthur attempts to deal with the situation by law rather than force, providing a guard to ensure that Guinevere is not rescued from the fire. Two of the guards are Gareth and Gaherys, unarmed sympathisers with Lancelot's cause, whom he kills without even knowing he has done so, for he *saw them nat ... among the thyckyste of the prees*

(20.8). He is now a killing machine rather than an upholder of right, of chivalry, or even of humanity (see Lynch 2000).

The rest of the story lurches from one failed reconciliation to another. Lancelot brings Guinevere back to Arthur in a pageant which parallels the London pageants of the fifteenth century, several of which tried to heal the wounds of civil war (see Bliss 2000, and p. 36 above). However, Gawain's revenge for his dead brother Gareth is intransigent, and he forces Arthur to continue the war into France, allowing Mordred to assemble his own troops against his father. The ensuing civil war is much bloodier than any of the previous battles or tournaments, and Field (2000) suggests that (as well as following several sources including Geoffrey of Monmouth) Malory may have been remembering his own experience of the Wars of the Roses, and in particular the Battle of Towton of 1461. This was the bloodiest battle ever fought on British soil, after which at least 28,000 bodies were buried, and during the fighting the men left alive were impeded by heaps of dead men (Hicks 2003, p. 87). In Malory's final battle only four men are left from 100,000, and one of them, Arthur, kills another, Mordred, amid *a grete hepe of dede men* (20.4). Malory is showing the disintegration of the chivalric ideal as much as the fate of his heroes; indeed, he conveys a sense of an inevitable tragedy for the whole Arthurian society and perhaps his own society as well. This makes his book a good text on which to end this survey of Medieval English literature.

Questions on Malory's *Morte Darthur*

- To what extent are each of the major figures involved responsible for the fall of the Round Table (see Benson 1996)?
- Compare the three women in Lancelot's life: Elaine of Corbin (mother of Galahad, see Bk 12), Elaine of Astolat (see Bks 18.8–20) and Guinevere (particularly in Bks 19–20). Changes to his sources can be illuminating (see McCarthy 'Sources' on Elaine of Astolat, and Benson 'Ending' on Guinevere: both in Archibald and Edwards 1996), as is contextualising the women in the story legally and socially (see Cherewatuk 2006).
- Using the famous passage from 18.25 as a starting point (with perhaps 19.6 as a contrast), how would you define Malory's

notion of 'virtuous love'? Critics vary in their judgement of what the essential virtue is, suggesting among other things chastity, loyalty, or long-suffering (see the round-up of critics in Benson 1996, pp. 337–9; Waldron 1992; McCarthy 1988, pp. 69–72). What is your opinion?
- How are the values, which the Fellowship of the Round Table has upheld, in conflict in Malory's last Book (20–21 in Caxton)? The values themselves are articulated in Caxton's preface, by Arthur in 3.15, by Bors in 20.5–6, in Ector's panegyric on Lancelot 21.13, among other places. Do you feel that the Fellowship fails because the knights fail to be true to these values, or because the values are themselves flawed?
- The *Morte Darthur*, even more than Chaucer's *Troilus and Criseyde*, can claim to be the first English novel. This is largely because it is written in prose, so that the action is described rather as in a chronicle, and the dialogue can feel very naturalistic. Is it therefore appropriate to use modern critical methods of analysing novels on Malory's text?

Texts, Sources and Further Reading

Texts

Armitage, Simon (transl.) (2009) *Sir Gawain and the Green Knight* (Faber).

Benson, L. D. (1986) *King Arthur's Death: Stanzaic Morte Arthur and Alliterative Morte Arthure* (University of Exeter Press).

Benson, L. D. (ed.) and Foster, E. (rev.) (1994) *The Stanzaic Morte Arthur and Alliterative Morte Arthure* (TEAMS Middle English Texts, http://d.lib.rochester.edu/teams/text/benson-and-foster-king-arthurs-death-stanzaic-morte-arthur-part-iii). This is the text used for quotation.

Christine de Pisan (1408–9) *The Book of Fayttes of Armes of Chyualrye*, (translated and printed by W. Caxton in 1480), ed. Byles, A. T. P. (Early English Text Society, EETS o.s. 189, 1932). Passage reprinted in Allmand, C. (ed.), *Society at War: Experience of England and France during the 100 Years War* (Boydell and Brewer, 1998).

Cowen, J. (ed.) (2004) *Sir Thomas Malory: Le Morte Darthur* (2 vols, Penguin Classics). This is a reprint of Penguin's 1966 edition of Caxton's version.

Lull, R. (1826) *Book of the Order of Chivalry*, transl. W. Caxton, ed. A. T. P. Byles (Early English Text Society, EETS, o.s. 168).
Sands, D. (ed.) (1986) *Middle English Verse Romances* (Exeter Unversity Press).
Schmidt, A. (1980) *Medieval English Romances*, 2 vols (Medieval and Renaissance Series, Hodder and Stoughton). These are abridged versions: Part 1 includes *Havelock*, *Athelston*, and *Sir Orfeo*; Part 2 includes *Ywain and Gawain*, *The Alliterative Morte Arthure* and the *Stanzaic Morte Arthur*.
Thorpe, L. (transl.) (1966) *Geoffrey of Monmouth* (Penguin Classics).
Tolkien, J. R. R. and Gordon, E. (1963) *Sir Gawain and the Green Knight* (University of Michigan electronic texts, http://quod.lib.umich.edu/c/cme/Gawain?rgn=main;view=fulltext). This is the text used for quotation.
Vinaver, E. (1959) *The Works of Sir Thomas Malory* (Oxford University Press).

History of society at war
Allmand, C. (1998) *The Hundred Years War* (Cambridge University Press).
Allmand, C. (ed.) (1998) *Society at War: Experience of England and France during the Hundred Years War* (Boydell Press).
Clark, L. (ed.) (2007) *Conflicts, Consequences and the Crown in the Late Middle Ages* (Boydell Press).
Hicks, M. (2003) *The Wars of the Roses* (Open University Press).
Lander, J. R. (1977) *Conflict and Stability in Fifteenth Century England* (Hutchinson).
Mercer, M. (2010) *The Medieval Gentry: Power, Leadership, and Choice during the Wars of the Roses* (Continuum).
Robbins, R. H. (ed.) (1959) *Historical Poems of the XIVth and XVth Centuries* (Columbia University Press).
Saunders, C., Le Saux, F., and Thomas, N. (eds) (2004) *Writing War: Medieval Literary Responses to Warfare* (D. S. Brewer).

Early Arthurian Romance
Field, P. J. C. (1998) *Malory: Texts and Sources* (D. S. Brewer).
Fulton, H. (ed.) (2012) *A Companion to Arthurian Literature* (Blackwell).

Jankulak, K. (2010) *Geoffrey of Monmouth* (University of Wales Press).
Krueger, R. L. (2000) *Cambridge Companion to Medieval Romance* (Cambridge University Press).
Lacy, N. (ed.) (2008) *The Grail, The Quest, and the World of Arthur* (D. S. Brewer).
Lacy, N. J. and Grimbert, J. T. (eds) (2005) *A Companion to Chrétien de Troyes* (D. S. Brewer).
Mahoney, D. B. (ed.) (2000) *The Grail: A Casebook* (Garland Press).
Norris, R. (2008) *Malory's Library: The Sources of the Morte Darthur* (D. S. Brewer).
Pearsall, D. (2003) *Arthurian Romance: A Short Introduction* (Blackwell).
Tether, L. (2012) *The Continuations of Chrétien's Percival: Content and Construction, Extension and Ending* (D. S. Brewer).

Yvain, the *Stanzaic Morte Arthur* and the *Alliterative Morte Arthure*

Archibald, E. (2004) 'Lancelot as lover in the English tradition before Malory', in Wheeler, B. (ed.), *Arthurian Studies in Honour of P. J. C. Field* (D. S. Brewer).
Brewer, D. (1988) *Studies in Medieval English Romance: Some New Approaches* (D. S. Brewer).
Cherewatuk, K. and Whetter, K. S. (eds) (2009) *The Arthurian Way of Death: The English Tradition* (D. S. Brewer).
DeMarco, P. (2005) 'An Arthur for the Ricardian age: Crown, Nobility, and the Alliterative *Morte Arthure*', *Speculum*, 80, pp. 464–93.
Fein, S. and Johnston, M. (eds) (2014) *Robert Thornton and his Books: Essays on the Lincoln and London Thornton Manuscripts* (York Medieval Press).
Findon, J. (2005) 'The other story: female friendship in the Middle English *Ywain and Gawain*', *Paragon*, 22, pp. 71–94.
Hamilton, G. K. (1976) 'The breaking of the troth in *Ywain and Gawain*', *Mediaevalia*, 2, pp. 111–35.
Kennedy, E. D. (2004) 'Sir Thomas Malory's (French) Romance and (English) Chronicle', in Wheeler, B. (ed.), *Arthurian Studies in Honour of P. J. C. Field* (D. S. Brewer).

Knepper, J. (2001) 'A bad girl will love you to death: excessive love in the Stanzaic *Morte Arthur* and Malory', in Wheeler, B. and Tolhurst, F. (eds), *On Arthurian Women: Essays in Memory of Maureen Fries* (Scriptorium Press).

Lawlor, J. (1966) *Patterns of Love and Courtesy: Essays in Memory of C. S. Lewis* (Edward Arnold).

Moll, R. J. (2003) *Before Malory: Reading Arthur in Later Medieval England* (University of Toronto Press).

Pearsall, D. (1977) *Old English and Middle English Poetry* (Routledge).

Schmidt, A. (1980) 'Introduction', in *Medieval English Romances*, Vol. 2 (Medieval and Renaissance Series, Hodder and Stoughton).

Whetter, K. S. (2002) 'The Stanzaic *Morte Arthur* and Medieval Tragedy', *Reading Medieval Studies*, 28, pp. 87–111.

Sir Gawain and the Green Knight

Anderson, J. J. (2005) *Language and Imagination in the Gawain-poems* (Manchester University Press).

Andrew, M. (1997) 'Theories of authorship', in Brewer, D. and Gibson, J. (eds), *A Companion to the Gawain-Poet* (D. S. Brewer).

Benson, L. (1965) *Art and Tradition in Sir Gawain and the Green Knight* (Rutgers University Press).

Blanch, R. J. (ed.) (1971) *Sir Gawain and Pearl: Critical Essays* (Indiana University Press).

Brewer, D. (1966) 'Courtesy and the Gawain poet', in Lawlor, J. (ed.), *Patterns of Love and Courtesy: Essays in Memory of C. S. Lewis* (Edward Arnold).

Brewer, D. (1997) 'The sources of *Sir Gawain and the Green Knight*', in Brewer, D. and Gibson, J. (eds), *A Companion to the Gawain-Poet* (D. S. Brewer), pp. 243–56.

Brewer, D. and Gibson, J. (eds) (1997) *A Companion to the Gawain-Poet* (D. S. Brewer).

Brewer, E. (1973) *From Cuchulainn to Gawain* (D. S. Brewer).

Brewer, E. (ed.) (1992) *Sir Gawain and the Green Knight: Sources and Analogues* (Boydell and Brewer).

Burrow, J. (1966; repr. 1971) 'The two confession scenes in *Sir Gawain and the Green Knight*', in Blanch, R. J. (ed.), *Sir Gawain and Pearl: Critical Essays* (Indiana University Press).

Craymer, S. (1999) 'Signifying chivalric identities: armour and clothing in *Sir Gawain and the Green Knight*', *Medieval Perspectives*, 14, pp. 50–60.

Elliott, R. (1997) 'Landscape and geography', in Brewer, D. and Gibson, J. (eds) *A Companion to the Gawain-Poet* (D. S. Brewer).

Green, R. H. (1966) 'Gawain's shield and the quest for perfection', in Blanch, R. J. (ed.), *Sir Gawain and Pearl: Critical Essays* (Indiana University Press).

Howard, D. (1964) 'Structure and symbolism in *Gawain and the Green Knight*', *Speculum*, 39, pp. 325–83; repr. in Blanch, R. J. (ed.) (1971), *Sir Gawain and Pearl: Critical Essays* (Indiana University Press).

Knight, R. (2003) 'All dressed up with someplace to go: regional identity in *Sir Gawain and the Green Knight*', *Studies in the Age of Chaucer*, 25, pp. 259–84.

Martin, P. (1997) 'Allegory and Symbolism', in Brewer, D. and Gibson, J. (eds), *A Companion to the Gawain-Poet* (D. S. Brewer).

McCarthy, C. (2001) '*Sir Gawain and the Green Knight* and the Sign of Trawthe', *Neophilologus*, 85, pp. 297–308.

Mills, M. (1968) 'Christian significance and Romance tradition', in Howard, D. R. and Zacher, C. (eds), *Critical Studies of Sir Gawain and the Green Knight* (University of Notre Dame Press).

Morgan, G. (1979) 'The significance of the Pentangle symbolism in *Sir Gawain and the Green Knight*', *Modern Language Review*, 74, pp. 769–90.

Pearsall, D. (1997) 'The order of shame and the invention of embarrassment', in Brewer, D. and Gibson, J. (eds), *A Companion to the Gawain-Poet* (D. S. Brewer).

Prior, S. P. (1996) *The Pearl-Poet Revisited* (Maxwell Macmillan International).

Putter, A. (1995) *Sir Gawain and the Green Knight and French Arthurian Romance* (Clarendon).

Putter, A. (1996) *An Introduction to the Pearl-Poet* (Longman).

Rooney, A. (1997) 'The hunts in *Gawain and the Green Knight*', in Brewer, D. and Gibson, J. (eds), *A Companion to the Gawain-Poet* (D. S. Brewer).

Rushton, C. (2007) 'The lady's man: Gawain as lover in Middle English literature', in Hopkins, A. and Rushton, C. J. (eds), *The Erotic in the Literature of Medieval Britain* (D. S. Brewer).

Sadowski, P. (1996) *The Knight on His Quest: Patterns of Transition in Sir Gawain and the Green Knight* (Associated University Presses).
Scattergood, J. (1981) 'Sir Gawain and the sins of the flesh', *Tradutio*, 37, pp. 347–71.
Spiers, J. (1957) *Medieval English Poetry: The Non-Chaucerian Tradition* (Faber and Faber).
Stanbury, S. (1991) *Seeing the Gawain-Poet: Description and the Act of Perception* (University of Pennsylvania Press).
Stevens, M. (1972) 'Laughter and game in *Sir Gawain and the Green Knight*', *Speculum*, 47, pp. 65–78.
Twomey, D. (2009) '"Hadet with an aluisch mon" and "britned to noght": *Sir Gawain and the Green Knight*, Death, and the Devil', in Cherewatuk, K. and Whetter, K. S. (eds), *The Arthurian Way of Death: The English Tradition* (D. S. Brewer).

Lydgate and Malory

Archibald, E. (1989) 'Arthur and Mordred: variations on an incest theme', *Arthurian Literature*, 8, pp. 1–27.
Archibald, E. and Edwards, A. S. G. (1996) *A Companion to Malory* (D. S. Brewer).
Armstrong, D. (2003) *Gender and the Chivalric Community in Malory's Morte D'Arthur* (University of Florida Press).
Barber, R. (1996) 'Chivalry and the *Morte Darthur*', in Archibald, E. and Edwards, A. S. G. (eds), *A Companion to Malory* (D. S. Brewer).
Batt, C. (2002) *Malory's Morte Darthur: Remaking Arthurian Tradition* (Palgrave Macmillan).
Benson, L. D. (1996) 'The ending of the Morte Darthur', in Archibald, E. and Edwards, A. S. G. (eds), *A Companion to Malory* (D. S. Brewer).
Bliss, A. (2000) 'The symbolic importance of processions in Malory's *Morte Darthur* and fifteenth-century England', in Hanks, T. and Brogdon, J. (eds), *The Social and Literary Contexts of Malory's Morte Darthur* (D. S. Brewer).
Cherewatuk, K. (2005) 'Malory's "Grete Boke"', in Whetter, K. S. and Radulescu, R. (eds), *Re-viewing Le Morte Darthur: Texts and Contexts, Characters and Themes* (D. S. Brewer).
Cherewatuk, K. (2006) *Marriage, Adultery, and Inheritance in Malory's Morte Darthur* (D. S. Brewer).

Cherewatuk, K. and Whetter, K. S. (eds) (2009) *The Arthurian Way of Death: The English Tradition* (D. S. Brewer).
Clark, D. et al. (eds) (2011) *Blood, Sex, Malory: Essays on the Morte Darthur* (D. S. Brewer).
Field, P. (1993) *The Life and Times of Sir Thomas Malory* (D. S. Brewer).
Field, P. (1998) *Malory: Texts and Sources* (D. S. Brewer).
Field, P. (2000) 'Malory and the Battle of Towton', in Hanks, D. T. and Brogdon, J. (eds), *The Social and Literary Contexts of Malory's Morte Darthur* (D. S. Brewer).
Francis, C. (2011) 'Reading Malory's bloody bedrooms', in Clark, D. et al. (eds), *Blood, Sex, Malory: Essays on the Morte Darthur* (D. S. Brewer).
Goodman, J. (1985) 'Malory and Caxton's chivalric series', in Spisak, J. W. (ed.), *Studies in Malory* (Medieval Institute Publications, Western Michigan University).
Hanks, T. (1992) 'The Mortes and the confrontation in Guinevere's bedchamber', in Hanks, T. (ed.), *Thomas Malory: Views and Re-views* (AMS Press).
Hanks, T. (ed.) (1992) *Thomas Malory: Views and Re-views* (AMS Press).
Hanks, T. and Brogdon, J. (2000) *The Social and Literary Contexts of Malory's Morte Darthur* (D. S. Brewer).
Hardyment, C. (2006) *Malory: The Life and Times of Arthur's Chronicler* (Harper Perennial).
Kelly, H. A. (1997) *Chaucerian Tragedy* (D. S. Brewer).
Kelly, R. L. (1985) 'Wounds, healing and knighthood in Malory's Tale of Lancelot and Guinevere', in Spisak J. W. (ed.), *Studies in Malory* (Medieval Institute Publications, Western Michigan University).
Lexton, R. (2011) 'Kingship in Malory's *Morte Darthur*', *Journal of English and Germanic Philology*, 110, pp. 173–201.
Lynch, A. (2000) '"Thou woll never have done": ideology, context and excess in Malory's war', in Hanks, D. T. and Brogdon, J. (eds), *The Social and Literary Contexts of Malory's Morte Darthur* (D. S. Brewer).
Martin, M. (2010) *Vision and Gender in Malory's Morte Darthur* (D. S. Brewer).
McCarthy, T. (1988) *An Introduction to Malory* (D. S. Brewer).
McCarthy, T. (1996) 'Malory and his sources', in Archibald, E. and Edwards, A. (eds), *A Companion to Malory* (D. S. Brewer).

Pearsall, D. (1970) *John Lydgate* (Routledge).
Pearsall, D. (2003) *Arthurian Romance: A Short Introduction* (Blackwell).
Radulescu, R. L. (2003) *The Gentry Context for Malory's Morte Darthur* (D. S. Brewer).
Radulescu, R. L. (2005) '"Oute of mesure": violence and knighthood in Malory's Morte Darthur', in Whetter, K. S. and Radulescu, R. L. (eds), *Re-viewing Le Morte Darthur* (D. S. Brewer).
Riddy, F. (1987) *Sir Thomas Malory* (Brill).
Robeson, L. (2005) 'Women's worship: female versions of chivalric honour', in Whetter, K. and Radulescu, R. L., *Re-viewing Le Morte Darthur* (D. S. Brewer).
Scanlon, L. (ed.) (2009) *The Cambridge Companion to Medieval English Literature 1100–1500* (Cambridge University Press).
Scanlon, L. and Simpson, J. (eds) (2006) *John Lydgate: Poetry, Culture and Lancastrian England* (University of Notre Dame Press).
Simpson, J. (2009) 'John Lydgate', in Scanlon, L. (ed.), *The Cambridge Companion to Medieval English Literature 1100–1500* (Cambridge University Press).
Spisak, J. W. (1985) *Studies in Malory* (Medieval Institute Publications, Western Michigan University).
Sweeney, M. (2006) 'Divine love or loving divinely: the ending of Malory's *Morte Darthur*', *Arthuriana*, 16, pp. 73–7.
Waldron, P. (1992) 'Virtuous love and adulterous lovers', in Hanks, T. (ed.), *Thomas Malory: Views and Re-views* (AMS Press).
Walsh, J. (1985) 'Malory's "Very Mater of La Cheualer du haryot": characterisation and structure', in Spisak, J. (ed.), *Studies in Malory* (Medieval Institute Publications, Western Michigan University).
Whetter, K. (2008) *Understanding Genre and Medieval Romance* (Ashgate).
Whetter, K. S. and Radulescu, R. L. (eds) (2005) *Re-Viewing Le Morte Darthur: Texts and Contexts, Characters and Themes* (D. S. Brewer).

Index

Texts are listed where possible under their authors, and topics and genres are described as they appear in the book. Critics and historians are not listed.

Ailred of Rievaulx   126
affective devotion   26–7, 131, 137, 148
Alain of Lille (*The Complaint of Nature*)   202, 212, 214–15
alliterative metre   25–6, 29, 90, 160, 176–7, 185, 88–190, 209, 244, 247, 247, 250–1, 253, 252
'Alliterative Revival'   5, 25, 76
Alliterative Morte Arthure   5, 26, 244, 246, 248, 250–1, 253, 262–3
Andreas Capellanus (*Ars Amandi*)   200, 202–3
Anne of Bohemia (Queen of Richard II)   5, 35, 212
anti-feminism   107–10, 112, 222, 227
anti-Semitism   159–60
Aristotle   85
Arundel, Richard (Lord Appellant)   64
Arundel, Thomas (Archbishop)   51, 54, 147
audiences   1, 13, 27; Arthurian Romance 139–40; Chaucer's 72, 104; Courtly love 198; Hilton's 132–3; Popular Romance 165; Rolle's 124, 130; *Wynnere and Wastoure* 76
see also readers
'autobiography'   86, 125, 143, 147, 175–6, 218

Ball, John   16–17
Bartholomeus Anglicanus   102
beggars   *see* social classes
Benoit de St Maure
  Roman de Troie   220, 222, 244
  Roman de Theyes   260
Bible   46, 143, 156, 176–7, 185, 186, 188–90, 256; *Gospel of Nicodemus* 28, 31
  translations, Rolle's   125, 130; Wycliffite 45, 51–2, 173

Black Death   15, 21, 130
Boccaccio, Giovanni   205, 217, 259
  Decameron   103, 168, 180, 221
  Filocolo   168, 220
  Filostrato   206, 220, 221, 222–8 *passim*
  Teseida   206, 213, 220
body   34, 131–3, 148, 158–9, 209, 219, 266
Boethius (*Consolation of Philosophy*)   188, 201, 212, 218, 221, 223–5, 227
Bokenham, Osbern   156, 158, 160–1, 162–4
Bouchier, Isobel (sister of Duke of York)   160
Breton Lay   167–8, 208
Brut, Walter   157
Brut   *see* Layamon and Wace
Bury St Edmund's Abbey   36, 160, 216–17

Cade, Jack   242
Cain and Abel (Wakefield Pageant)   25, 28, 29–32
Cambridge   34, 36
Capgrave, John   158, 160–1, 169
Cardinal Virtues   23, 85, 87
Castle of Perseverance   33, 34
Caxton, William   2, 6, 240, 260–1, 262
Charles d'Orléans   210, 215
Chaucer, Geoffrey   1, 5–6, 64, 69, 203–4, 205, 221
  Book of the Duchess   69
  Canterbury Tales in general   7, 47, 66, 70, 104–7
  Clerk's Tale   107, 180–183
  Chaucer's own tales   86 (*Melibee*), 167, 242 (*Sir Thopas*)
  General Prologue   63, 68–73, 104, 162, 307
  Franklyn's Tale   107, 114–15, 168–9, 222

277

Friar's Tale 116
Knight's Tale 116, 218, 221, 222, 224, 260
Legend of Good Women 5, 104, 159, 212
Man of Law's Tale 170–3, 207
Merchant's Tale 106, 107, 111–13
Miller's Tale 116–18, 198, 203
Pardoner's Prologue and Tale 108; *Pardoner's Tale* 174
Parliament of Fowls 70, 76, 186, 207, 211–14, 221, 222
Parson's Tale 46, 175
Physician's Tale 159
Reeve's Tale 117–18
Retraction 206
Romance of the Rose translation 203
Second Nun's Tale 159, 162–4
Shipman's Tale 107, 110
Shorter Poems 210
Summoner's Tale 46, 116
Troilus and Criseyde 70, 105, 305, 222–8, 252, 258, 267
Wife of Bath's Prologue and Tale 106, 107–11, 181
Chester Cycle 27–28, 33
Chrétien de Troyes 244–5, 248, 256
Christine de Pisan 87
chronicles and chroniclers 7, 16–17, 26, 106
  see also Hardyng; Trivet; Walsingham
Clanvowe, John (*The Cuckoo and the Nightingale*) 76, 215–16
Cloud of Unknowing 132–3, 134–6
Complaint Poetry 83–4

Dante Alighieri 205
Death and Life 26, 76, 186
Debate Poetry 26, 56, 75–6, 212–15, 184, 187, 212, 214, 216, 242
Deguileville, Guillaume de 167, 217
Deschamps, Eustace 205
Despenser, Henry de 138
Digby MS 102 (Political Poems) 63, 89
Drama 26–35, 106, 116 (farce)
  Doctrine Plays 32–33
  Folk Plays (*Robin Hood*) 37
  Interludes ('Mumming') 36, 75, 217
  Morality Plays 33

Mummers' Plays (*St George*) 37
Mystery Plays 27–32, 118
Royal Pageants 36, 65, 217, 268
Saints' Plays 32, 35
Dream Visions 75, 230
  love 202–7, 215–19
  religious 184–190; defined 185
Dunbar, William 25, 128, 204, 216, 219

East Anglia 14, 32, 34
Edward II 74, 85
Edward III 3, 64, 77–8; his son Clarence 69
Edward IV 239, 243, 261
Émaré 168, 170–3, 177, 208
Estates
  satire on 20, 22, 65–73, 78, 79
  sermons on 48
  theory of 2–3, 66, 68
  see also social classes
Everyman 33, 35
Exempla (Moral Examples) 172–83

fabliaux 37, 101, 115–19, 174
Faith and Faithkeeping *see* Truth
Fasciculi Morum 47
Floris and Blanchfleur 167
Floure and the Lefe 218
folk tales 48, 165–70, 181, 247, 252–3
Fortune 21, 182, 200, 201, 205, 219, 221, 224, 227, 229, 231, 251, 264
  Remede de Fortune 205
Freud, Sigmund 205
Friars 46, 47, 48, 55–6, 76, 79
  see also Bokenham; Capgrave
Froissart, Jean 205, 211, 241

Game of Chess Moralised see Jacobus de Cressolis
Gamelyn 167
Gaunt, John of (Duke of Lancaster) *see* John of Gaunt
Gawain and the Green Knight see Sir Gawain and the Green Knight
Gawain-poet *see Pearl*-poet
Geoffrey of Monmouth (*Historia Regum Britanniae*) 243, 248, 249, 250, 253
Gesta Romanorum 47–8, 174
Giles of Rome 85, 242

Gilte Legende 156, 161
Golden Legend *see* Jacobus de Voragine; *Gilte Legende*
Gottfried von Strasburg (*Tristram and Isolde*) 245, 246
Gower, John 1, 5–6, 17, 19, 102
   Confessio Amantis 5, 66, 85–6, 102–4, 105, 170
   In Praise of Peace 242
   Miroir de l'omme 71, 102
   Vox Clamantis 102
Great Rising 13–15, 16–17, 38, 50, 53, 102
   see also Cade; Oldcastle
Great Schism *see* Pope
Grimestone, John 48, 127
Grosseteste, Robert (*Cursor Mundi*) 174, 187
Guido de Collonne (*Historia Destructionis Troiae*) 217, 220, 222, 259–60
guilds 26, 27, 28, 32, 62, 64, 108, 156, 217
   Minstrels 208
   parish 36, 63, 72
   St George 32
   Stationers 5–6
Guillaume de Loris *see Romance of the Rose*
Guillaume de Machaut *see* Machaut
Guy of Warwick 167

Hardyng, John 247, 262
Harley Lyrics 309–10
Havelock the Dane 166–7
Henry IV (Bolingbroke, Earl of Derby) 64–5, 85, 88, 103, 241; his sons 7
Henry V 160, 241, 260
Henry VI 160, 216, 242, 243
Henry VII 36, 133, 260
Henryson, Robert 216, 219, 221, 227
   Testament of Cressid 229–32
hermits 20, 67
Hilton, Walter 7, 132
   Testament of Cressid 133–4
Hoccleve, Thomas 19, 86–7
   Regement of Princes 87–8, 242
homiletic texts 45–7
Humphrey of Gloucester 160, 217

Isumbras 169

Jacobus de Cressolis (*Game of Chess*) 65–6, 85
Jacobus de Voragine (*Golden Legend*) 156, 159, 161, 162, 164
James I King of Scotland (*Kingis Quair*) 7, 215, 218–19
Jean de Meun *see Romance of the Rose*
John of Gaunt (Duke of Lancaster) 17, 64, 65; with Blanche 69
John of Howden 127
jongleurs *see* minstrels
Julian of Norwich 54, 133, 137–44
Justice 68; opposed by maintenance 80–2
   see also Truth
justices (judges) 22, 31, 36, 69; Chaucer 70

Katherine Group 156
Kempe, Margery 54, 138, 144–9, 158
King Horn 169
King of Tares 169
Knight of La Tour-Landry 100, 157

Lancelot, French prose 263, 265, 266
Langland, William 5–6, 19–20, 37, 84, 90–1, 186–8, 216
   Piers Plowman: whole text 8, 46, 242
   B-text, B.Prologue 35, 66–8; B.2–4 79–82, 88–9, 242; B.6 18–21; B.16 140; B.18 76, 173; B.19 22–4; B.20 24
   C-text C.5 19
languages and dialects 1, 3, 5; Chaucer's 69; *Pearl*-poet's 176, 251
lawyers *see* social classes
Layamon (*Brut*) 244, 250, 253
literacy 2, 13, 44–5, 51, 62, 137, 147, 158
Lollards (Wycliffites) 2, 17, 24, 33, 38, 48, 51–5, 68, 138, 157–8, 173, 242
   Margery Kempe 146–7
   Lollard poems 2, 55, 90–4
   see also Ball; Bible; Brut (Walter); Wycliffe
London 5, 19, 79, 80; City of 63–4; Mayor of 80; Westminster 64–5, 80, 86
Love 18, 103, 134, 136, 139, Ch. 7 *passim*; of Jesus as mother 142–4; secular love definitions 199–200

Love, Nicholas (*Mirror of the Blessed Life*)   126, 148, 161
Lull, Raymundus   242, 261
Lydgate, John   36, 54, 216–17, 240
  Fall of Princes   217, 259
  hagiographies   160–1
  Debate of Horse Goose and Sheep   242
  Siege of Thebes   259–60
  Temple of Glass   216–18, 219
  Troy Book   216–17, 259
Lynn (King's Lynn)   144–5, 147, 149, 158, 160
lyrics
  love lyrics   208–11
  religious lyrics   127–9

Machaut, Guillaume de   205, 211
Macrobius (*Commentary on Dream of Scipio*)   185–6, 201, 212–13
maistrie (mastery)   110, 114
Malory, Sir Thomas   220, 239, 60–2
  Morte Darthur   2, 5, 8, 246, 249, 260–8
  sources   243–7, 249–51, 247–8
Mankind   33, 34–35
Mannyng of Brunne, Robert (*Manuel des Péchés*)   101, 103
manuscripts   4–8, 44, 63, 190, 260
  Boethius   201
  Chaucer   105–6, 162, 224
  courtly Romance   240
  Geoffrey of Monmouth   243
  Gower   102
  hagiography   154, 156
  Langland   19, 186
  Lydgate   160–1, 260
  lyrics   128, 208–11
  Malory   262
  mystics   131, 134, 138
  Pearl-poet   163
  Piers Plowman   19, 186
  Prikke of Conscience   46
  political texts   85, 89, 92, 89
  Popular Romances   166, 242, 169
  Romance of the Rose   203
  Wycliffite Bible   51
Margaret, Queen of Henry VI   27, 243
Marie de Champagne   202, 244
Marie de France (*Lays*)   167–8

marriage   107–19, 181, 202–3, 215, 219, 264; mystical 146
Meditations on the Life of Christ (attrib. Bonaventura)   126, 130, 156, 161
  see also   Love, Nicholas
minstrels and jongleurs   67, 208
monks and monasteries   4–7, 71, 76, 102, 124; Cistercians 126, 245
  see also   Hilton; Lydgate; *Cloud of Unknowing*
Mort Artu   246, 249, 266
Morte Darthur   see Malory
Mummers' Plays   see Drama
Myrc, John
  Festial   156
  Instructions   46

narrators   103, 117, 216, 220; in Chaucer 105–7
Negative Way   132–6
  see also   pseudo-Dionysius
Neville, Lady Cecily   7
Neville, Richard Duke of Warwick   217, 243, 261
Norwich   188
N-Town Cycle   27–8

Octavian   169
Oldcastle, John   53, 146
Ovid   300
Owl and the Nightingale, The   76, 214
Oxford   36

pagans (including Muslims)   163, 169, 170–1, 263
pardoners   67, 73, 108, 174
parliament   64–5, 81, 91, 239
Parliament of Three Ages   26, 77
Paston family   6, 37
Patience   176–9, 256
patience (*suffraunce*)   114–15, 155, 168, 169, 172–3, 175–83, 191, 225, 256
  defined   176–7, 180
Peace (as character and concept)   81, 86, 242, 260
Pearl-poet   175
  Pearl   25, 188–90, 217, 257
  see also   *Patience*; *Sir Gawain*; *St Erkenwald*

peasants *see* social classes
Peasants' Revolt *see* Great Rising
Pecock (Peacock), Reginald   54
penance and confession   46–7, 52, 55, 178, 257
Perrers, Alice   64, 69, 80
Petrarch, Francesco   168, 180, 182, 205
Piers Plowman see Langland
  'Piers Plowman letters'   17
  Piers the Plowman's Crede   55–8, 117
  Ploughman's Tale   55–8
plays *see* Drama
Political Advice   80–1, 84–94
Political Prophecy   83–4
Poll Taxes   16
Pope   5, 23, 67, 76, 78
  Papal Schism   19
Pride of Life (Morality Play)   33
Prikke of Conscience   46
printing   2, 240, 260–1
  see Caxton
pseudo-Dionysius   132, 134

readers and reading habits   6–9, 19, 63, 65, 100, 130–3, 105, 154–5, 156, 165, 198, 239–40
realism   72, 100, 108, 116–17, 189, 220, 223, 249, 253, 258
Reason (as a character)   82, 204
rhymed forms   206–7, 209, 212, 226, 250; in *Gawain* 262; in lyrics 170; in *Stanzaic Morte Arthur* 247; *rhyme royal* 112, 160–2, 222, 229, 260; tail rhyme 170; villanelle 215
Richard II   2, 3, 5, 16, 35–6, 64–5, 81, 85, 87, 89, 90–3, 103, 175, 176, 212, 251, 252; coronation 68
Robin Hood (plays and ballads)   37–8, 100
Rolle, Richard   129–32, 133, 148
  Ego Dormio   129
  Form of Living   130
  Lyrics   129
  Meditations on the Passion   131
  Psalms translation   46, 125, 130
Roman de Brut see Wace
Roman de Fauvel   74
Roman de Troie see Benoit de St Maure
Romances   165–72, 220–32, Ch. 8 *passim*

French Vulgate Cycle   246–7, 262, 263–6
Grail stories   245–7, 252, 256
Matter of Antiquity   26, 247
  (Alexander)   239 (courtly)
Matter of Britain   167 and 247 (non-courtly)
values of Chivalric Romance   240, 244–5, 247–69, 253–4, 261, 264
  see also Alliterative Morte, Layamon, Malory, Mort Artu, Sir Gawain, Stanzaic Morte, Suite de Merlin, Truth, *Yvain,* Wace
Romance of the Rose   71, 108, 110, 66, 108, 185, 200, 202, 203–4, 209, 212, 213, 218, 223–4, 225

Saints
  Ambrose   156; Invocation to the Virgin 162
  Augustine, Rule   71; On the Trinity 133, 141–2
  Bernard of Clairvaux   126
  Bonaventura   126
    (*see also Meditations*)
  Bridget of Sweden   146
  Edmund Rich   126
  Elizabeth of Hungary   158
  Francis   56
  George   32, 37
  Jerome   109, 110, 181
  Mary Magdalene   32
  Paul   32; on marriage 109–10, 157
  Peter   22
  see also   Virgin Mary
St Erkenwald   160, 175
Saints' Lives (hagiography)   144, 155–64, 173
Scogan, Henry   7
schools   15, 44
Scotland   7, 84
  see also   James I
Second Shepherds' Play   28, 32
Secreta Secretorum   85
serfdom   2, 14, 15–17, 20, 22, 30
sermons   47–51
  see also   Wycliffe
Shakespeare, William   35, 103, 223, 230
Simonie, The   74–5

sins   23, 34, 46–7, 257, 263; in Gower 103; in Julian 139
Sir Gawain and the Green Knight   4–5, 26, 47, 175, 176, 240, 241, 248, 251–9
Sir Orfeo   168, 207, 248
social classes   1, 62–3, 5–6, 62, 72–3, 77–8, 104, 107, 110, 117; in *Parliament of Fowls* 214
  aristocracy   198, 239–40, 243
  beggars   21
  civil servants   86
  lawyers   16, 36, 76
  merchants   62, 80
  peasants and urban poor   13–17, 22, 29–31, 48–9, 55–8, 66, 91
  see also   audiences, estates, towns
soldiers   76, 84, 242–3; Britoners 21
Song of the Husbandman   75, 83, 209
South English Legendary   156
Stanzaic Morte Arthur   246, 247, 249–50, 251, 254, 262, 265, 267
Statutes of Labourers   15, 21–2
suffraunce   *see* patience
Suite de Merlin   246, 263
Swarte-smeked smethes   26, 211

Towneley Cycle   27–9, 33
towns and townspeople   2–33, 13–16, 29, 45, 51–4, 69–72, 108, 117, 154–5, 198, 207, 231, 239, 243
  see also   London; Lynn; Norwich
Trevisa, John   85
Trivet, Nicholas   106, 170
Truth and Faithkeeping   18, 23–4, 34, 85, 87, 89–90, 93–3, 168–9, 172, 231–2, 248, 254; as a character 20–2; truth-telling 89–93, 229; with *leaute* 68

Venality Satire   20, 74–83
Vere, Elizabeth   160
Virgil   224

Virgin Mary   28, 148, 256–7; miracles 159; plays about 32; poems about 128–9

Wace (*Roman de Brut*)   244
'Wakefield Master'   28–9
  see also   Cain and Abel
Walsingham, Thomas of (*Chronicle*)   50, 53
Wars
  Hundred Years War   241–2
  literature of war   242, 250
  Wars of the Roses   65, 42–3, 83, 242–3, 268
Wars of Alexander   26, 247
Waster (as a character)   20–1, 66
Westminster   *see* London
wills   5, 100
Wisdom (Interlude)   36
women
  behaviour norms   101
  in Chivalric Romances   232, 250, 264–5
  in *Clerk's Tale*   181–3
  Criseyde   227–8
  God as woman   142–3
  in Love Romances   171
  reading hagiography   149, 156–8, 160–2
  reading Rolle   130–2
  in towns   7, 63–4, 108
  widows   64
  wife of Chaucer   69
  writing style   137
  see also   anti-feminism; audiences; Julian of Norwich; Margery Kempe; marriage; readers
Wycliffe, John   45, 49–53, 157
  Of Servants and Lords   49–51
Wycliffites   *see* Lollards
Wynnere and Wastoure   5, 26, 75–9, 91

York Cycle   27–9, 32–3
Yvain   167, 248, 254